Mechanistic Realism and US Foreign Policy

This book aims to invigorate realist international relations theory by developing a catalogue of micro-mechanisms able to explain security policy decision-making.

Typically, realism discounts the role of individuals and uses states as the unit of analysis. By examining instead the mental operations of those who act on behalf of the state, a better understanding of security policy formation is attainable. The book demonstrates how realism can be translated from a systemic "grand theory" into a catalogue of psychologically plausible mechanisms applicable to individual decision-makers. This catalogue, here called "Mechanistic Realism", may be employed to investigate the cognitive precursors to security policy.

The explanatory power of Mechanistic Realism is demonstrated through a meticulous analysis of what transpired inside the George W. Bush administration, as its members forged a response to the 2001 terrorist attacks. Through the exploration of individual-level data, Mechanistic Realism provides a more comprehensive analysis of the US response. The book concludes that international relations (IR) scholars would benefit analytically by assembling the most pertinent mechanisms into an explanatory toolbox rather than developing and applying grand theories. Mechanistic Realism is a first step in this direction.

This book should be of great interest to students of IR, foreign policy, American politics, and security studies in general.

Johannes Gullestad Rø is Associate Professor at the Norwegian Institute for Defence Studies and head of the Centre for Transatlantic Relations.

Contemporary Security Studies
Series Editors:
James Gow and Rachel Kerr
King's College London

This series focuses on new research across the spectrum of international peace and security, in an era where each year throws up multiple examples of conflicts that present new security challenges in the world around them.

NATO's Secret Armies
Operation Gladio and terrorism in Western Europe
Daniele Ganser

The US, NATO and Military Burden-sharing
Peter Kent Forster and Stephen J. Cimbala

Russian Governance in the Twenty-First Century
Geo-strategy, geopolitics and governance
Irina Isakova

The Foreign Office and Finland 1938–1940
Diplomatic sideshow
Craig Gerrard

Rethinking the Nature of War
Edited by Isabelle Duyvesteyn and Jan Angstrom

Perception and Reality in the Modern Yugoslav Conflict
Myth, falsehood and deceit 1991–1995
Brendan O'Shea

The Political Economy of Peacebuilding in Post-Dayton Bosnia
Tim Donais

The Distracted Eagle
The rift between America and Old Europe
Peter H. Merkl

The Iraq War
European perspectives on politics, strategy and operations
Edited by Jan Hallenberg and Håkan Karlsson

Strategic Contest
Weapons proliferation and war in the Greater Middle East
Richard L. Russell

Propaganda, the Press and Conflict
The Gulf War and Kosovo
David R. Willcox

Missile Defence
International, regional and national implications
Edited by Bertel Heurlin and Sten Rynning

Globalising Justice for Mass Atrocities
A revolution in accountability
Chandra Lekha Sriram

Ethnic Conflict and Terrorism
The origins and dynamics of civil wars
Joseph L. Soeters

Globalisation and the Future of Terrorism
Patterns and predictions
Brynjar Lia

Nuclear Weapons and Strategy
The evolution of American nuclear policy
Stephen J. Cimbala

Nasser and the Missile Age in the Middle East
Owen L. Sirrs

War as Risk Management
Strategy and conflict in an age of globalised risks
Yee-Kuang Heng

Military Nanotechnology
Potential applications and preventive arms control
Jurgen Altmann

NATO and Weapons of Mass Destruction
Regional alliance, global threats
Eric R. Terzuolo

Europeanisation of National Security Identity
The EU and the changing security identities of the Nordic states
Pernille Rieker

Conflict Prevention and Peacebuilding in Post-War Societies
Sustaining the peace
Edited by T. David Mason and James D. Meernik

Controlling the Weapons of War
Politics, persuasion, and the prohibition of inhumanity
Brian Rappert

Changing Transatlantic Security Relations
Do the US, the EU and Russia form a new strategic triangle?
Edited by Jan Hallenberg and Håkan Karlsson

Theoretical Roots of US Foreign Policy
Machiavelli and American unilateralism
Thomas M. Kane

Corporate Soldiers and International Security
The rise of private military companies
Christopher Kinsey

Transforming European Militaries
Coalition operations and the technology gap
Gordon Adams and Guy Ben-Ari

Globalization and Conflict
National security in a 'new' strategic era
Edited by Robert G. Patman

Military Forces in 21st Century Peace Operations
No job for a soldier?
James V. Arbuckle

The Political Road to War with Iraq
Bush, 9/11 and the drive to overthrow Saddam
Nick Ritchie and Paul Rogers

Bosnian Security after Dayton
New perspectives
Edited by Michael A. Innes

Kennedy, Johnson and NATO
Britain, America and the dynamics of alliance, 1962–68
Andrew Priest

Small Arms and Security
New emerging international norms
Denise Garcia

The United States and Europe
Beyond the neo-conservative divide?
Edited by John Baylis and Jon Roper

Russia, NATO and Cooperative Security
Bridging the gap
Lionel Ponsard

International Law and International Relations
Bridging theory and practice
Edited by Tom Bierstecker, Peter Spiro, Chandra Lekha Sriram and Veronica Raffo

Deterring International Terrorism and Rogue States
US national security policy after 9/11
James H. Lebovic

Vietnam in Iraq
Tactics, lessons, legacies and ghosts
Edited by John Dumbrell and David Ryan

Understanding Victory and Defeat in Contemporary War
Edited by Jan Angstrom and Isabelle Duyvesteyn

Propaganda and Information Warfare in the Twenty-First Century
Altered images and deception operations
Scot Macdonald

Governance in Post-Conflict Societies
Rebuilding fragile states
Edited by Derick W. Brinkerhoff

European Security in the Twenty-First Century
The challenge of multipolarity
Adrian Hyde-Price

Ethics, Technology and the American Way of War
Cruise missiles and US security policy
Reuben E. Brigety II

International Law and the Use of Armed Force
The UN charter and the major powers
Joel H. Westra

Disease and Security
Natural plagues and biological weapons in East Asia
Christian Enermark

Explaining War and Peace
Case studies and necessary condition counterfactuals
Jack Levy and Gary Goertz

War, Image and Legitimacy
Viewing contemporary conflict
James Gow and Milena Michalski

Information Strategy and Warfare
A guide to theory and practice
John Arquilla and Douglas A. Borer

Countering the Proliferation of Weapons of Mass Destruction
NATO and EU options in the Mediterranean and the Middle East
Thanos P. Dokos

Security and the War on Terror
Edited by Alex J. Bellamy, Roland Bleiker, Sara E. Davies and Richard Devetak

The European Union and Strategy
An emerging actor
Edited by Jan Hallenberg and Kjell Engelbrekt

Causes and Consequences of International Conflict
Data, methods and theory
Edited by Glenn Palmer

Russian Energy Policy and Military Power
Putin's quest for greatness
Pavel Baev

The Baltic Question during the Cold War
Edited by John Hiden, Vahur Made and David J. Smith

America, the EU and Strategic Culture
Renegotiating the transatlantic bargain
Asle Toje

Afghanistan, Arms and Conflict
Armed groups, disarmament and security in a post-war society
Michael Bhatia and Mark Sedra

Punishment, Justice and International Relations
Ethics and order after the Cold War
Anthony F. Lang, Jr.

Intra-State Conflict, Governments and Security
Dilemmas of deterrence and assurance
Edited by Stephen M. Saideman and Marie-Joëlle J. Zahar

Democracy and Security
Preferences, norms and policy-making
Edited by Matthew Evangelista, Harald Müller and Niklas Schörnig

The Homeland Security Dilemma
Fear, failure and the future of American security
Frank P. Harvey

Military Transformation and Strategy
Revolutions in military affairs and small states
Edited by Bernard Loo

Peace Operations and International Criminal Justice
Building peace after mass atrocities
Majbritt Lyck

NATO, Security and Risk Management
From Kosovo to Khandahar
M. J. Williams

Cyber Conflict and Global Politics
Edited by Athina Karatzogianni

Globalisation and Defence in the Asia-Pacific
Arms across Asia
Edited by Geoffrey Till, Emrys Chew and Joshua Ho

Security Strategies and American World Order
Lost power
Birthe Hansen, Peter Toft and Anders Wivel

War, Torture and Terrorism
Rethinking the rules of international security
Edited by Anthony F. Lang, Jr. and Amanda Russell Beattie

America and Iraq
Policy-making, intervention and regional politics
Edited by David Ryan and Patrick Kiely

European Security in a Global Context
Internal and external dynamics
Edited by Thierry Tardy

Women and Political Violence
Female combatants in ethno-national conflict
Miranda H. Alison

Justice, Intervention and Force in International Relations
Reassessing just war theory in the 21st century
Kimberley A. Hudson

Clinton's Foreign Policy
Between the Bushes, 1992–2000
John Dumbrell

Aggression, Crime and International Security
Moral, political and legal dimensions of international relations
Page Wilson

European Security Governance
The European Union in a Westphalian world
Charlotte Wagnsson, James Sperling and Jan Hallenberg

Private Security and the Reconstruction of Iraq
Christopher Kinsey

US Foreign Policy and Iran
American–Iranian relations since the Islamic revolution
Donette Murray

Legitimising the Use of Force in International Relations
Kosovo, Iraq and the ethics of intervention
Corneliu Bjola

The EU and European Security Order
Interfacing security actors
Rikard Bengtsson

US Counter-terrorism Strategy and al-Qaeda
Signalling and the terrorist world-view
Joshua Alexander Geltzer

Global Biosecurity
Threats and responses
Edited by Peter Katona, John P. Sullivan and Michael D. Intriligator

US Hegemony and International Legitimacy
Norms, power and followership in the wars on Iraq
Lavina Lee

Private Security Contractors and New Wars
Risk, law, and ethics
Kateri Carmola

Russia's Foreign Security Policy in the 21st Century
Putin, Medvedev and beyond
Marcel de Haas

Rethinking Security Governance
The problem of unintended consequences
Edited by Christopher Daase and Cornelius Friesendorf

Territory, War, and Peace
John A. Vasquez and Marie T. Henehan

Justifying America's Wars
The conduct and practice of US military intervention
Nicholas Kerton-Johnson

Legitimacy and the Use of Armed Force
Stability missions in the post-Cold War era
Chiyuki Aoi

Women, Peace and Security
Translating policy into practice
Edited by Funmi Olonisakin, Karen Barnes and Ekaette Ikpe

War, Ethics and Justice
New perspectives on a post-9/11 world
Edited by Annika Bergman-Rosamond and Mark Phythian

Transitional Justice, Peace and Accountability
Outreach and the role of international courts after conflict
Jessica Lincoln

International Law, Security and Ethics
Policy challenges in the post-9/11 world
Edited by Aidan Hehir, Matasha Kuhrt and Andrew Mumford

Multipolarity in the 21st Century
A new world order
Edited by David Brown and Donette Murray

European Homeland Security
A European strategy in the making?
Edited by Christian Kaunert, Sarah Léonard and Patryk Pawlak

Transatlantic Relations in the 21st Century
Europe, America and the rise of the rest
Erwan Lagadec

The EU, the UN and Collective Security
Making multilateralism effective
Edited by Joachim Krause and Natalino Ronzitti

Understanding Emerging Security Challenges
Threats and opportunities
Ashok Swain

Crime-Terror Alliances and the State
Ethnonationalist and Islamist challenges to regional security
Lyubov Grigorova Mincheva and Ted Robert Gurr

Understanding NATO in the 21st Century
Alliance strategies, security and global governance
Edited by Graeme P. Herd and John Kriendler

Ethics and the Laws of War
The moral justification of legal norms
Antony Lamb

Militancy and Violence in West Africa
Religion, politics and radicalisation
*Edited by Ernst Dijxhoorn,
James Gow and Funmi Olonisakin*

Mechanistic Realism and US Foreign Policy
A new framework for analysis
Johannes Gullestad Rø

Mechanistic Realism and US Foreign Policy
A new framework for analysis

Johannes Gullestad Rø

LONDON AND NEW YORK

First published 2013 by Routledge

2 Park Square, Milton Park, Abingdon, Oxfordshire OX14 4RN
711 Third Avenue, New York, NY 10017

Routledge is an imprint of the Taylor & Francis Group, an informa business

First issued in paperback 2018

Copyright © 2013 Johannes Gullestad Rø

The right of Johannes Gullestad Rø to be identified as author of this work has been asserted by him in accordance with sections 77 and 78 of the Copyright, Designs and Patents Act 1988.

All rights reserved. No part of this book may be reprinted or reproduced or utilised in any form or by any electronic, mechanical, or other means, now known or hereafter invented, including photocopying and recording, or in any information storage or retrieval system, without permission in writing from the publishers.

Notice:
Product or corporate names may be trademarks or registered trademarks, and are used only for identification and explanation without intent to infringe.

British Library Cataloguing in Publication Data
A catalogue record for this book is available from the British Library

Library of Congress Cataloging-in-Publication Data
Rø, Johannes, 1980–
Mechanistic realism and US foreign policy : a new framework for analysis / Johannes Rø.
  pages cm. – (Contemporary security studies)
  Includes bibliographical references and index.
  1. United States–Foreign relations–2001–2009. 2. Security, International. I. Title.
  JZ1480.R6 2013
  327.73001–dc23   2012050442

ISBN: 978-0-415-63539-4 (hbk)
ISBN: 978-1-138-37709-7 (pbk)

Typeset in Times
by Wearset Ltd, Boldon, Tyne and Wear

Contents

1 Introduction 1

PART I
Assumptions and theory 19

2 Foundations for social analysis 21

3 Mechanistic Realism 39

PART II
The empirical merit of Mechanistic Realism 67

4 The explanatory power of Mechanistic Realism 69

5 Idealism 117

6 Conclusion 141

Notes 151
Bibliography 160
Index 171

1 Introduction

1.1 The aims of the book

The first aim of this book is to invigorate realist-inspired analysis of international relations (IR) by utilizing the idea of *explanation by mechanisms*.[1] The book shows how realism can be translated from a systemic grand theory into a repertoire of detailed mechanisms accounting for the cognitive operations that are assumed to determine the conduct of individual men and women who make security policy decisions. I shall call the catalogue of mechanisms resulting from this micro-analytical revamp *Mechanistic Realism*. Because the catalogued mechanisms expose in detail the mental processes under influence of which decision-makers are expected to act, the framework is more apt to individual-level analysis of political psychology than other realist renditions. The book outlines, elaborates on, and demonstrates the explanatory potential of this versatile framework. Informing the argument of the entire book is the view that a mechanism-centered research program is more alluring than a continued attempt to refine abstract and law-like IR theories, such as realism.

The second aim of the book is to demonstrate the explanatory power of Mechanistic Realism. By invoking the mechanisms in the catalogue, our understanding of the Bush administration's security polices in the aftermath of the terrorist attacks on New York and Washington DC on September 11, 2001, (hereafter 9/11), would be improved. The empirical sections of the book vouch that Mechanistic Realism offers a more plausible, a more intelligible and an intellectually more satisfactory rendering of US responses than other available explanatory candidates, the most prominent alternative being that neoconservative ideologues hold sway of the response (cf. Greenwald 2007; Hersh 2004). There is one reservation though. The massive presence of evidence according a causal role to idealist ideas and sentiments indicates that the premise of national egoism, on which Mechanistic Realism is built, is moot. The book therefore includes a meticulous evaluation of the merit of various idealist explanations as well, to gauge whether any of these can stand.

By introducing Mechanistic Realism and vouching for its explanatory power in the case of US policies after 9/11, I impugn two influential stances in the contemporary IR debate. In the first place, I take issue with those analysts who have proclaimed sea change in the wake of the unprecedented and specific assertions that we have entered a new era of globalization, post-modernity, risks, networks or securitization in which theories and knowledge from the past have little to teach us (cf. Buzan *et al.* 1998; Beck 2005; Rasmussen 2006). Impugning the views of the social science iconoclasts, who insist on "[o]verturning conventional logic and historical patterns" and on the need for a "new vocabulary" (Heng 2006: 1, 3), this book builds on the presumption that certain psychological and behavioral regularities remain influential in international politics despite changing circumstances.

The degree of continuity in international politics, illustrated by the recurrence of war and the importance of fear as precursors to state action, supports the suggestion that some features of individual statesmanship are permanent, perhaps because of underlying determinants of the international system. In contrast to the numerous assertions that US response to 9/11 departed fundamentally from patterns that run through much political history and represented "revolutionary change" (Daalder and Lindsey 2005), that "9/11 did indeed force us to recognize that everything had changed" (Coker 2009: 132), it will be accentuated in the following how important features of the US response conformed to well-known patterns of political thinking, reasoning and behavior comprehended by realist insights.

In the second place, this book expresses an equally strong incredulity with proponents of deterministic and mono-causal theories of international relations, often associated with the realist label. At times these proponents seem too concerned with continuity, permanence, "the irresistible strength of existing forces and the inevitable character of existing tendencies" (Carr 1946: 10). Although wedded to realist insights, the following exploration will demonstrate how acclaimed analysts unwarrantedly gloss over important nuances and contradictory tendencies in the name of analytical parsimony and theoretical coherence.[2] There is a misguided tendency among realist scholars to rely too heavily on the assumption that balance of power considerations, presumably elicited by a systemic pressure towards equilibrium, are the essential instigation of state action in the international system (cf. Waltz 2008: Chapters 13 and 15). Despite the aptitude of realist insights for being true, their truth claims have repeatedly been shown to be empirically weak. The common assertion, for example, that "the objective [of the Iraq war] was to preserve the existing balance of power in the Persian Gulf" and "preserving American military hegemony in the Persian Gulf" (Record 2004: 67), needs careful empirical scrutiny, and cannot simply be assumed to be and accepted as "the undeclared war aim" (ibid.).

Throughout this book I hope to display the inadequacies of the two stances of the sea change protagonists and the permanence protagonists by introducing what I believe to be a sounder analytical approach grounded in an understanding of causal mechanisms, methodological individualism and the philosophical position known as scientific realism. Anchored in these fundamental assumptions, the book will, by appealing to Mechanistic Realism, demonstrate the claims of erupting discontinuity and fixed continuity as equally in need of qualification.

I conclude the book by addressing the important ongoing meta-debate about the "future of theory" in IR studies and I shall argue that we need to rethink the role and use of theory in the discipline.[3] In particular, I call into question the widespread instrumentalist view of theory and the suggestion that critical and cumulative revisions of abstract theories will improve our ability to explain the events we encounter. Given a commitment to a categorical truth concern and acknowledging the complex nature and relationship of the causal forces at play in international politics, we would be better off analytically, that is, better able to make sense of international politics, by assembling mechanisms into an explanatory toolbox instead of continuing to develop grand theories of the category to which realism belongs.

That this argument ultimately dissolves realism as a grand theory is arguably compensated for by the higher measure of understanding we gain by subsuming observation under the detailed mechanisms that can be derived from it. Furthermore, the complexity of international politics, to which the empirical case in this book testifies, suggests that our current division of the IR field into supposedly irreconcilable theoretical schools or "paradigms" is inexpedient. The book intends to show how mechanisms from opposing theory traditions can work in concert. The distinctive feature of a mechanism-centered research strategy is its ability to comprehend contradictory tendencies that cut across competing paradigms without degenerating into to vacuous eclecticism.

1.2 Realism and the US response to 9/11

If we were to summarize realism in one sentence, writes Malnes (1993: 23), "it would be that international relations are characterized by a struggle for power and permanent risk of war". While it is true that realism is no unified theory (Dunne and Schmidt 2001: 147–148), but rather a family of differently formulated variations of the above sentence, it is still rash to conclude, as Legro and Moravcsik (1999: 7) memorably did, that "realists lack an explicit nontrivial set of core assumptions". Realism is, despite numerous nuances among its advocates, at its core a theory about political motivation. In its purest outline, it postulates that states put a high premium on security and act self-interestedly because of the non-existence of a central authority above all states. This ordering condition, referred to as a structural anarchy, constrains states considerably and leaves them with extremely limited scope for choice: States are, we are told, like "prisoners trapped in an iron cage" (Mearsheimer 2001: 12), and the anarchic structure is an immutable and relentless "force that shapes and shoves the units" (Waltz 2008: 78). A fixed set of motives, including reasons and psychological inclinations, ensue that impel a distinct pattern of behavior. Eager only to survive, rational states are prompted to constantly struggle for power and relative advantage. This pursuit is triggered by mutual uncertainty, distrust and fear (Jervis 1976: 62–67). Since states in the international system potentially are revisionist, power competition is near unavoidable and the threat of interstate violence is continuously on call. Offensive measures, often military, are to be expected and war is a possible outcome, ultimately explainable as pursuit of self-defense.

Although contested for several reasons, this is a coherent, distinct, and yet an extremely parsimonious theory which, judged by how frequent its precepts are invoked in security analysis, has an undeniable analytical allure. In spite of its simplicity, it has proved able to inform interpretations and to dispel empirical puzzles. Notably, in the case under scrutiny in this book, realism has the merit of correctly predicting, after the fact, US policies in the wake of 9/11, i.e., the offensive projection of military power to increase own security. The US attack on Iraq, for example, seemingly bore out the proposition that powerful states concerned with own security and under sway of fear defy international law and customs and struggle for power by military means, behavior indeed falling squarely on the above outline. The old realist adage that "the best defense is a good offense" was even invoked verbatim in official US strategy documents after 9/11. Based on such observations, acclaimed analysts, such as Robert Jervis, have vouched the validity of realism in this case.

> [T]he American stance toward Iraq, and the Bush doctrine in general, follows from the realist generalization that a state's definition of its interest will expand as its power does. More specifically, Offensive Realism perhaps provides the best explanation for what the US is doing because it sees states as always wanting more power in order to try to gain more security for an uncertain future.
>
> (Jervis 2003c: 2)

Kenneth Waltz (2002), another prominent realist, also defended realism in the wake of 9/11. "New challenges [i.e., international terrorism]", he argued, "have not changed old habits".

> The terrorist act of September 11 has prompted the United States to enlarge its already bloated military forces and to extend its influence into parts of the world that its tentacles had not already reached. Fortunately or not, terrorists contribute to the continuity of international politics. They further trends already in motion.
>
> (Ibid.: 352–353)

Colin Gray (2002), another realist, argued that "realism was vindicated" after 9/11 and that "the eternal lore of statecraft still holds" (ibid.: 226).

> The reason, of course, is that old-fashioned geopolitics and geostrategy continue to comprise the serious business of national security policy ... the prudent realists who now command the American ship of state are not confused over the distinction between first- and second-order perils.
>
> (Ibid.: 229)

Together, the military offensive and power-amassing US stance after 9/11 and the cited scholarly conclusions would arguably appear to give some reason for believing realism is true.

However, whether realist theory has explanatory power in the case of the crucial decisions made after 9/11 is far from a clear conclusion. In fact, the most significant contributors to realist thinking in the US publicly opposed the Bush administration's foreign policy as it took shape. Notably, on September 26, 2002, thirty-three members of the so-called Coalition for a Realistic Foreign Policy paid for an advertisement in the *New York Times* arguing that a war with Iraq was inadvisable as it did not advance the "national interest".[4] As advertisements by definition are terse, realist scholars such as John Mearsheimer and Stephen Walt (2003) expanded on the realist critique in a much-cited article arguing that Bush strayed from realist principles and that the Iraq war was "unnecessary".

The US administration's decision to go to war with Iraq six months after the petition was published and in defiance of the scholarly advice, could reasonably be taken to imply that realist scholars subscribed to a theory that failed to predict reliably and describe realistically the policy of the most important great power in the system. Assuming the scholars derived their prescriptions and accompanying critique from realist theory, it is hard to interpret Bush's defiance of their advice as anything but a blow to the validity of realism.

In short, the utility of realist theory did not seem to parse. On the one hand, several scholars promoted realism as providing the best possible explanation for the policies pursued after 9/11. On the other hand, acclaimed realist scholars, sometimes even the very same scholars, have argued against Bush's policies because, they insisted, they did not enhance the US national interest.

Surprisingly however, very few of those who suggested Bush had strayed from realist thinking or any of those who insisted that realism explained Bush's choices have taken great care to examine whether evidence from within the administration squared with realist propositions. Indeed, in-depth empirical scrutiny of the processes leading up to Bush's decision, not least in debt scrutiny of the psychological precursors to Bush's actions, has been conspicuous by its absence. The realists who opposed Bush's policies did not inquire whether any or some elements of realist propositions shaped Bush thinking. Illustratively, without having analyzed micro-level evidence, one prominent realist simply averred that "Iraq has turned into a debacle for the United States, which is powerful evidence – at least for me – that the realists were right [in opposing the war] and the neoconservatives were wrong [in favoring it]" (Mearsheimer 2005: 6). Elsewhere the same author concludes that "Iraq doesn't fit my theory" on the basis that he knew the war was "bound to turn out to be a disaster" (Mearsheimer 2006: 115). Without more astute attentiveness to empirical data from the processes that preceded the decision to invade Iraq, such arguments are empirically weak and strain credulity. It is intellectually dubious to make judgments about the character of causal precursors to action based on the consequences of the same actions.

Likewise, those who have argued for realism's explanatory merit have typically invoked its tenets in a somewhat cliché-like fashion, underscoring the fit between theoretical implications and observations without taking care to document possible concurrence between Bush's thinking and all components of the theory, nor pondering the extent to which there were other precursors to Bush decisions than those brought up by realism.

Ascribing merit to a theory based on successful predictions does not subdue our concern for truth. In order to justify the tentative judgment of realism as the best truth candidate available, one has to demonstrate empirically whether the theory identifies the actual causal factors responsible for the observed policy. This requires scrutiny of the states of mind of the responsible decision-makers. But realists have not conducted this kind of analysis. Rather, the debate about whether Bush's polices substantiated realism or not testified to the cavalier fashion with which realist scholars attended to the mechanisms on which their theory rested.

One possible reason why realist judgments were not derived from a scrutiny of the mechanisms responsible for Bush's decisions is that these mechanisms are often not spelled out in as much detail as realist theory permits. This book attempts to rectify this analytical deficiency by translating realism's abstract and deterministic propositions into a catalogue of micro-mechanisms accounting for the mental operations that are assumed to determine the conduct of individuals making foreign policy decisions. In contrast to other realist rendering, this catalogue allows for, even explicitly stimulates, micro analysis of decisions pertaining to foreign conduct, such as those made by the Bush administration after 9/11. After outlining the mechanisms in the catalogue, I will apply them to the case and confront the mechanisms, one by one, with the evidence of what happened. The procedure should produce a qualified, tentative judgment of the validity of realism's various components and thereby contribute to the scholarly debate.

1.3 Why Mechanistic Realism?

Frustration with the undue attention realists pay to the micro-foundations of their theory and intellectual dissatisfaction with how realists have analyzed the US response to 9/11 elicit a call for a new realist framework and for an alternative interpretation of US policies in the wake of 9/11 based on that framework. By utilizing the idea of explanation by causal mechanism this book will carve out such an alternative. Roughly speaking, "mechanisms are frequently occurring and easily recognizable causal patterns" (Elster 1999: 1) that allow us to explain empirical puzzles. There are three reasons that explain the considerable potential of a research strategy centered on mechanisms to enrich both realist thinking and our understanding of the Bush administration response to 9/11.

In the first place, mechanistic explanation is a sound via media between, on the one hand, the idea of making sense of the Bush administration's policies after 9/11 by detailed historical description and, on the other, the idea of making sense of the same policies by invoking law-like generalizations anchored in realist theory. Although both ideographic and nomological attempts at coming to terms with US policies after 9/11 have offered valuable insights, there are also shortcomings attached to both approaches. While narrative accounts fasten on too much detail with the effect of failing to separate decisive from indecisive causal factors affecting the administration, the nomological accounts emphasize general regularities and enduring causal factors to the effect of ignoring the individual decision-makers and the quandaries with which they grappled. Between the analytical extremes of inclusive description and deterministic theoretical proposition there is scope for the study of the causal mechanisms under whose influence individual decision-makers within the Bush administration forged US foreign policies. The ensuing knowledge is more general than mere descriptions, but less general than proposed laws.

In the second place, a mechanism-centered research strategy offers a persuasive alternative to the acclaimed, but highly problematic, instrumentalist ideal according to which the theories' prime purpose is to be a useful tool for understanding, rather than aspiring to provide a truthful rendering of the phenomenon of one's interest. The instrumentalist denial that the truth or falsity of theoretical assumptions and implied causal micro-processes has a bearing on the theories' merit has led much IR theorizing astray, including, I should add, realism. By ascribing merit to a theory, in this case Mechanistic Realism, for its aptness to correctly capture the operating causal mechanism, intellectually more fulfilling insights can be gained, primarily because the risk of spuriousness is reduced. The philosophy of science tag associated with this anti-instrumentalist position is *scientific realism* and arguments comprising this position will inform the design of Mechanistic Realism and the execution of this case study.

In the third place, mechanism-based explanations in the social sciences apply to individuals, and as such contribute to the program of *methodological individualism*, according to which "a satisfactory explanation must ultimately be anchored in hypothesis about individual behaviour" (Elster 2007: 36). This program is apt to rectify the liability of many realist analysts to account for state behavior by referring to passive explanatory abstractions such as "forces of anarchy", "security dilemma" and "balance of power". Invocations of such abstractions only advance our understanding when they can be empirically grounded, that is, translated into hypotheses about discernible individual processes. One important aim of this study is to explore how well the abstractions invoked by realism beget hypotheses about individual psychology and behavior that concur with empirical findings.

1.3.1 The first reason expanded: between detailed descriptions and general theories

The 9/11 events were seminal and the US response to them has elicited much analytical pondering. Ideographic contributions consist of chronologically or episodically organized descriptions of US policy evolution following the events. This historical accounting can be read as a collective enterprise pushed forward by journalists, commentators, involved decision-makers, contemporary historians, and social scientists attempting to provide a detailed historical account of the opening phase of the so-called "global war on terror". The depth and detail of these narratives are generally impressive and indeed valuable in conveying the chronology of the events, though their lack of access to certain relevant sources, an occasional partisan tone, scapegoat tenor, and sporadic lack of scientific rigor sometimes make one wonder how reliable they are as examples of history writing (cf. Richs 2007). The underlying premise of the ideographic reconstruction is that if we just get all the details exposed, if we get complete knowledge about exactly who told whom what, and at what time, if we simply exhaust the empirical universe, reveal all the facts, grasp "wie es eigentlich gewesen", then we have finally made sense of what happened.

Fidelity to the ideographic method has no doubt brought information to the fore, in the absence of which understanding the US response to 9/11 would have been impossible. Yet the available descriptions nevertheless fail to provide what Thomas Hobbes (in Heilke 2004: 123) thought Thucydides managed in his *History of the Peloponnesian War*. According to Hobbes, "the narration itself doth secretly instruct the reader, and more effectively than can be done by precept". The description available of the "war on terror", however, does not by itself adequately alert readers to the recurring patterns of thinking and behavior relating to statesmanship. While the immediate occasion for the "war on terror" campaign is clear, the causal factors responsible for the policies are neither appropriately comprehended nor transparently exhibited. Crucially, the detailed descriptions fail to distinguish the more important from the less important factors shaping US policy. Moreover, even accurate retellings are unable to suggest plausible explanations of *why* the elicited events played out as they did.

On this score, the nomological contributions deliver better. General IR theories, such as realism, aspire to posit the decisive causal forces presumably shaping state conduct. Additionally, by making claims about enduring regularities, theories are able to suggest answers to otherwise tricky "why" questions. By defying the plethora of detail and attending instead to the general patterns of behavior, theories supposedly provide a more rewarding way of making sense of the US policies. Underpinning the nomological explanations is the presumption that abstract modeling, theoretical constructs and identification of law-like regularities help us understand how events play out better than detailed historical descriptions. Kenneth Waltz (1979: 65) famously developed this line of argument:

> If the aims, policies, and actions of states become matters of exclusive attention or even central concern, then we are forced back to the descriptive level; and from simple descriptions no valid generalizations can logically be drawn.

The Bush administration's policies in the wake of 9/11 readily lend themselves to nomological analysis. Robert Jervis (2003a: 2), for example, makes sense of Bush policies in the wake of 9/11 utilizing nomological insights.

The forceful and unilateral exercise of US power is not simply the by-product of September 11, the Bush administration, or some neoconservative cabal – it is the logical outcome of the current US position in the international system.

Elsewhere Jervis (2003b: 383) writes:

[I]n order to protect itself, the United States is impelled to act in a way that will increase, or at least bring to the surface, conflict with others. Even if the prevailing situation is satisfactory, it cannot be maintained by purely defensive measures.

By relating the Bush administration's foreign policy to the generalized proposition that great powers tend to expand, Jervis dispels, however crudely, the oddity of the policies pursued. Jervis's "logical" derivation is well suited to an interpretation anchored in realism. On this account, the administration's decisions were fundamentally driven by features of the international system, first and foremost the anarchical conditions and the power distribution among states in the system. The puzzle of why the US favored expansive policies in the wake of 9/11 is explained by relating it to the law-like regularity with which powerful states in anarchy strive to increase relative advantage.

The view that there are two separate analytical realms, one descriptive and one theoretical, with different aspirations, namely accuracy and parsimony, upholds the separation of labor between historians and political scientists, between ideographic and nomological sciences. A central argument of this book and the intellectual impetus for Mechanistic Realism is that this dualist epistemology is an obstacle to improved understating of international politics in general and the decisions of the Bush administrations in particular. A viable alternative to this dualism is suggested by Jon Elster (1993: 1–34 and 1999: Chapter 1). He pleas for a research agenda exploring the *intermediary* between laws and descriptions, an analytical realm which scholars adhering strictly to either the ideographic or the nomothetic approaches fail to acknowledge.

Despite widespread belief to the contrary, the alternative to nomological thinking is not a merely descriptive or narrative ideographic method. Between these extremes there is place and need for the study of mechanisms.

(Elster 1993: 2–3)

On the one hand, there is reason to believe that mechanisms with prospective explanatory power can be derived from a theory claiming to have covered general laws of international relations. These laws can be disaggregated into a repertoire of recognizable and frequently occurring causal patterns. This way of benefiting from theoretical knowledge amounts to a reductionist strategy. Although realism is nomological at its core and does not explicitly seek to explain the finer detail of political deliberation, its validity is nevertheless dependent on accurately identifying the causal mechanisms under whose influence foreign policy comes about. In order to exploit the theory's fullest explanatory potential, it is therefore necessary to take the theory apart, identify the mechanisms it implies, and subsequently explore the extent to which the single mechanisms can account for individual decision-makers' responses to 9/11. This endeavor requires one, admittedly somewhat irreverently, to translate realism's broad and abstract structural arguments, briefly sketched above, into a detailed and psychologically plausible framework for analysis of individual agency.

But abstract theories are not the only source from which causal mechanisms can be extrapolated. Mechanisms can also be extracted inductively from detailed descriptions, even if this is an extremely challenging task. Utilizing descriptive knowledge this way amounts to a generalizing strategy. Arguably the available descriptions of the inner workings within the Bush administration offer a rich reservoir from which the mechanisms influencing foreign policy decision-making can be extracted. Such inductively inferred mechanisms can benefit considerably from knowledge from other fields and theory traditions that have set store by regularities departing from those implied by realism. Chapter 5 of this book includes examples of idealist mechanisms shaping US polices which suggested themselves after careful engagement with the data, demonstrating that Mechanistic Realism is incomplete.

By utilizing both the reductionist and the generalizing strategy, I can compile a preliminary catalogue of frequently occurring causal patterns that presumably operate somewhere between proposed laws and suggested descriptions. Genuine *realism* implies that any causal mechanism that demonstrably shapes US policy arguably deserves a place in the toolbox of possible components in foreign policy explanations. The resulting catalogue is less than a full-fleshed theory, but more than simply a new description. It resembles what Robert Merton (in Hedström and Swedberg 1998: 6) calls middle-range theorizing. The repertoire enables me to account for, clarify and (sometimes) understand the US response to 9/11 in a way that neither loses sight of the individuals by being wedded to deterministic theoretical abstraction nor becomes overwhelmed by the detail of all-inclusive narratives. Although realism as a grand theory breaks down as a result of this, the accumulation of mechanisms to which it contributed still count, when empirically supported, as valid knowledge with an "intermediate degree of generality" (Elster 1993: 24).

1.3.2 The second reason expanded: defying instrumentalism, endorsing scientific realism

Apart from being a via media between ideographic and nomological approaches, the mechanism-based research strategy that informs Mechanistic Realism is an alluring alternative to analysis informed by the instrumentalist view by which theories are useful tools of comprehension (Hacking 1983: 63). Of the kinds of merit one may ascribe to theories, instrumentalists seize, not on truth, but on predictive power and usefulness. This view is adopted and expressed straightforwardly by Kenneth Waltz, probably the most influential structural realist. He argues:

> The question, as ever with theories, is not whether the isolation of a realm is realistic, but whether it is useful. And usefulness is judged by the explanatory powers of the theory that may be fashioned.... Explanatory power is gained by moving away from "reality," not by staying close to it. A full description would be of least explanatory power; an elegant theory, of most.
> (Waltz 1979: 8, 9)

In the article *Realist Thought and Neorealist Theory*, Waltz (2008: Chapter 5) explains why he rejects the idea that theories ought to correspond with empirical reality and why only simplifying approximations are useful. "Theory is artifice" (ibid.: 68), he writes.

> Descriptions strive for accuracy; assumptions are brazenly false. The assumptions on which theories are built are radical simplifications of the world and are useful only because they are such. Any radical simplification conveys a false impression of the world ... theory cannot fit the facts or correspond with events it seeks to explain.
> (Ibid.: 72, 75)

The principal deficiency of instrumentalism is its lack of concern with truth.[5] According to the contrasting doctrine of scientific realism, the only feature of a theory that makes it worthy of merit is its aptness for being true. A theory's aptness for being true is ultimately a judgment call. When a theory receives so much empirical support that we are justified in judging it to be the best truth candidate available, that is, when we have no sound reason for discarding it, we call it *validation*. Validation, however, is always tentative, and the judgment is continuously subject to withdrawal or correction upon the emergence of reasons, typically new evidence, that impugn it. Importantly, talking of validation is not a way to deflect attention from talk of truth, but since the epistemic position of *being sure* is practically unattainable, we need a term which denotes our best judgment under the present epistemological circumstances, and that term is validation.

This principal deficiency of instrumentalism is illustrated by the case pondered in this book. On the face of it, it is hard to deny the *usefulness* of realist theory as it appears to elucidate the US response to 9/11. The two ensuing wars, for instance, can be taken as confirmation of the theory's main prediction as they fall into an expected pattern of constant urge for maximum power, projected unilaterally by military means. For an instrumentalist, these observations would count as solid evidence of the theory's predictive power and verification of its usefulness. So long as the theory produces efficient predictions it is irrelevant for an instrumentalist whether the factors bringing about the effect are included in the theory, which is another way of saying that the risk of spuriousness is downplayed as trivial.

However, as *validation of theory* successful prediction is clearly insufficient. A theory that off-hand seems right on the mark because its theoretically derived predictions concurred with observed behavior, need not, on closer inspection, have captured the processes responsible for the outcome. Indeed, realism may have failed to identify the efficacious causal mechanism shaping the Bush administration's conduct, while the mechanisms actually responsible for the observations may, for all that is known, depart completely from those theoretically implied. Probing that eventuality, while irrelevant to an instrumentalist, would appear to be crucial from the point of view of the scientific realist. In fact, validation of the theory requires a credible account of the causal mechanisms responsible for the administration's conduct and it is for this reason the mechanism-based research program and Mechanistic Realism is so apt.

In contrast to a theory-testing procedure conducted in the instrumentalist spirit, which is how structural realist theory typically is put on trial, I shall therefore not judge the validity of realism by comparing theoretically derived predictions with observed behavior. Rather, in line with the mechanism-based strategy, my sole interest is the extent to which the theory has identified causal mechanisms that demonstrably bring about the effects we observe. Nor, then, am I interested in the usefulness of the theory in yielding crude and unspecific predictions based on "as if" assumptions, but rather in establishing to what extent it has succeeded, by invoking structural variables, in identifying true underlying causal mechanisms influencing the policymakers in the decision-making situation.

This procedure should put me in a better position to make an informed judgment about the validity of realism's psychological underpinnings. Besides, peering inside the black box could also reveal the theoretically omitted, but causally decisive, links in the causal chain leading to decisions we seek to understand. The aim of this study is also to identify some of these, thereby contributing to the project of accumulating mechanisms for the explanatory toolbox.

1.3.3 The third reason expanded: the program of methodological individualism

The third allure of a mechanism-centered exploration of the Bush administration is Mechanistic Realism's implied commitment to the program of methodological individualism, arguably the program that contributes most to the improvement of social scientific knowledge (Boudon 2006). In principle, mechanisms need not reside in individuals. The explanation, for example, on which some versions of balance of power theories rest, i.e., that all systems favor equilibrium, is also, although abstract, a mechanistic explanation as it invokes the frequently occurring phenomenon known as the "invisible force", or some other mechanism, which somehow kicks in whenever systemic imbalance occurs, to restore it (Wolfers 1962: 122; Jervis 1997: Chapter 4). The problem with this type of mechanistic explanation, however, is that the detailed sequence between the independent variable (systemic imbalance) and dependent variable (restored balance) remains hidden and perplexing.

In order to make balance of power theory credible, as Wolfers (1962: 9) notes, "one cannot escape an examination of the psychology of individuals". This relates to the more general proposition that in the social sciences, where mental processes, such as thoughts and feelings, stand in the forefront, there is every reason to think that the relevant explanatory mechanisms reside in individuals, i.e., refer to individual motives and choices. "As far as the social sciences are concerned, the elementary causes of any social phenomenon are obviously human individual actions" (Boudon 2006: 25).

Consequently, by centering attention on the mental mechanisms under whose influence decision-makers act, Mechanistic Realism is likely to improve the credibility of realist explanation simply by virtue of being individually anchored. Commonly, analysis inspired by structural theories is "so abstract that actual states and leaders do not get mentioned" (Boot and Wheeler 2008: 294) and events are accounted for in passive tense by invocation of amorphous explanatory abstractions such as "forces of anarchy", "dynamics of power", "national interest", "security dilemma", "spheres of influence", and "balance of power".

However, since history unfolds because individuals *decide* to act in a certain way, not because disembodied and amorphous anarchic forces, obscure ideas of systemic equilibrium or some purposive dialectics of history are at play, the above abstractions are only credible candidates of validation when anchored in individuals. If the mechanisms contained in Mechanistic Realism are to be validated, it is therefore crucial for the individuals within the Bush administration to demonstrably act under their influence. Material conditions, such as anarchy, power distribution, geography, become effective only through the cognitive apparatus of their interpreters as a "human decision to act in a specific way, an event that occurs in the psyche of man, necessarily [representing] the last link in the chain of antecedents of any act of policy" (Wolfers 1962: 42). An important aim of this study is to get a clearer understanding of these antecedents with respect to the Bush administration and for that aim the mechanism-based program, and Mechanistic Realism, are viable.

1.4 Mechanistic Realism: a new framework of analysis

Adherence to above principles of explanation suggest an analytical mode of operation with considerable potential to utilize the insights contained in realism in a way that reduces the risk of spurious explanations. By taking realism apart, disclosing the mental mechanisms that are hidden within the theory and confronting these mechanisms with empirical evidence from historical cases, it should be possible to ascertain which, if any, of the mechanisms implied by realism is validated, and hence, deserving a place in the mechanistic toolbox of foreign policy explanations. Applied to the US policies in the wake of 9/11, neither the suggestion that Bush's decision-making utterly refuted realism, nor that it is, in all respects, the best available conveyor of truth, have to be correct. The truth of the matter could be that some of the mechanisms implied by the theory failed to account for Bush administration policies, while others did. Exploring this would both enhance our understanding of the validity of realism and nuance our understanding of the case studied.

Being a repertoire of distinct micro-mechanisms rather than a sterling theoretical model, Mechanistic Realism does not establish invariable propositions as other versions of realism do. Rather, the causal mechanisms identified are contingent and their explanatory merit must be judged by their confined applicability, not as part of a coherent system of thought. They conceptualize and structure a set of plausible cognitive precursors to foreign policy decisions that may operate in a wide range of contexts, without claiming to have exhausted the potential impetuses of statesmanship.

In essence, Mechanistic Realism outlines the building blocks of a psychological theory of foreign policy decision-making by exhibiting twelve mental operations that are assumed to affect foreign policy decision-makers. The benefit of the catalogued mechanisms compared to its theoretical ancestor is that it offers a more precise picture of the various mental sequences by which decision-makers formulate foreign policy. By exposing these sequences one gets a more transparent and more detailed grasp of *what* is driving foreign policy decision-making and *how* it is driven. Thanks to the explication of the mechanisms in the catalogue and the concern with micro-foundations, the time lag between explanans and explanandum in the realist causal story is reduced (cf. Elster 1983: 24).

The presentation of the entire catalogue must wait till Chapter 3. Yet, the account proposed by Mechanistic Realism of how fear enters decision-makers' heads and eventually becomes the prime motive behind their foreign conduct is a telling illustration of the catalogue's explanatory utility. Whereas realism restrictively asserts that fear coupled with the motive to survive spurs foreign policy decisions, Mechanistic Realism spells out in detail four distinct and psychologically plausible causal patterns by which fear ensues. Mechanistic Realism proposes that fear results both from rational evaluation of threatening signals, from uncertainty about others' intentions, from imperfect epistemological circumstances and from counter-wishful thinking. Since these four mechanisms exhibit more specific causal patterns, an intellectually more fulfilling account of the role of fear in foreign policy decision-making can be given.

Consider an example: reading the memoir of the CIA Director, George Tenet (2007), one is struck by the extent to which his account is "quivering with emotion" (ibid.: 115). A leitmotiv of the memoir is how the constant exposure to new intelligence instilled a "palpable fear" (ibid.: 230), which Tenet conveyed to the president in his daily intelligence briefs causing Bush "to wake up in the middle of the night worried about what I had read" (Bush 2010: 153). Upon careful reading, the memoir is evidence to suggest that Tenet's fear had multiple sources corresponding to the four fear-fostering psychological patterns suggested by Mechanistic Realism. That individual-level data found in Tenet's memoir can be subsumed under the mechanisms identified by Mechanistic Realism, corroborates their causal significance on the individual level. Consequently the content of Tenet's mental life is better understood. Since fear, according to realism, is presumed to be the main psychosocial precursor to foreign policy decisions, it is intellectually rewarding to know in more detail how it enters into decision-makers' heads. It gives a higher measure of understanding and suggests that this particular psychological component of the causal story told by realism has empirical merit.

Some have argued that realist scholars have failed to study the impact of emotions, in particular fear, *systematically*. Crawford (2000) asserts that fear, although accepted as an important state motive and crucial for several theories of international politics, is often only implicitly assumed and supposedly "unexamined", "underproblematized" and "undertheorized" (ibid.: 118–119). "This taken for-for-granted-status, especially of fear, has particularly pernicious effects" (Crawford 2000: 118). By way of contributing to theorizing fear, Mechanistic Realism renders this critique less pertinent, as the above example highlights. Awareness of the ways fear comes about, suggests that Tenet's fearfulness is no coincidence, but rather explicable.

Furthermore, the higher measure of specification offered by Mechanistic Realism, for example of the role of fear, makes epistemological evaluation of empirical merit easier. The "critical rationalist" view, associated with Karl Popper (2009: Chapter1), whereby knowledge advances through the *testing* of claims, is arguably a viable way to probe the validity of all types of theoretical claims. Popper's hypothetical deductive method requires researchers to work out testable empirical implications of a given theory and observe the fit between the implications and observations. Supposedly, when theoretical deductions fit empirical findings there are grounds for strengthened confidence in the explanation suggested. While any claim is subject to withdrawal upon the emergence of contrary evidence, claims that endure continuous falsification attempts aspire to be the best truth candidate available.

But even if observations fit theoretical deductions, as seems to be the case of US policies after 9/11 and realism, prudent skeptics would still be concerned with the possibility of spuriousness, i.e., that the fit between the observations and the theoretical deductions could be due to a third factor, not acknowledged by the theory. This skepticism invites theoretical deductions of the lowest levels of abstraction that a theory permits. Taking this into account, instead of exploring the crude and unspecific fits between realist predictions and US behavior, Mechanistic Realism opts to explore whether the intervening causal mechanisms implied by realism are operative in the case of concern. This is to follow Popper's (2009: 20) recommendation to expose a theory to falsification "in every conceivable way" and to "the fiercest struggle for survival".

Failure of attempts to show that the mechanisms comprising Mechanistic Realism are not causally effective inspires more confidence that the mechanism mirrors the real causal process, i.e., that responsible for the outcome. The mechanisms in the repertoire that are not rebutted, but rather, like in the above example, seem to account for how observations at the decision-making level fit together, provide an explanation because they are more general than the phenomenon they subsume (see Elster 1999: 6). Mechanisms of this kind arguably deserve a place in the toolbox of possible foreign policy explanations.

Yet engagement with the available data suggests the existence of additional mechanisms, related and unrelated to Mechanistic Realism. One advantage of attempting to subsume what happened under the mechanisms included in Mechanistic Realism is to reveal non-subsumable information, suggesting a need for additional mechanisms in order to account for the residual oddity. By engaging with the "superfluous" data directly, mechanisms can be inductively *suggested*. It is sometimes possible to relate seemingly relevant aspects of the descriptions to mechanisms invoked by theory traditions other than realism. The conspicuous presence of idealist rhetoric after 9/11 is a case in point. These observations defy Mechanistic Realism. Yet since they relate to more general ideas of human motivation, this suggests that incidents in which self-interest appears to be superseded can be subsumed under a regularly occurring pattern of unselfishness. While the epistemological challenge of demonstrating the causal power of idealism is profound, mental patterns occurring with demonstrable frequency in foreign policy decision-making, such as idealist motives, may help dispel new puzzles, even if these explanations probably require refinement. In Chapter 5 I shall attempt to spell out and probe the validity of idealist mechanisms as meticulously as possible, to the effect of expanding the repertoire of mechanisms necessary to dispel the puzzles surrounding the Bush administration's decisions after 9/11.

1.5 Outline of the book

What I offer in the following is a new framework for realist analysis. Although Mechanistic Realism in principle is applicable to any case, I shall demonstrate its explanatory utility by investigating whether members of the Bush administration in the time span between 9/11 and the invasions of Iraq, acted in line with the detailed causal mechanisms it espouses. The book is separated into two parts.

Part I deals with assumptions and theory. Chapter 2 gives an account of the three principles of social science informing both how I develop Mechanistic Realism and how I analyze the empirical data. This includes an elaboration of scientific realism, mechanism-centered research strategy, and methodological individualism. The chapter also devotes considerable attention to the difficulty of distinguishing mechanisms from mere descriptions and to the task of avoiding theory-laden conclusions when utilizing mechanism for explanatory purposes.

Next, in Chapter 3, I outline the tenets of one acclaimed realist rendering before using this benchmark to translate its propositions into a catalogue of mechanisms applicable to observations inside any black box, that is, any state. The resulting catalogue of mechanisms is what I shall refer to as Mechanistic Realism. Since the precision in the description of the causal processes affecting foreign policy decision-makers is at the cognitive level, the framework aspires to outline the building blocks of a psychological theory of foreign policy decision-making. Thirdly, in the conclusion of the chapter, I call attention to some distinctive allures of the framework.

Part II of the book presents evidence in support of and evidence defying Mechanistic Realism. In Chapter 4 I ask whether each and every mechanism in the catalogue squares with findings from the decision-making process within the Bush administration after 9/11. After a brief account of the most common interpretation of the Bush administration's conduct and its shortcomings, I document that several mechanisms in the catalogue help make sense of the response, but I also point to nuances and hint at observations suggesting that contradictory tendencies are in play.

In Chapter 5 I recommend mechanisms with explanatory power that are not part of the Mechanistic Realism toolbox. In particular, I probe the validity of five different idealist explanations and conclude, cautiously, that idealist motives may have played a causal role, despite the empirical weakness of the suggestions. This conclusion implies that while some of the mechanisms of Mechanistic Realism are valid as far as they go, the catalogue all the same may be incomplete as it leaves out something important.

Finally, in Chapter 6, I review the main findings of the book. I conclude by voicing the idea that a program of accumulating causal mechanisms explaining foreign policy choice should replace the quest for general IR theories and argue that the mechanisms deserving a place in this toolbox cut across supposedly incompatible theoretical paradigms such as realism and idealism.

Part I
Assumptions and theory

2 Foundations for social analysis

The aim of this chapter is to explicate the assumptions on which the forthcoming theoretical exploration and the empirical analysis will rest. In order to appreciate my vouch for Mechanistic Realism and how I approach the empirical data, acquaintance with my positions on three matters regarding social scientific inquiry is required. I shall make the case for scientific realism, a mechanism-centered research strategy, and methodological individualism and argue that these precepts are intertwined. They invite a distinct way of contributing to the realist tradition and making sense of US foreign policy after 9/11. The chapter's final section will account for how mechanisms can be distinguished from mere descriptions and how mechanistic analysis steers clear of theory-laden conclusions.

Although this chapter raises deep philosophical questions, it is beyond the scope of this book to provide a philosophical justification for or to discuss all adequate reservations to these assumptions. Even if they concur with what influential philosophers of science have written (cf. George and Bennett 2005), the chapter is neither an exploration of philosophy of science nor intended as a contribution to it. Orthodox skeptics can without difficulty dispute these assumptions, despite the sound reasons and critical scrutiny that lend them credence (cf. Dancy 1998: Chapter 1). Although not immune to critique, an analysis based on these assumptions has considerable potential to enhance our understanding of international politics and fares better than available alternatives.

2.1 Scientific realism

The view of truth as a relation between a description and the object of the description is referred to as the "correspondence theory of truth" (Malnes 2002: Chapter 9). On this view, a belief is true provided there exists a fact corresponding to it (Audi 1999: 930). Yet the correspondence theory of truth is compatible with the view that the very same phenomenon can be truthfully described in more ways than one (cf. Hacking 1983: 143); that a true description of a phenomenon need not be a complete description (Føllesdal 2006: 79); and that some phenomena, such as beliefs, are ontologically subjective but epistemologically objective (Hacking 1999: 22).

For all intents and purposes this theory of truth merges with common sense. A description of a phenomenon, say an arms race between two states, is true only if systematic inquiry reveals concordance between the description and the state of affairs. Evidence implying that causally relevant factors are unaccounted for in a description of a phenomenon, say that prestige is overlooked as a precursor to armament, when observations indicate that pride evidently is an important driver, would require the description to be *corrected* in order to narrow the gap between description and fact. Consequently, a virtue of any description is that it is correctable in light of new and reliable findings (Popper 2009).

The correspondence theory of truth has been criticized by social scientists armed with the idea that beliefs about the world are *socially constructed* and constrained by the way we inter-subjectively represent phenomena discursively rather than by empirical references (Rorty 1989: 6–7; Hacking 1999). This idea has caught on in the IR field too. Christopher Hill (2003: 9), among others, expresses sympathy with the view that

> there is little point in attempting to work scientifically towards a "truthful" picture of human behaviour. This is because politics is constituted by language, ideas and values. We cannot stand outside ourselves and make neutral judgements.[1]

Apart from being logically inconsistent (if truths are unattainable, how can Hill's own postulate be true?), it appears that even analysts who explicitly reject being concerned with "truthfulness" or "objective reality", cannot in practice, at least implicitly, escape adhering to the correspondence theory of truth inasmuch as they often maintain that established knowledge needs either revision or correction. And anyone arguing that an account can be corrected adheres to the correspondence theory of truth, even when they do their best to deny this.[2]

The correspondence theory of truth applies not only to descriptions, but also to theories and claims about causal relationships. The theoretically informed claim, say that the lack of sovereign authority causes wars of aggression between rational sovereign states, is a candidate for a true, but rather unspecified, causal relationship. It may also be wrong or correctable. That high unemployment rates within states cause wars of aggression is an alternative, also rather unspecified, candidate for truth, suggesting a very different causal history. Both suggestions can be true accounts of why two different wars of aggression come about, but both suggestions cannot both be true for the very same war. Consequently, true beliefs can be locally confined and need not necessarily be subsumed under the same general theory.

Scientific realism is a position at par with the correspondence theory of truth. While the correspondence theory of truth answers what truth is, scientific realism addresses what we should demand of scientific constructs and theories. The essence of the doctrine is that theoretical constructs and theories aim at truth and refer to ontological entities that exist independent of the observer (Hacking 1983: Chapter 1). It is, in the words of Searle (1990: 16), the "view that there exists a reality independent of our representations of it".[3]

This view departs from *positivism*, which says that only propositions based on observables are candidates for truth (Hacking 1983: Chapter 3). Scientific realists think, in contrast, that phenomena defying direct observation, say metal phenomena, ought to be the subject of scientific inquiry. The doctrine also departs, as noted in the Introduction, from *instrumentalism*, the view that theoretical constructs or statements need *not* be candidates for truth as long as they are useful tools providing sound predictions. According to scientific realists, in contrast, theories earn merit only to the extent that a literal understanding of their constructs and implied causal relationships correspond to reality. To satisfy the demands of scientific realism, theoretical entities, say states, must refer to real and existing entities; implied causal relationships, as captured by the dictum "uncertainty fosters fear", must describe the actual psychological reactions of agents; and theoretical assumptions, such as the rational actor premise, must be causally responsible for the decisions made.

The last point clearly illustrates the disparity between scientific realism and instrumentalism, insofar as the two doctrines construe a theoretical premise, such as that of rationality, differently. Instrumentalists take the premise to be useful as a simplifying device. Whether an agent conforms to standards of rationality is irrelevant, as long as the inclusion of the premise in the theory contributes to the production of accurate predictions. If a theory of state behavior, premised on individual rationality, yields sound predictions about interstate discord, it is unimportant whether the protagonists actually fail to satisfy the standards of rationality. According to instrumentalists the value of a theory is not dependent on the truth and falsity of its premises: effectiveness is what matters. Friedman's anti-realist dictum (in Bennett 2003: 14) is an (in)famous summation of this position: "[T]he relevant question to ask about the 'assumptions' of a theory is not whether they are descriptively 'realistic,' for they never are, but whether they are sufficiently good approximation to the purpose in hand".

A scientific realist regards, in contrast, theoretical premises as aspiring candidates for truth.[4] The premise of rationality, viewed as a distinct procedure of due consideration, is only appropriately included as a theoretical premise if the agents in question conform to this distinctively specified procedure. A scientific realist would not validate a theory assuming rationality unless it is documented that rational deliberations are causally responsible for the outcomes. Usefulness is of negligible value if the outcomes turn out to be coincidences of sorts.

Furthermore, a scientific realist would want accounts to capture the finest details of causal processes, even if these details sometimes are unobservable. Thus, a sound theory must ideally include all details in the causal chain that are causally responsible for the observations one wants to understand. It follows that the sole aim of science is to reduce the disparity between our interpretations of the world and the real state of affairs as much as possible.

Some argue that scientific realism is unsustainable when applied to theories, as the essential idea behind theoretical modeling is simplification. A common view is that theories are not *supposed* to give as accurate a picture of reality as possible. The goal is instead to cut to the core – to simplify, to focus on what is driving things, to bring out what was really important.

(Trachtenberg 2006: 40–41)

Trachtenberg is correct that models and theories cut to the core in the sense that they extract the presumptive significant features of a phenomenon. Even extractions that do not capture a phenomenon in full, and are by that measure incomplete, may justify a validating judgment if what they say is demonstrably in accordance with the facts. But it is hard to understand how simplifications can be validated unless it can be demonstrated empirically that the "core" supposedly "driving things" translates into accurate real-world observations. Ultimately, even what we think of as simplifications are worth credit only by virtue of the fact that there are features of the world to which the simplification corresponds (cf. Searle 1990: 14).

2.2 A mechanism-centered research strategy

A mechanisms-centered research strategy commits to two distinct goals. The first is to disclose the causal chains that are "hidden" inside statements about general causal regularities. This is what is referred to as "opening up the black box". The second is to identify the causal mechanism responsible for observations of interest. This amounts to an effort to accumulate a catalogue of causal mechanisms, more general than descriptions, but less general than laws, with the capacity to *explain* by subsuming observations under more familiar causal patterns (cf. Elster 1983, 1989, 1993, 1999, 2007). Both goals sit well with the doctrine of scientific realism as they aspire to provide truthful explanations based on micro-process with purchase in the real world.

How is the first goal of a mechanistic research program realized? Consider the statement "poison kills". Even if it corresponded to reality, this law-like regularity would not satisfy a true scientific realist, because the causal links between the explanans (poison) and explanandum (death) are not stipulated. Something is hidden inside the regularity which makes it a paradigmatic black box statement. A scientific realist adhering to a mechanism-centered research strategy would prefer to know the causal processes that made it a true statement, that is, know how exactly poison causes death. For that, the causal chains hidden inside the statistical statement must be explicated. Accounts exhibiting more causal links are more convincing candidates for truth as they stipulate the causal processes producing the strong correlation. This causal account, for example, gives a glimpse inside the black box statement "poison kills":

> Poison deprives the blood of oxygen, leading to cellular brain damage, leading to non-transmission of neural messages across synapses, leading to cessation of breathing and the stoppage of the heart, in the absence of which life is not possible.
>
> (Kaplan 1971: 18–19)

Thus formulated, the regularity between intake of poison and death is less opaque. When it is specified *how* poison kills, we can feel more assured that the relationship is not a coincidental correlation, but that the ingestion of poison is the genuine impetus of the causal chain that leads to death. Knowing this is arguably intellectually more satisfying, because it makes us more *certain* that we are approaching an accurate account of the effect of poison on humans. The chances of spuriousness, i.e., the possibility that an unrelated third cause is responsible for the outcome, are therefore reduced. The "better we focus the causal story, the easier it is to make sure that we are not dealing with mere correlation" (Elster 2007: 35). One can discuss ad infinitum the degree of specification needed to overcome a critical threshold and achieve certainty, but the crux is that certainty is a matter of degree, and causal specification typically heightens it by reducing the danger of unnoticed "third factors".

The main reasons to decompose realism by specifying the causal relationships it implies are that it diminishes the opaqueness of the theory, increases our degree of certainty and reduces the danger of spuriousness. A causally specified version of the theory allows examination of whether its successful predictions are due to accurately posited micro-processes. Whereas the original theory is analogous to the statement "poison kills", the specified repertoire of mechanisms, what I refer to as Mechanistic Realism, aspires to resemble the specification of how poison kills quoted above. It remains an open question whether the specified mechanisms fit the empirical data, but it would anyhow be rash, according to a mechanism-based research program, to validate a theory predicting *macro*-level outcomes before it is documented whether the causal *micro*-processes implied by the theory were acting causally.

The effort to specify and elucidate abstractions is closely related to the reductionist program of "seek[ing] an explanation at a lower level than the explanandum" (Elster 1983: 23). Reductionism implies abstract theories are in trouble if the causal chains they imply at lower levels of abstraction are inconsistent with observations (George and Bennett 2005: 141). Identifying the correct micro-processes is, on this view, crucial since "adequate explanation requires also the specification of hypothesis about causal processes that brought about the observed correlation" (ibid.: 140).

The second goal of a mechanistic research program, namely to accumulate explanatory mechanisms able to dispel observational puzzles, is achieved by distinguishing mechanisms that are recurring causal patterns from laws. Instead of resting explanations on laws of which there are few in the social sciences anyway, mechanisms "explain behaviour by showing it to be an instance of a general causal pattern.... [T]o subsume an individual instance under a more general causal pattern is also to explain it" (Elster 2007: 37). Explanation by mechanisms, at best, suggests both *how* (the dynamic in itself) and *why* (the conditions for its activation) phenomena occur. Since both how and why questions are at the core of the scientific enterprise, it provides a strong argument for a research strategy centered on mechanisms.

While definitions of social mechanism abound, for the purpose of the present study it suffices to say that a causal mechanism is a plausible account of how a cause and effect are linked together (Hedström and Swedberg 1998: 7). A mechanism provides an account of the sequence between two occurrences to the effect of dispelling the puzzle of how the second occurrence came about. Preferably, a mechanistic explanation includes knowledge about the conditions under which one mechanism and not an alternative mechanism was triggered, but this is an ambitious, perhaps a too ambitious, requirement.[5]

Consider an example: realists maintain that states in anarchy are prompted to struggle for power. This regularity rests on the micro-foundation that *uncertainty fosters fear*. Since this is a frequently occurring causal pattern it amounts to a mechanism that sits inside the black box statement that anarchy causes states to struggle for power. Confronted with an individual instance of a decision-maker, faced with uncertainty about other states' motives, who subsequently experiences fear, we can presume we know something about why. The fact that we can subsume the observation under a more general and psychologically plausible causal pattern removes the oddity from the observation and effects an explanation of why fear came about. When the mechanism operates in this manner, it makes the initial realist presumption less opaque.

According to some realists, the mechanism whereby uncertainty fosters fear is not contingent, but closer to a deterministic regularity. However, as has been suggested by other scholars, decision-makers facing uncertainty, rather than experiencing fear, may become complacent. This amounts to a different mechanism, suggesting the same state of mind can trigger a different response. Elster has pointed out that mechanisms often come in mutually exclusive pairs (Elster 2006: 37). The two mechanisms answer how fear and complacency respectively come about after the fact, but since both mechanisms appear plausible, they do not allow us to predict.

Accordingly, prediction requires knowledge about which conditions increase the likelihood of the activation of one or the other mechanism. Historical experience could, for example, be a condition which affects the activation of either mechanism or knowing a decision-maker is inclined towards optimism or pessimism is a type of contextual information that can facilitate prediction. Yet, as uncertainty appears capable of triggering mutually incompatible effects (both fear and complacency), causal mechanisms are not, contrary to laws, sufficient for prediction, enabling explanations only in hindsight.

While Elster welcomes all kinds of mechanistic explanation, others have argued that one type of mechanistic explanation is particularly alluring (Boudon 1998; Malnes 2006). That is the so-called *reason-explanation*.

> Reason-explanations cast light on links in the causal chain that lead to an action – typically desires that make someone crave or care for something and beliefs that draw the agent's attention to specific ways and means of fulfilling her desires.
>
> (Malnes 2006: 182–183)

Reasons meet the definitional requirement of a mechanism: providing a plausible account of how cause and effect are linked. On consideration, there is hardly a better ground for dispelling observational puzzles than reasons because when a "phenomenon is made the outcome of individual reasons, one does not need to ask further questions" (Boudon 1998: 177).[6] Again it is desirable to know something about the conditions under which particular reasons are invoked. This obviously is an insurmountable goal, given the variety of reasons humans offer as grounds for action. Yet, as we shall see in the next chapter, and this is not a far-fetched argument, realism suggests the diversity of reasons is severely constrained by circumstances. Under anarchical circumstances certain reasons are presumably apt to prevail.[7] There are limits to this argument as material conditions are often such that several reasons would suggest themselves. Yet individual reasoning, even if diverse, is still not beyond our conception if we know much about circumstances in which individuals operate, conditioned, of course, by the presumption that the individuals in question are of a rational bent.

If they are, we know a lot about how they typically go about. We know approximately how they collect information, how they form beliefs, how they cope with problems and how they make decisions. This allows us to use ourselves as instruments of comprehension, performing what Schelling (1978/2006: 18) calls the "method of vicarious problem solving". The method is also favored by Holsti (1995: 251), who describes how researchers can come to terms with how political leaders reach decisions:

> In searching for explanations, then, we must place us in the position of the policy makers and try to understand their intentions and purposes, and then understand why they chose various strategies and actions to sustain or achieve them.
>
> (Ibid.)

This method can only indicate how mental states fit together, but constrained by other sources of evidence, it is more fulfilling to make sense of other people's behavior in terms of reasons than in terms of other less transparent cognitive mechanisms since they "impinge on what we do in a transparent manner" and because "acting on a reason is a staple experience" (Malnes 2006: 186).

An example illustrates the point. The number of troops deployed to the Iraq war puzzled many as it, compared to military operations of similar scope, was conspicuously lower. Why? It has been suggested that the mechanism known as wishful thinking can dispel the puzzle. Wishful thinking refers to the recurring phenomenon that a person's desire impinges on her beliefs behind her back. Somehow, to relieve the discomfort generated by realizing the looming challenges and costs of war, it is argued, the Bush administration came to believe that a relatively smaller troop contingent could suffice for the task. They believed wishfully that "once a people is liberated from tyranny, it will automatically endorse democracy irrespective of regional, religious and cultural variations, because liberty is a universal aspiration" (Miller 2010: 60).

Wishful thinking offers an explanation of the puzzle. We know this deviation from rationality from other social situations and know from "vicarious" introspection that dissonance reduction from time to time can (somehow) manifest itself as wishful thinking. But despite being a recurring causal pattern, the mechanism does not dispel the puzzle completely, as we immediately come to wonder how particular cases of self-deceit occur. On consideration, the mechanism of wishful thinking is almost as puzzling as the phenomenon it seeks to explain.

In contrast, an explanation of the puzzle anchored in reasons brings about more complete understanding. The low number of troops was due to new thinking within the military, embodied by the Defense Minister, it has been suggested (Kaplan 2008: 49). The troop estimates were developed from the assumption that advanced technology and blitzing speed reduced the need for manpower (Ricks 2007: 34). This explanation resting on reasons dispels the puzzle more completely, because it also makes sense of the action. Compared to recurring patterns beyond full comprehension, such as wishful thinking, alluding to reasons makes us fully satisfied with the explanation, as equally perplexing follow-up questions do not arise.

In what follows, I will utilize mechanistic explanations anchored in reason, but not stray from non-reason mechanisms. Having said that, in the latter case I will strive to account for, often drawing on theoretical knowledge, why the regularity in question comes about and makes the invoked mechanism, to the extent possible, not as strange as the puzzle it is meant to dispel.

Let me finally underline two additional attractions of a mechanistic-centered research program. First, centering attention on presumptive mechanisms makes it easier to embark on empirical scrutiny. This is fundamentally an epistemological feature of mechanisms. They are, by Elster's definition, "easily recognizable". The mechanism alluded to earlier, i.e., uncertainty fosters fear, which is capable of dispelling the puzzle of why limited information generates alarm, is, for example, relatively recognizable. While there are exceptions to this rule, mechanisms are effective guides to empirical investigation as they lend focus to empirical scrutiny by suggesting what to ponder and where to start looking in the historical material.[8]

Yet, the extent to which mechanisms are "easily recognizable" arguably varies depending on the subject matter being studied. Both the task to isolate a distinct mechanism and the task of specifying the conditions under which a mechanism is activated are typically made more challenging by complexity. Therefore, cases in which the level of complexity is reduced by features of the situation are attractive for mechanistic analysis. The situation in the US after 9/11 is such a case. It is apt for mechanistic analysis of security reasoning precisely because the context was *synoptic* in the sense of isolating the very variables that influence security reasoning and revealing how decision-makers reasoned under precarious circumstances. Otherwise, disguised mechanisms under the influence of which security policy is shaped would presumably be easier to recognize after a security crisis such as 9/11, providing an epistemological reason for applying Mechanistic Realism to this case.

Second, a mechanism-centered research strategy can resolve indeterminacies within a theory and disputes between competing theories. Some realists find states facing uncertainty about the motives of other states more prone to worst-case thinking. Simultaneously, they suggest states are rational agents, which implies that they act on estimates of average utility. These two claims are incompatible. You cannot, as a state leader, both assume the worst and try to figure out the likelihood of others doing you harm. Instead of criticizing realists for inconsistency in holding both positions, we could instead interpret them as suggesting that two mechanisms are existing but activated under different conditions. Sometimes worst-case considerations prevail, sometimes calculated expected utility holds sway.

Likewise, theoretical disputes can be resolved by allowing for the existence of more, even contrary, mechanisms. Within the realist theory tradition there are competing accounts of the behavioral consequences of fear. Offensive Realists, like Mearsheimer, hold that fear typically elicits expansionist behavior while defensive realists, like Kenneth Waltz, maintain in contrast that fear typically triggers defensive behavior. Instead of viewing Mearsheimer's and Waltz's accounts as incompatible one may interpret the dispute as implying that either mechanism can be triggered, but on different occasions. A mechanism-centered approach would assume that both mechanisms deserve a place in the toolbox and would recommend attempts to identify the conditions under which one or the other mechanism is activated instead of engaging in unfruitful debates that basically see the proposals as irreconcilable.

More generally, the accumulation of explanatory mechanism is principally agnostic about schools of thought, the one often pitted against the other as if competing for primacy. The toolbox of mechanisms will likely draw on theoretical insights that typically are considered impossible to merge. Katzenstein and Okawara (2001/2002: 154) write:

> The complex links between power, interests, and norms defy analytical capture by any one paradigm. They are made more intelligible by drawing selectively on different paradigms – that is, by analytical eclecticisms, not parsimony.

A mechanism-centered research strategy is a fruitful way of heeding this call. The separation of the IR field into contending schools of thought does not sit well with an emphasis on explanation via causal mechanisms that may cut across these schools (George and Bennett 2005: 127–128).

2.3 Methodological individualism

Adherence to scientific realism and mechanism-based explanations entails a commitment to the doctrine of *reductionism*, which, roughly speaking, is the view that complex phenomena are reducible and larger phenomena can be explained by simpler ones (Elster 1983: 23). For the IR sciences, the doctrine of reductionism presumably leads all the way from the systemic level down to the level of chemical reactions in the brains of decision-makers. For the foreseeable future it is impossible to conduct political analysis at the neuro-scientific level as we lack proper instruments and mature measurement techniques. Currently, individuals and their psychology arguably comprise the appropriate unit of explanation of state conduct. Although this may sound trite, it is worth accentuating simply because many IR scholars are generally reticent on this point. Alexander Wendt (1999: 10), for instance, holds "that states are actors with more or less human qualities: intentionality, rationality, interests, etc. ... I shall argue that states *really are* agents".

The view according to which, at one point or another, all social macro phenomena, such as arms races, balance of power politics, revolutions, power maximizing and wars of aggression, can be reduced to individual human action is known as *methodological individualism* (Elster 1989: 13). This program is inspired by how other sciences have made progress. Identifying the elementary units responsible for observed phenomena characterizes the procedure of all sciences and, as far as the social sciences are concerned, individuals comprise the elementary unit (Boudon 2006: 25).

Sometimes, however, individuals face physical as well as manmade constraints of such formidable proportions, they would arguably overwhelm the significance of other variables. This leads some social scientists to conclude that it is more important to understand constraints than to understand the cast of mind of the individuals facing them (Satz and Ferejohn 1994). Realism is a case in point as the theory assumes that structural constraints are causally more relevant than state or particular characteristics in international politics:

> Structural factors ... are what matter most for explaining international politics. The theory pays little attention to individuals and domestic political considerations.
>
> (Mearsheimer 2001: 10–11)

This view, however, is no rejection of methodological individualism. It claims, rather, that constraints have more explanatory relevance than variables at other levels of analysis. The above quote suggests that the conditions under which international politics take place limit the opportunity sets of individual decision-makers to such a degree that there is virtually no room left for other variables to shape the policies. Although controversial, the simplification sits well with the view that individuals, typically those with executive power, are ontologically speaking the acting agents. Even if the anarchic structure is the most causally effective variable in foreign policy decision-making, it must still operate through considerations of individuals.

Throughout the book from which the above quote is taken, especially in the empirical parts of it, the commitment to individual anchoring becomes apparent. The following quotes are illustrative:

Foundations for social analysis 31

> There should be little evidence of *policymakers* saying that they are satisfied with their share of world power ... we should always find *leaders* thinking it is imperative to gain more power to enhance their state's prospects for survival.
>
> (Ibid.: 169 my italics)

> [T]here is considerable evidence that *policymakers* in these states talked and thought like offensive realists ... [and] hard to find evidence of *key leaders* expressing satisfaction with the existing balance of power.
>
> (Ibid.: 170 my italics)

> Italian policymakers were motivated to be aggressive in large part by balance of power considerations.
>
> (Ibid.: 171)

Mearsheimer sometimes even demonstrates his commitment to methodological individualism by invoking psychological discomfort on the part of the decision-makers as a precursor to behavior conforming to his theory. When defending the proposition that concerns with narrow self-interest trump idealist concerns, he brings up an incident in Somalia in 1992–1993, where eighteen US soldiers were killed in action on a so-called humanitarian mission. As this mission did not pay off well from a national security perspective, the incident "so *traumatized American policymakers* that they immediately pulled all US troops out of Somalia" (ibid.: 47, my italics).

Such evidence squares well with the program of methodological individualism in its attempts to make explicit the mental states that caused a consequential decision. In acknowledging that individual policymakers and their state of mind constitute the impetus of state action, Mearsheimer demonstrates an understanding on his part that the validity of his theory is dependent on the extent to which the psychological reactions of the policymakers are congruent with what his theory implies. Giving attention to the state of mind of US decision-makers as they reacted to the incident in Somalia nicely shows how individual anchoring works as a bulwark against structural explanations unconcerned with individual motivation. Believing some factors are explanatorily relevant, gives no warrant to escape individually anchored justifications as "there can be no 'state behavior' except as the term is used to describe the combined behavior of individual human beings organized into the state" (Wolfers 1962: 8).

Moreover, the example demonstrates there is nothing intrinsically wrong with arguments suggesting constraints are explananda (the most relevant explanatory factor or independent variable), and the individual decisions the explanans (what one wants explained or the dependent variable), as long as it is stipulated why and how constraints explain individual actions. But seeing outcomes as preordained by constraints is unwarranted if it cannot be documented empirically whether individuals in fact are regulated by the constraints. Analysts, say, relying on the explanatory capacity of the logic of the security dilemma, must, if state A arms, still verify that individuals within state A decided to do so in response to equalize the armament of state B. Someone within state A must demonstrably desire more arms because state B has acquired them and have the opportunities to bring that desire to fruition. Without individual anchoring the logic of the security dilemma is just speculation. Claiming that arms races are explained by the fact that all social systems favor *equilibrium*, thereby implying that one state's armament inevitably instigates armament on the part of another to restore the equilibrium, is no viable alternative as functionalist explanations (suggesting the consequences explain the cause) are of little worth as a "goal without a subject for whom it is a goal is an incoherent notion" (Elster 1981).

The conception of individual action as a function of the conditions raises questions about the link between environmental constraints and individual cognition. One may ask whether it is justified to maintain that structures regulate behavior if the individuals in question are unaware of the constraints. The answer, it seems, depends on the nature of the constraint.

Some constraints are regulative regardless of individual cognition. Playing the bar game "Fussball" on a heavily tilted play-board determines the result of the game. The perceptions of the players have no bearing on the course of events or result. Likewise, the finite number of American soldiers constrains the President's freedom of troop deployment as troop numbers are not contingent on his thoughts or perceptions. Such material facts remain what they are even if individuals think of them differently.

Then there are manmade constraints, such as social norms, regulating behavior even when individual cognition appears negligible. The regulating force is often conditioned on a tacit internalized habit nurtured by the unpleasant experience of formal or informal sanctions unleashed when the norms are defied. Although these structures sometimes appear independent of cognition, they are, on inspection, dependent on it. They cease to exist as regulators if individuals start to think of them differently and aberration from the norms is no longer sanctioned.

Then there are structures that unquestionably are real, but still depend on cognition to regulate behavior. Consider a burning building (Wolfers 1962: 13). It constitutes an external compulsion on individuals. Regardless of psychological idiosyncrasies, the external condition prompts all rational individuals to seek an exit. But unlike material barriers such as number of soldiers or tilted playing field, a house on fire is only an effective material regulator if the individuals inside conceive of the structure as compelling a certain action. There needs to be a link that connects the structure to the human cognition. Without that link the structure would presumably be an ineffective instigator of actions. A sleeping person would not regard the situation as a threat and would likely burn inside.

Realists appear to see the anarchic structure of the international system as a regulating factor on a par with a burning house. States are prompted to maximize power because their security is always at risk in an environment of offensive military capacities, potentially hostile intentions and no higher authority on which to call for help. But for anarchy to be a determining factor the situation has to be perceived as perilous and the decision-makers have to interpret the material reality of anarchy as compelling certain actions. If that link exists, we are correct to assume that structures instigate individual actions. If not, the idea is in trouble.

While anarchy is an ordering structure independent of how it is perceived, and while the perceptions have no bearing on whether a system has a higher authority or not, the consequences of anarchy are nevertheless affected by how the anarchic social ordering is conceived by the involved agents. The consequences of anarchy must therefore clearly depend on how the affected individuals experience the situation. Even if the range of possible beliefs about factual matters can be very wide indeed, one would think the chance of anyone vested with political power in the world arriving at a belief that the international system is not an anarchy, but rather resembles a well-ordered state, is negligible. Obviously, the agents vested with political power need not describe the structure and the external compulsion with the analytical clarity of realists. One would expect social scientists to have an edge on precision. All the commitment to the principle of methodological individualism entails is for the motives, reasons, desires and beliefs which the policymakers view as compelling in this situation, to relate to the external social order in a manner consistent with what realism implies.

2.4 Conducting mechanistic analysis

While alluring in principle, identifying causal mechanisms empirically is obviously challenging as causal connections, what Hume (in Audi 1999: 125) famously called "the cement of the universe", are not directly observable. One difficulty is to know when a mechanism springs out from detailed descriptions of causal relations. How are we, in short, to distinguish mechanisms from mere descriptions? George and Bennett (2005) suggest a method called *process tracing* is apt. They expand on the method thus:

> In process-tracing, the researcher examines histories, archival documents, interview transcripts, and other sources to see whether the causal process a theory hypothesizes or implies in a case is in fact evident in the sequence and values of intervening variables in that case.
>
> (Ibid.: 6)

Process tracing appears to be an appropriate methodological procedure for attempting to verify causal mechanisms. At some point, it seems, meticulous storytelling warrants inference of a maxim. However, while the method surely highlights how careful scrutiny of the available data can narrow the list of efficacious explanatory factors, it is reticent about at which point the examination of the *process* allows us to infer the existence of an explanatory mechanism. George and Bennett's employment of the verb "see" suggests they underestimate the difficulty of the task, as the distinct feature of causality is exactly that it cannot be seen.

On this score, Elster's (2007: 37) suggestion, while struggling with the same difficulty, is more elaborate. Showing a description to be an instance of a more general and recurring causal pattern removes, in his view, some of the opaqueness of the description, although complete intellectual satisfaction remains a vain hope since it is difficult to give a complete account of why a certain pattern occurs. Throughout this book I have followed Elster in attempting to examine whether the detailed sequence of events (i.e., processes) inside the Bush administration can be subsumed under the more general and frequently occurring causal patterns suggested by Mechanistic Realism. The viability of this approach rests on Elster's premise that "to subsume an individual instance under a more general pattern is also to provide an explanation" (Elster 2007: 37). When, for example, examination of the historical record reveals individuals for whom "the absence of solid information on additional threats was terrifying" (Tenet 2007: 342), this individual observation can be subsumed under the fear-fostering mechanism included in Mechanistic Realism whereby "uncertainty fosters fear". That being the case, the observation's opacity is diminished according to Elster's argument.

However, one may reasonably object that without documenting why a mechanism occurs and what condition triggers it we have not provided an explanation, but rather an empty statement iterating the observation in more general terms. After all, one could argue that the "observation that an action is somehow typical – that it falls into a pattern – sheds light on it only if the pattern is not equally in need of explanation" (Malnes 2006: 184). The objection is indeed warranted. Yet three arguments reduce its sting.

First, although descriptions provide us with the empirical sequence suggesting "what" happened, a satisfying explanation would also require an indication of what *connected* the data points in the sequence, that is, "why" one event followed the other. Mechanisms, in Elster's definition, offer these connections by appealing to the somewhat imprecise notion of *familiarity*. Even if appeals to the sense that a causal connection fits into a *familiar* pattern are not completely satisfactory, invocation of a frequently observed connection is still apt to stop an inquirer from asking further questions. By knowing that two events have previously been repeatedly connected in a particular way, such as uncertainty and fear, we can feel more confident in our supposition that the observations we now encounter are connected, and thus explained, in the same way. Accordingly, equipped with a repertoire of familiar mechanisms, we can more confidently make causal assumptions about the psychological reactions of decision-makers precisely because we have noticed the efficacy of these mechanisms form similar cases previously. Without knowledge of the pre-existing mechanism, we would have greater doubts regarding our causal hypothesis. This higher degree of confidence is why mechanistic explanations add value compared to mere descriptions, even if the mechanism invoked defies our full grasp.

Second, because there are innumerable observations that might be considered causally significant in a given case, the clutter that accompanies a detailed historical retelling can hinder comprehension of complex events. The empirical richness of some narratives is simply overwhelming. However, by invoking mechanisms it becomes easier to distill the observations that are fundamental and pertinent to causality from the rich detail of the descriptions. Because mechanisms provide a means of sorting the empirical data and reducing the details to the significant core, they facilitate understanding. Accordingly, noticing from the plethora of details that individuals experienced the "absence of solid information on additional threats as terrifying" becomes a more important piece of empirical data once the causal mechanism "uncertainty fosters fear" is known and invoked.

Third, since the mechanisms contained in Mechanistic Realism are translated from more fundamental premises about the character of the international system, the causal patterns invoked have been accounted for and are therefore not *equally* in need of explanation. Mechanistic Realism is apt to explain precisely because the assumptions from which the mechanisms are derived require less explanation than the observations on which they shed light. That the causal patterns of Mechanistic Realism are wedded to a more general theory gives a tiny assurance that the occurrence of the mechanism is no coincidence. It provides us with an account of why seemingly inexplicable causal patterns, such as uncertainty fosters fear, emerge in the first place and therefore facilitates a higher degree of comprehension. While the assurance may be frail, it is still better than no assurance.

Another challenge of mechanistic analysis, which occurs after a mechanism is identified, is that of "confirmation bias" (George and Bennett 2005: 217). The criteria used for including an observation as *evidence* of a mechanism may shape the conclusions one arrives at. The malpractice of cherry-picking evidence to confirm posited mechanisms will lead researchers to overstate the causal weight accorded to it. This danger is particularly salient since mechanisms, as noted above, are apt to sort the messy empirical data. Bryman (in Silverman 2008: 211) points out how

> Brief conversation, snippets from unstructured interviews ... are used to provide evidence of a particular contention. There are grounds for disquiet in that the representativeness or generality of these fragments are rarely addressed.

The bulwark against confirmation bias is to uphold the ideal of representativeness, an ideal achieved if the conclusions drawn from the sampled data would have been similar if the entire universe of data had been studied. Representativeness is distorted if anecdotal examples that concur with preconceived beliefs or fit a purpose other than truthfulness are taken to connote the entire universe. The problem of selection bias is possibly most acute in theoretically informed studies. Admittedly, Mechanistic Realism directs attention to a limited set of variables which need not, in a given case, be the decisive ones. This potential inferential trap therefore deserves special comment.

Few would dispute that objective knowledge is the goal of science. For sure, some object to this. Trachtenberg (2006: 7–14), discussing the so-called "constructionist challenge", refers to Hayden White for whom there is no difference between history writing and myth making. In White's view, historians perform "an essentially poetic act" (ibid.: 8), which obviously deprives any historical description of a claim to objectivity. These positions are exceptional, however. As Hacking (1999: 4) concludes, unconditional statements of relativism, i.e., the view that truth only resides in the eye of the beholder, "are hard to find". Yet, questions of objectivity often surface when theories are utilized for analytical purposes. But does it harm objectivity to utilize theoretical knowledge, in this case Mechanistic Realism, for empirical analysis?

Some clearly think so. David Silverman (2008) is arguing that the theory one chooses is bound to be confirmed.

> [M]odels, concepts and theories are self-confirming in that they instruct us to look at phenomena in particular ways. This means that they can never be disproved but only found to be more or less useful.
>
> (Ibid.: 99)

Under this view the use of theories cannot be reconciled with an ideal of objectivity. The theory you pick determines the conclusion you reach as it inevitably leads the researcher to confirming evidence. Accordingly, theories are never discarded. In order to understand why a researcher arrives at a certain conclusion rather than confront her evidence, one should analyze her initial choice of theory. This is hardly a defendable view, as it suggests the hypothetical deductive method is never practiced with success. As Popper (2007: 144) points out, the public character of science and the fact that ideas are constantly criticized "imposes a mental discipline on the individual scientist". Ideas at odds with evidence will have a short life in a critical environment, especially when they smack of prejudice and theoretical fidelity.

A more moderate rejection of objectivity finds observations not so much self-confirming as "theory-laden". This is the view of Alexander Wendt (1999), who thinks prejudice is always involved when mechanisms, what he calls "unobservables", are interpreted.

> In the long run, empirical work may help us decide which conceptualization [of the world] is best, but the "observation" of unobservables is always theory-laden, involving an inherent gap between theory and reality.
>
> (Ibid.: 5)

Wendt's view is widespread. Many scholars who reject relativism still argue that observations are theory-laden. Jack Levy (1997: 26), for example, takes this to be conventional wisdom.

> The argument that all empirical observations are filtered through a priori mental frameworks and that explanations are necessarily based on underlying theoretical assumptions and concepts is now conventional wisdom in both political science and history.

Haber *et al.* (1997: 37) maintain likewise that this is the consensus view.

[M]ost would not resist the claim that their observations are theory laden....
Naïve positivism, in which the world is assumed simply to speak for itself,
is not one of the claims of contemporary social science.

However, the view that all observations are theory-laden is, as Malnes (2008: 9) points out, hard to reconcile with ordinary experience. When I observe someone crying and infer that she is sad, neither the observation nor my assumption is laden with much theory (ibid.). Although the tendency to attach particular weight to observations that support pre-existing beliefs and to ignore inconvenient evidence is a problem with empirical merit, it must not be exaggerated. The social world is frequently merciless to theory-laden conclusions by displaying facts which are impossible to ignore and impossible to reconcile with simplistic views.

To take an example. Beliefs are apt to differ among scholars adhering to different IR theories when it comes to things that render the international system different from a pure anarchy. It could be the role played by international law and organizations like the UN (United Nations). Variations on this score reflect the plurality of reasonable interpretations to which the overall evidence is amenable. Yet it is impossible to take the observation that the US ignored the UN Security Council before the Iraq war as anything but an indication that the international system in important respects differs from a well-ordered state. Any theory-laden attempt to arrive at a different conclusion is bound to fail as researchers steeped in norms of accountability and trained to counteract intellectual imperfections would refuse to stand by a belief shown to be false by contradictory evidence. In that sense, theoretical beliefs are self-corrigible even if observations are bound up with theoretical expectations.

This study is a case in point. Even if Mechanistic Realism leaves no room for idealism to influence the formulation of foreign policy, the number of statements made by members of the administration and scholars invoking this fact as important makes it impossible to scrutinize the case without probing the validity of idealist explanations. Any scholar failing to discuss idealism in this case will struggle to ward off the criticism that he has ignored a potentially important causal factor. In that sense, evidence asserts a profound influence of what ought to be discussed.

This is not to deny the origin of most explorations in a preconceived and consciously chosen point of view – for which there exist alternatives. Popper (2007) writes:

> For in theoretical science laws act, among other things, as centres of interest to which observations are related, or as points of view from which observations are made.... This does not mean that we may twist the facts until they fit into a framework of preconceived ideas, or that we may neglect the facts that do not fit. On the contrary, all available evidence which has bearing on our point of view should be considered carefully and objectively.... But it means that we need not worry about all those facts and

aspects which have no bearing upon our point of view and which therefore do not interest us.

(Ibid.: 138–139)

A point of view adopted to help navigate the sea of empirical data will influence an analysis, as it narrows the list of causal processes of presumed importance. Take the motive of fear. Following Mechanistic Realism, understanding fear is a necessary requirement to understanding foreign policy decisions. Evidence ascribing causal weight to fear will have a bearing on the point of view of Mechanistic Realism, and this presumption will make me fasten on evidence to this effect. However, demonstrating empirically that fear was a motivating factor amounts only to a tentative judgment that must be confronted with an objectivity test to ensure that the judgment is not theory-laden. One such test is introduced by Dagfinn Føllesdal (2006: 78):

> Something is objective if the answer to the following question is no: "Is there information/data ... that are not included, but which, if they had been included would have changed the beliefs and attitudes of the receiver?"

If there exists information that would have corrected the tentative judgment that fear was a motivating factor, it must be brought to the fore. If not, the conclusion fails the objectivity test.

Typically, however, there will be room for scholarly controversy and many interpretations will remain moot and open to dispute. Lack of consensus, though, does not owe so much to theory-laden observation (the fact, say, that a researcher fastens onto occurrences in which fear appeared to sway decisions), or lack of objectivity (failure to comment on features that would have changed the belief of a receiver), as to the fact that the evidence is open to different but equally reasonable interpretations. Because imputation of motives and reasons is central to most social science, and also required to verify Mechanistic Realism, and because such imputations are always only suggestive, the research community is likely to remain in epistemological limbo. That does not denote a failure of objectivity, but underscores that ultimate verification is an unattainable goal for social sciences and that in the end, the "game of science is, in principle, without end" (Popper 2009: 32).

2.5 Conclusion

The above arguments point to the same conclusion about how realism ought to be utilized for empirical investigation. Only through a decomposition of this structural theory can one hope to stay true to the assumptions spelled out in this chapter. The interpretation of realism that I am about to offer carves out a *repertoire of causal mechanisms* affecting *individual decision-makers* that supposedly *correspond to the political reality*. It is to the rendering of Mechanistic Realism that I now turn.

3 Mechanistic Realism

The aim of this chapter is to make use of the precepts explicated in the previous chapter to derive a catalogue of realist mechanisms. The following exploration starts from the supposition that while realism in its traditional formulation contains valid propositions, it remains incomplete or preliminary in the sense that its premises permit us to say more about individual-level psychology than is commonly done. The added value of Mechanistic Realism is to spell out the more fine-grained implications that realist premises permit to the effect of making realism more specific, less opaque and empirically more incisive.

In order to do so, I shall use John Mearsheimer's version of realism, known as Offensive Realism, as a point of reference. There are several reasons for this choice. First, Mearsheimer's is the newest formulation in the annals of realism, and his 2001 book *The Tragedy of Great Power Politics* was "immediately hailed as a classic that deserved to supersede the works of Morgenthau and Waltz in the core canon of realist literature" (Little 2007: 213). Clearly, since the book is considered a "major theoretical advance" (Snyder 2002: 150), with "striking operational clarity" (Boot and Wheeler 2008: 35), any attempt to invigorate realism would have to engage Mearsheimer's rendition.

Second, Mearsheimer's version of realism is not only a systemic theory of international politics that explains "why a certain similarity of behavior is expected from similarly situated states" (Waltz 1979: 122), but also a theory of foreign policy that explains state action by accounting for, sometimes rather crudely, how decision-makers think and act. As Little (2007: 217) rightly observes, "whereas Waltz acknowledges that his theory can only throw light on systemic processes, Mearsheimer insists that his theory helps to illuminate the foreign policy orientation of individual states". It is, in short, less abstract – indeed a valuable feature given my ambition to take realism to the lowest level of abstraction possible. To the extent that the ambition to come to terms with the causal and intentional links at the individual level, i.e., the mental precursor of actions, is worth pursuing, Mearsheimer is a better point of reference than Waltz, whose theory is concerned with "outcomes" rather than decision-making.

Third, although realism is a school of thought of which there exist numerous instructive syntheses that could have been used as reference points, some detail is typically lost in such integrative renderings. That being the case, it is analytically rewarding to embark on a theoretical revamp from a *pure benchmark*. Offensive Realism stands out as the most viable benchmark as it is the most logically coherent version of realism available in the sense that it begets *conclusive* propositions. By conclusiveness I refer to how readily theoretical assumptions can, by performing the operations built into the model, be translated into operational terms (cf. Underdal 1984: 73), and Offensive Realism scores high on that criterion. Ultimately, however, being a catalogue of mechanism rather than a general theory, Mechanistic Realism will be equally irreverent to all types of realism, as it fundamentally rejects the grand theory aspirations of the realist tradition in favor of the more modest attempt at collecting plausible, explanatory and promising, but still contingent, mechanisms to a toolbox.

For these reasons, the first part of the chapter accounts for the bedrock assumptions of Offensive Realism, displays the notional implications of these assumptions for state behavior and outlines the presumed consequences for international politics. For an oversight of the theory, I present it in its most condensed form, as a set of terse propositions. While the facsimile indeed mirrors Mearsheimer's original statement, it is not redundant as I both elaborate on the premises and identify some points of contestation.

Following this, I will spell out as detailed an account of the mental mechanisms that are assumed to determine the conduct of foreign policy decision-makers as the realist premises permit. Although the catalogue is intellectually indebted to Offensive Realism, the content and plausibility of the mechanisms will throughout be judged on their own merit. Importantly, as I have no scruples about being unfaithful to the theoretical benchmark, this judgment sometimes leads me to suggest the inclusion of mechanisms that stray from the premises of Offensive Realism.

Crucially, Mechanistic Realism is more apt for individual-level analysis than any other formulation of realism. It exposes the causal micro-processes expected to permeate the thinking and psychological life of the decision-makers of any state, hereby disclosing what sits inside statistical black-box statements proposed by realists, the most prominent being that fearful states in anarchy struggle for power. This exposition focuses the realist causal story and reduces the spatial and temporal sequence between the assumptions of realism and state behavior and displays the mechanisms responsible for a state's behavior in a sharper light. Herein lies the value added of the framework. Although one could always wish for even finer specification, the catalogued mechanisms render the abstract features of realism more concrete, allowing for in-depth analysis of psychological processes taking place among individual decision-makers inside the black box.

3.1 Offensive Realism

Offensive Realism aspires to explain the foreign policies of all states, but explaining the conduct of those "with the greatest capability", the so-called great powers, is the theory's prime concern.[1]

Mearsheimer (2011: 11) maintains Offensive Realism "is mainly a descriptive theory. It explains how great powers have behaved in the past and how they are likely to behave in the future". He further asserts, "it is also a prescriptive theory. States *should* behave according to the dictates of offensive realism, because it outlines the best way to survive in a dangerous world" (ibid.: 11). I will be viewing the theory not "mainly", but *solely* as a descriptive theory. This view is, on closer consideration, more consistent. In fact, the theory cannot, strictly speaking, be both. Ultimately, the theory's descriptive validity hinges on the premise that states need no encouragement (for example from Mearsheimer) in order to abide by it. One essential precept is exactly that states are *prompted* by anarchy to act more or less concordant with the theory. If states' international conduct had corresponded to the theory because of a desire on the part of the politicians to abide by the theory, not because of the enunciated structural constraints, it would have suggested another causal story and, hence, invalidated the original theory. If, against all odds, Offensive Realism was proven correct because policymakers of powerful states chose to conform to Mearsheimer's ideas, it would have been a sensational example of a self-fulfilling prophesy, unheard of, as far as I know, in the annals of political science.

Five bedrock assumptions comprise the axioms from which all empirical expectations flow: (1) the international system is anarchic; (2) states possess offensive military capability; (3) states are uncertain about other states' intentions; (4) survival is the primary goal of states; and (5) states are rational actors (Mearsheimer 2001: 30–31). The substance of each assumption deserves comment.

1 Contrary to common parlance, anarchy is not synonymous with conflict or chaos: it is an ordering principle of units within a system. A system is anarchically ordered if there is no governing authority above the units, in which case the system would have been hierarchically ordered. States are the units of the international system and sovereignty inheres only in them. Since no authority or government exists above states, the system is anarchic. Although the consequences of this order can be reasonably debated, its existence cannot. Anarchy is a matter of fact regardless of perceptions, and cognitions have no bearing on the material reality of this particular social order, even if some have suggested otherwise (Wendt 1992).

Were a supra-state authority established, anarchy would dissolve, that is, if the "the states that make up the system agree to form a world government" (Mearsheimer 2001: xii). Such an establishment would convert the international system into a social system resembling a well-ordered state. Alternatively, anarchy ceases to be an ordering principle if one state takes control of the entire system against the wishes of all other states, in which case a world hegemon would have been established. Until one of these transformations occurs, anarchy remains a structuring condition of international politics.

2 Possession of offensive military capability denotes a state's wherewithal to harm other states, force them into compliance, wage war and annex other states' territory. Indeed, states can rely on several resources to get their way.

Although Offensive Realism implies that all resources at a state's disposal are utilized to promote its security interests, the theory purports offensive military capability to be the most important means to this effect. Military capability gives destructive power to force other states to sacrifice values they cherish, the most important being security. Mearsheimer (2001: 55) maintains that "a state's effective power is ultimately a function of its military forces and how they compare with the military forces of other rival states". Moreover, using military force to achieve intended effects "is considered an acceptable instrument of statecraft" (ibid.: 18). As capabilities are the most reliable indicator of power, states pay careful attention to other states' possession thereof.

Even though defensive and offensive weapons differ in principle, what the difference comprises is often vague, and hence, hard to pin down. Moreover, arms procured for defensive purposes, say a shield, often enhance the state's offensive capacity as well. Mearsheimer echoes here a point often ascribed to Jervis (1976: 69): even if the distinction between defensive and offensive weapons is clear and definite from the point of view of those who build up armaments, the distinction is not that obvious to observers in other states. Therefore, there is no way to draw infallible inferences about defensive motivation based on observations of presumably defensive weapons. In Mearsheimer's (2006: 123) formulation it is impossible to "signal type": perceived military capability, even if procured for self-protective purposes only, is viewed as offensive in scope.

3 Uncertainty about the intentions of others refers to the impossibility of ascertaining the beliefs underlying such considerations that are taking place in the minds of decision-makers in other states. This irresolvable uncertainty is often referred to as "the other mind problem" (Boot and Wheeler 2008: 4). Although it is possible to increase confidence by exchanging signals of amity to the effect of marginalizing the uncertainty, the crux of this assumption remains the impossibility of eliminating the chance that ostensibly friendly signals are actually deceptive and aimed to conceal and/or temporarily disguise enmity: "Specifically, no state can be sure that another state will not use its offensive military capability to attack the first state" (Mearsheimer 2001: 31).

This irresolvable uncertainty does not mean that a state's intentions will always be hostile, but that as long there is ground for uncertainty, it would be imprudent for states to work from sanguine assumptions as they may be wrong. Even more so as intentions can change. A treaty of non-aggression that is agreed upon one day, may conceivably be violated the next. Uncertainty is therefore an inevitable feature of interstate politics and makes states liable to make *worst-case assumptions* about the other states' intent. As Boot and Wheeler (2008: 37) note, for Mearsheimer "the dilemma of interpretation must be resolved fatalistically by assuming the worst about the intentions of those that can do harm".

4 Survival refers to a state's material interest in continued existence. That survival is the primary motive of states is tantamount to saying that survival

ranks highest in the hierarchy of state goals. This harmless motive is what elicits concerns with security. Protecting the state's sovereignty and territorial integrity trumps all other motives in motivational conflicts: all other conceivable state objectives are subordinated to, and at the same time also dependent on, states never putting their survival at risk.

Mearsheimer recognizes that states at times pursue non-security goals and cherish values other than security, such as ideology, national unification, social welfare or human rights, but the realization of non-security goals is always subordinate to that of survival and will only be pursued when requisite actions do not conflict with power calculations. Hence, concerns about security get first priority, whereas other goals, if at all pursued, have secondary status. Mearsheimer, however, does not explain how non-security motives enter into decision-makers' minds.

5   Without the rational choice assumption, Offensive Realism would not have had much to say about state behavior as it is a necessary component of any structural explanation (Parsons 2007: 52–56). As Thomas Schelling (1960/1980: 4) notes: "The premise of 'rational behavior' is a potent one for the production of theory". Indeed, the rational actor assumption accompanies (almost) all empirical deductions from the theory. I put "almost" in brackets because Offensive Realism can also be interpreted in terms of genuine situational determinism under which the anarchical constraints reduce the options available to states to one only. In this case, of course, the rational choice assumption would be redundant because there would be no *choice* to be made. More realistically, the number of options is limited by constraints, but never to such an extreme. The rational actor premise is therefore crucial.

The rationality assumption can be described and explained in detail. For now, let a general characterization of rational agency suffice. An agent is rational to the extent that he chooses the action that best realizes his desires, given his beliefs, which are constrained by available and often imperfect information. That is, states consider duly how to survive in the international system in the long and short term and they choose actions that maximize the expected payoff, given their desires.[2]

The rational agent which Mearsheimer purports has some important characteristics that influence how decision-makers cope with ambiguous signals of dangers. Mearsheimer imperceptibly suggests that anarchy mandates a pessimistic and notoriously suspicious style of rational judgment, clearly an inclination with causal impact as it causes decision-makers to favor some reasonable interpretations, typically those with a dismal cast, over others.

There is, therefore, a noteworthy difference between Mearsheimer's and traditional accounts of rationality. Mearsheimer maintains that states scrutinize and keep track of the current balance of power. This is done, we are told, by collecting information about other states' capabilities. Intentions are indeed relevant, but since they are always uncertain, states do not give them much scrutiny, according to Mearsheimer. They simply presuppose they are hostile. Consequently, the *probability* of conflict with a certain country is not given much consideration, compared to the concern with capabilities. This view, of course, runs counter to most versions of rational choice theory, for which the probability of an eventuality is measured carefully and is an important premise for action (cf. Alexander 2007: 43).

By marrying these five assumptions, Mearsheimer (2001: 29) concludes that every state in the system has "considerable reason to think and sometimes behave aggressively". Prompted by the structural conditions, states constantly look for opportunities to take the offensive and maximize relative power as they realize that this is the best survival strategy. In effect, Mearsheimer's extrapolation from the bedrock assumptions amounts to a semi-deterministic account of the consequences of anarchy. I say "semi-deterministic" because Mearsheimer is inconsistent on this issue. Sometimes he maintains that the system leaves states no choice but to behave aggressively if they want to survive. This is pure determinism. At others he maintains that anarchy creates powerful incentives for aggressive behavior. This is a weaker version of structural determinism.

> In sum, my argument is that the structure of the international system, not the particular characteristics of individual great powers, causes them to think and act offensively and to seek hegemony.
>
> (Ibid.: 53)

This war-driving logic is "tragic" because power maximizing and the resulting interstate conflicts run counter to a state's desire for survival. States do not want the conflicts they help create as they simply prefer security. They are neither evil nor possessed by an intrinsic will to power, but merely worried about their continued existence. The security competition and the continuous threat of war are ultimately *suboptimal* to all states in the system. It is an unintended fact of international politics that "survival mandates aggressive behavior ... [and that states] have to seek more power if they want to maximize their odds of survival" (Mearsheimer 2001: 21).

> [T]he structure of the international system forces states which seek only to be secure nonetheless to act aggressively toward each other.... Great powers that have no reason to fight each other – that are merely concerned with their own survival – nevertheless have little choice but to pursue power and to seek to dominate the other states in the system.
>
> (Ibid.: 3)

Although tragic, little can be done to amend the situation. The lack of a sovereign authority with a mandate and the capacity to check offensive behavior prescribes continued uncertainty. Had the states been assured of being rescued in case of foreign aggression, they would have had little reason to fear for their security and future survival. But, contrary to the situation in a well-ordered state, the international system lacks an agency that penalizes state perpetrators. States can only rely on themselves, making the international system a "self-help" system (Mearsheimer 2001: 32).

Moreover, each state knows full well that other states have the capacity and knowledge to produce offensive military capabilities. As all states realize that "force is the *ulitma ratio* of international politics" (ibid.: 56), they come to appreciate the unique utility of military capacity. First, it deters other states from aggression as the costs may outweigh the prospective benefits. Second, it is a necessary instrument of defense if deterrence fails and an adversary attacks. Third, it is an effective means to acquire more power, either through blackmail, coercion or warfighting. As the prospect of survival depends on military possessions no state will fail to acquire them.

Uncertainty about other states bifurcates at this point. First, states become uncertain about how much military capability other states have procured. To mitigate this uncertainty states pay close attention to how capabilities are distributed throughout the system. They also keep a wary eye on other states' "latent power", a term that denotes a state's wealth and population size (Mearsheimer 2001: 55) – the two variables that best indicate potential growth of military power.

> When a state surveys its environment to determine which states pose a threat to its survival, it focuses mainly on the offensive *capabilities* of potential rivals...
>
> (Ibid.: 45)

Second, states become uncertain about the intentions of other states to employ the destructive means they possess. This uncertainty is more profound as it cannot be mitigated by rational vigilance. Since intentions are unknowable, states worried about their survival therefore "make worst case assumptions about their rival's intentions" (Mearsheimer 2001: 45).

The absence of central authority, the existence of offensive military capability, uncertainty about other states' intentions, and the drive to survive foster fear. This is a regularity of fundamental importance to Offensive Realism. Fear is the sole emotional catalyst in the international system. Fear causes states to strive to be as powerful as possible relative to all others. "Strength ensures safety, and the greatest strength is the greatest insurance of safety" (Mearsheimer 2001: xi). The ultimate safety guarantee is to become the hegemon in the system, which denotes a state "that is so powerful that it dominates all the other states in the system" (ibid.: 40). Hegemony is therefore the ultimate goal of every state.

The reasons supporting an expansionist strategy towards hegemony are straightforward. By being relatively more powerful, other states will be deterred from attacking you. If a state is powerful, but uncertainty nevertheless makes it fearsome, it has no compelling reasons to cease its unremitting bid for power until absolute security is reached. It follows there is no such thing as an *appropriate* amount of power, since there is no meaningful way of knowing when the level of appropriateness is reached. On the contrary, the appetite for power is insatiable. Small increments of relative power have equal value, independent of power already achieved, suggesting that states are insensitive to arguments about marginal gains. Even states in a position of considerable power advantage will be revisionist and crave for more. As Snyder (2002: 155) points out, "Mearsheimer's great powers require a surplus of power over 'appropriateness' to cover uncertainties, possible miscalculations, and future surprise".

An unintended consequence of the fact that every state wants to upset the balance of power to its own advantage is that a spiraling conflict of interest ensues.

> All states are influenced by this [power maximizing] logic, which means that not only do they look for opportunities to take advantage over one another, they also work to ensure that other states do not take advantage over them.
>
> (Mearsheimer 2001: 35)

In a system in which every state seeks domination, one state's loss is another state's gain. Power, accordingly, is the currency of a zero-sum game. The measures taken by state A to increase its security automatically decrease the security of the rival state B. This creates a powerful incentive for B to step up investments to acquire more power, creating in doing so the same incentive for A and precipitating a spiral of security competition often referred to as the logic of the security dilemma (somewhat inaccurately, since, as Boot and Wheeler (2008) point out, this is not a dilemma, but a paradox).

However, as Snyder (2002: 155) points out, it is "hard to see any 'dilemma'" since states, according to Mearsheimer (2001: 3), solve it by being "primed on offence". Considering how glad other states would be to take advantage of wanting vigilance and failure to respond in kind, states think "the best defense is a good offense" (ibid.: 36).

> Given the difficulty of determin[ing] how much power [i.e., capabilities] is enough for today and tomorrow, great powers recognize that the best way to ensure their security is to achieve hegemony now, thus *eliminating any possibility of a challenge* by another great power.
>
> (Ibid.: 35, my italics)

Consequently, states stay on the offensive "whenever they think it can be done at a reasonable price" (Mearsheimer 2001: 3). Power maximizing follows from precautionary security concerns, suggesting that the best way to provide security in anarchy is to amass power at others' expense, sometimes by using military means. In consequence, every state has similar preferences, spiraling conflicts become inevitable and the system is pervaded by, if not in a constant state of, war.

There are, however, four caveats which may tame the tendency of power maximization to escalate conflicts. First, states take timing into consideration. "At times, the costs and risks of trying to shift the balance of power are too great, forcing great powers to wait for more favorable circumstances" (Mearsheimer 2001: 3). Second, geography limits a state's power-projecting range. Specifically, Mearsheimer (2001: 40–42) notes "the stopping power of water" by which oceans act as geographical impediments to expansion. Accordingly, states surrounded by water are more status quo-oriented because they feel less threatened as they realize the looming challenge facing other states that consider amphibious power projections. This caveat to the theory is arguably problematic. If it were correct, states separated by oceans would not need to fear each other. Either the theory's validity is restricted to territorially connected states or it has a logical flaw. If it is impossible for states to attain power across water, one would have to wonder why states should worry about great powers far away (cf. Layne 2006: 126). Third, considerations about costs and benefits sometimes temper maximizing initiatives. Expansion is chosen only when the added relative security value exceeds the expected costs. These considerations are related to the nature of power's distribution in the system. Multi-polar systems are supposedly more likely to progress to conflict than bipolar systems, which suggests that individual states are more willing to embark on expansionist policies when power is scattered. Fourth, regional hegemons are reluctant to pursue power maximizing. Their main concern is to prevent other great powers from duplicating their success as regional hegemons in other corners of the world. Given these four caveats, states should be seen not as mindless, but rather "calculating aggressors" (Mearsheimer 2001: 37).

Nevertheless, the tendency certainly works against moderation. Typically a revisionist orientation trumps and "[p]eace, if one defines that concept as a state of tranquility or mutual harmony is not likely to break out in this world" (Mearsheimer 2001: 35).

It is instructive to formulate Offensive Realism as a set of propositions.[3]

1 The international system is anarchic
2 States are the units of the system and behave rationally
3 Survival is the primary goal of states
4 All states are uncertain about other states' intentions ("the other mind problem")
5 All states are aware of the destructiveness of military capabilities and pay close attention to other states' actual and potential military possessions, which they take as evidence of power
6 The combination of propositions 1, 3, 4 and 5 fosters fear, even if threatening signals are weak, inconclusive, virtually absent or open to interpretation
7 The combination of propositions 6 and 2, (i.e., fear and rationality), encourages states to look for opportunities to maximize their share of power, by military means if necessary, because greater power is believed to be the best way to secure own survival

48 *Assumptions and theory*

8 Since all states employ the same logic and prefer dominating the system, a power competition between states ensues
9 One state's gain in the power competition is another state's loss (zero-sum game)
10 Awareness of proposition 9 combined with a concern that other states will succeed in their quest for more power, compels states to pursue policies maximizing their relative power, tightening the spiral of competition
11 Use of military force is considered to be a useful and legitimate way of power maximizing
12 Consequently, the international system is on the brink, or in a state, of war.

3.2 Mechanistic Realism

The above outline describes a realist account of how states act in order to survive in a situation of international anarchy. Propositions 1 to 12 amount to an incisive realist benchmark. Although the decisive causal factors affecting states are exhibited, the outline is taciturn about how the structural constraints impact the mental operations of the decision-makers inside the units. Hovering above the state is a black box animated with human-like characteristics, such as motives, emotions and rational faculties. However, analyzing states *as if* they were agents able to intend, feel, reason and act is an instrumentalist approximation. It is worth asking if, as a scientific realist would prefer, it is possible to explain how the structural antecedents enter into the decision-makers' minds and affect their thinking.[4]

As realism, on the one hand, is committed to "explain events in the real world" (Mearsheimer 2001: 6), such as individual decisions, but, on the other, is not optimally contrived to enable individually anchored, in-depth analyses of the processes leading to state behavior, a theoretical rendering appears required. To the best of my knowledge, a rendering of realism able to guide individual-level analysis does not exist. A theory is only able to guide individual-level analysis if its inferred psychological operations lend themselves to plausible descriptions of frequently occurring causal patterns, or so, at least, I argued in Chapter 2. In this section on Mechanistic Realism I will therefore attempt to translate the realist theory of state behavior into what amounts to a delineation of the building blocks of a psychological theory of foreign policy decision-making. I shall attempt, in other words, to give a more detailed account of the mental mechanisms and the mental operations that are assumed to determine the conduct of individual men and women that act on behalf of their state.

The derived mechanisms arguably differ with respect to psychological plausibility, i.e., how well they conform to more general psychological insights. Some specifications refer to processes that quite obviously affect foreign policy decision-makers; vouching for their individual-level plausibility requires very limited elaboration. Some few of the mechanisms are admittedly little more than fleshed-out paraphrases of realist propositions and not readily corroborated by patterns of mental activity observed elsewhere. As they require a slight stretching of the imagination, they are amendable, and when justified, I shall suggest how they may be amended. Yet other specifications are more than paraphrases. They offer a more precise picture of the mental sequences by which the well-known realist assumptions achieve their effect.

In sum, the entire translation both substantiates the mechanism's micro-level plausibility and eases the task of deducing testable hypotheses. The explication of these frequently occurring causal patterns enables us moreover to account for observations of the processes, policies and actions in a way that removes some of their incipient oddity, and places us in a position to make more informed judgments about the validity of realism.

Mechanism 1: The primacy of security

In anarchy the motive to survive crystallizes as a principal preoccupation with national security and trumps any other potentially conflicting priority.

Survival ranks highest in the hierarchy of decision-makers' goals, implying that security considerations will permeate the thinking of the executives and outweigh all other priorities. Any indication of motivational conflict should have an easy solution: the preservation of national security holds sway. This mechanism is fundamental for all other second-order preferences; without a successful realization of this goal, the other preferences would not be felt. The implication of the mechanisms is for national security interests to dominate the reasoning inciting foreign conduct and a different order of priorities, say if idealist concerns or an ideological agenda rank higher, offers the clearest refutation of the importance of this mechanism.

Although merely rewording a core realist assumption, this mechanism is still strong with respect to psychological plausibility as it ties in with a fundamental human motivation and a primordial urge. It is simply rooted in the most potent human need (Krasner 1978: 341), and one need not invoke controversial anthropological assumptions of innate human evil or aggressiveness to agree that security is a sacred value. How intents that transcend the security interest, such as idealism, enter decision-makers' heads is a priori more curious. As Little (2007: 220) establishes, "it is generally accepted that it is uncontentious to suggest that states aim to survive (it is 'trivially true' according to Wendt)". The absence of contention should come as no surprise, in as far as the mechanism alludes to an *ultimate human aim* hard-wired into the brain by human evolution (Gat 2006: 667), suggesting that no mental exertion on the part of the decision-makers is required for this reason mechanism to determine their conduct when they act on behalf of the state.

Mechanism 2: Observation and fear

Observations taken as evidence of a counterpart's capability to inflict harm foster fear, owing to the decision-makers' rational disposition.

State leaders come to fear other states because they interpret certain events or states of affairs within those states as evidence of hostile intentions. Evidence can be found in, for instance, political statements, population growth, economic success, production of weapons, military exercises, increased military spending, alliance formations, assertive intelligence-gathering or mobilization. Observations taken as evidence of future hostility can arise as a result of conscious attempts, as when intelligence services collect information, or by ordinary vigilance. Whenever decision-makers perceive indications of danger, they become fearful as a result. This is a purely rational basis of fear.[5]

This fear-generating mechanism, famously identified by Thucydides (1954: 12), has been a premise of realist thinking since its first formulation:

> The real cause [of the Peloponnesian war], I consider to be the one which was formally most kept out of sight. The growth of the power of Athens, and the alarm[6] which this inspired in Lacedaemon, made war inevitable.

In accordance with Thucydides, fear ensues because observations indicate the power of a counterpart is on the rise. Decision-makers will pay attention to how power is distributed among the states and perceptual justifications work as testimonies to underpin the judgment of being in danger as being sound. In such cases observations, rationally, foster fear.

Receiving signals, forming beliefs of the likely actions or character traits of others and reacting emotionally to those beliefs is a staple experience. It refers to the most common mental path through which fear comes about, involving cognition, and suggests how intimately connected cognition is to emotion (Elster 1999: 249–271). That this cognitive pattern plays a role in foreign policy decision-makers' thinking and influences their behavior requires no further psychological justification.

It should be noted, however, that since fear induced by observations of events or states of affairs is mediated by beliefs about a factual matter, there is a risk, if the beliefs themselves are inaccurate, that the fearful state of mind is unwarranted. Mechanism 2 is accordingly highly dependent on proper rational belief formation based on the information available to the actors. Whenever the machinery of rationality breaks down, decision-makers are not acting under the sway of this mechanism. Still, forming a belief about something as elusive as a threat, would require ample scope for contrary beliefs, even if the assessment is constrained by largely rational procedures. Often several assessments of the same circumstances can stand to reason. Given the imperfections of evidence for hostile intention, it is therefore important to underscore the relatively wide range of reasonable beliefs that may induce fear. It would, for instance, be unreasonable to dismiss beliefs about threats which eventually turn out to be spurious, as aberrations from due considerations and this mechanism, as the epistemological circumstances of the assessment situation are imperfect.

Mechanism 3: Uncertainty and fear

Uncertainty about the genuine intentions of other statesmen and uncertainty caused by inconclusive evidence about the intent of others foster fear, owing to a psychological inclination to feel suspicion fomented by the anarchical conditions.

Decision-makers face two types of uncertainty. First, as they have no means of knowing the exact intentions of decision-makers in other states they cannot be certain about the character of such intentions. This is the "other mind problem". Ignorance of this kind constitutes a hermeneutic dilemma. Insofar as nothing is known about a counterpart's intent, ought one to believe the counterpart is bent on aggressive or friendly relations? Under this mechanism, decision-makers confronting this dilemma will tend to opt for the dismal interpretation. A different inclination could, rationally, have led to complacency, but anarchy gives decision-makers a suspicious cast of mind, swaying interpretations and giving them a sinister slant.

Second, decision-makers occasionally face inconclusive information about the intent of other state leaders. For instance, there may be no perceptible evidence of malign intent on the part of others, nor evidence of friendliness or indifference. Based on conscious attempts and ordinary vigilance, decision-makers have no basis for concluding whether hostility is in the offing or not. All the same, the absence of evidence fails to discount the possibility of being under threat. The real state of affairs, for all that is known, is equally likely to be one of danger or one of safety. This hermeneutic dilemma can, reasonably, give rise to both fear and complacency. According to this mechanism, this state of mind will foster fear rather than complacency. Decision-makers in anarchy are notoriously pessimistic when it comes to forming beliefs about threats, and their interpretations are systematically bent in a disheartening direction. Without the pessimistic inclination, they could have arrived at a brighter interpretation, in which case fear would have been a less salient emotion inside the heads of decision-makers.

This mechanism implies that fear comes about, not only after cognitive evaluation of evidence of an opponent's capabilities (mechanism 2), but also as a cognitive by-product of imperfect epistemological circumstances. With respect to psychological plausibility, some sense of probability (i.e., uncertainty) of danger is arguably a permissive condition for fear to emerge, as complete certainty of an undesired future event will typically trigger other emotions such as despair (Elster 2007: 150).

Having said that, the tendency to respond to uncertainty with fear still requires a suspicious mentality, as uncertainty can give a rational mind grounds for tranquility as well. That the external circumstances of anarchy tend to bring out this type of mentality, making decision-makers' psychological liability on this score entirely imputable, while debatable, is not beyond the bounds of plausibility, as the anarchical conditions give other states both the *opportunity* and the *desire* to perform acts of hostility. And while desire for hostility is expected to fluctuate, the opportunity will remain as long as the conditions remain anarchic. That the mere opportunity exists renders the suspicious attitude intelligible, although not beyond dispute. However, it stands to reason that the particular circumstances of anarchy will allay any idiosyncratic inclination to entertain a sense of optimism. The view that individual proclivities are muted or significantly shaped by conditions of anarchy is exactly the point of Waltz (2008: 59):

"the actors are usually suspicious ... even though by nature they may not be given to suspicion".

The fact that imperfect epistemological circumstances is a common feature of foreign policy decision-making suggests that this mechanism is widely and frequently applicable.

Mechanism 4: Counter-wishful thinking and fear

Observations of friendliness or indifference (somehow) cause fear to spread among decision-makers, owing to a liability for counter-wishful thinking caused by the anarchical conditions.

Decision-makers sometimes have evidence of friendliness, conciliation or indifference on the part of other states, like a conciliatory speech, a pacifying or cooperative gesture or unconditional aid. This ought, rationally, to make them complacent. However, owing to the sense of suspicion nurtured by anarchy, decision-makers are liable to think in a counter-wishful manner. They can put an interpretation on the signals as providing evidence of efforts by other states to lead them astray and lull them into complacency. Acting under the influence of counter-wishful thinking even friendly signals can be interpreted as deceptive Trojan horses. As a result, decision-makers become fearful in circumstances in which they ought to feel secure.

Suggesting that beliefs about other states' intentions tend to be more discouraging than the evidence warrants is counter-intuitive. Why would decision-makers think "today's alliance partner might be tomorrow's enemy" (Mearsheimer 2001: 33), if signals suggest otherwise? Why are they "suspicious of other states and reluctant to trust them" (ibid.: 32) if signals suggest friendliness? Why do they always "have ample reason not to trust other states and to be prepared for war" (ibid.: 32)?

These puzzles owe something no doubt to the liability for counter-wishful thinking. However, this mechanism itself needs explaining as it is almost as mysterious as the phenomenon it aspires to explain. A counter-wishful thinker is the negatively inclined sibling of the better known wishful thinker, the agent prone to believe whatever he desires. Counter-wishful thinking takes place when a contrary desire impacts an agent's belief. Unlike the wishful or the rational thinker, the counter-wishful thinker is neither dictated by the pleasure principle nor the reality principle. Rather, counter-wishful thinking occurs when evidence is systematically weighted with a negative bias, understood more negatively than the agent would like to be true and more negatively than a disinterested bystander would condone.

Since observations typically shape beliefs with inescapable force, this mechanism lacks prima facie plausibility. Yet it is hard to question the phenomenon's existence. It is evoked by the proverb "We easily believe what we fear" (Elster 2007: 384) and by the old adage stemming from the Trojan War, "beware of Greeks bearing gifts" (Boot and Wheeler 2008: 5–6). Clausewitz (1989: 117) famously pointed to the mechanism of counter-wishful thinking in his remarks about intelligence in war: "As a rule most men would rather believe bad news than good, and rather tend to exaggerate the bad news".

Some may even associate the mechanism of counter-wishful thinking with the so-called "inherent bad faith model", a term coined by Ole Holsti, describing US policymakers during the Cold War unable to interpret anything the Soviet Union did as conciliatory. "Such a mind-set rejects the possibility of knowledge that could invalidate" a conclusion that the Soviet Union had hostile intentions (Boot and Wheeler 2008: 65). "What happens" asks Holsti (in Finlay *et al.* 1967: 32), "when the other party is perceived to be acting in a conciliatory manner inconsistent with the enemy as evil?" According to Holsti, decision-makers respond to such overtures by developing a "number of strategies ... to reduce this discrepancy between affect and cognition" (Finlay *et al.* 1967: 32). As a result, the sinister attitude remains intact.

Indeed, the effects of the inherent bad faith model and counter-wishful thinking appear identical: even conciliatory signals are taken as evidence of hostility. But while Holsti's model presupposes an ideological insistence that some states are enemies simply by virtue of who they are, the mechanism of counter-wishful thinking presumably occurs even in the absence of ideological fundamentalism. It has, in other words, both a more curious nature and a more general applicability.

Although the counter-wishful thinking is inadequately understood and somewhat weak with respect to psychological plausibility, it is reasonable to expect it to bring about fear. Apparently, because "the stakes on questions of national security are so high, a degree of mistrust towards others has traditionally been considered to be the most prudent strategy. This being the case, *even* conciliatory gestures are met with suspicion" (Boot and Wheeler 2008: 5). As discussed in Chapter 2, one attraction of mechanism-based explanations is the allowance they provide for non-reason explanations even if the posited pattern remains beyond our full comprehension. This mechanism is of that kind.

Mechanism 5: (a) Power maximizing, (b) Power preservation and (c) Power amassment within reasonable limits

> 5a: Based on situational awareness, decision-makers seize any opportunity to *maximize* the power of their state.

Owing to the near impossibility of estimating what an appropriate amount of power would be, state leaders become revisionists, that is, they strive to balance the distribution of power in their own favor by initiating power-maximizing endeavors. Although security remains their sole concern, strategically calculating leaders will not only aim to protect their position in the system, but find themselves compelled to upset the status quo either by amassing latent power, such as military arms, or by externalized behavior designed to increase influence.

Aiming to be in charge of the most powerful state in the system, decision-makers seek under this mechanism advantage wherever they see an opportunity.

"Even when a great power achieves a distinct military advantage over its rivals, it continues looking for chances to gain more power" (Mearsheimer 2001: 34). Circumstantial analysis will never persuade decision-makers to be content with the present security level. Rather, power amassment will be justified by arguing more power is the best assurance of security in the long run.

Wolfers (1962: 92) anticipated this mechanism, and in his interpretation it amounts to a mental transformation: "Thus the quest for security ... can become so ambitious as to transform itself into a goal of unlimited self-extension". The accentuation of security-seeking states ultimately displaying aggressive intentions indeed suggests the occurrence of a motivational transformation. Yet, revisionism need not involve a motivational transformation; it can also be interpreted as a considered *decision*. Mearsheimer (2001: 43) suggests "a scared state will look especially hard for ways to enhance its security, and it will be disposed to pursue risky policies to achieve that end"; decision-makers then simply *decide* to be revisionist in proportion to the threats. That being the case, maximizing initiatives result from the judgment that more power is better because the assessment of appropriateness is difficult and it is hard to know what the future holds. Whether the revisionism follows from a mental transformation or from a considered decision, or both, the result is the same.

On the face of it, constant revisionism strains credulity, as insensitivity to marginal gains is strange. Following the so-called law of diminishing returns, the first sip of water is more valuable than the last, and one would think that the same dictum would apply to power as well. If so, the intensity of amassment would wane with success. Yet, mechanism 5 suggests the opposite. When it comes to the commodities of security and power, individuals become insatiable when they act on behalf of the state. Given an inch they will crave a mile. Some cravings are arguably such as to increase the craving after the object of the craving is acquired. Acquisition of knowledge, say, sometimes triggers a desire for more of the same; for some the quest is relentless. Power may be of an analogous kind. That, at least, is the view of Thomas Hobbes (1968: 161) who suggested that

> a perpetual and relentless desire for Power after power [is] ... a general inclination of all mankind.... And the cause of this, is not, always that a man hopes for a more intensive delight, than he has already attained to; or that he cannot be content with a moderate power: but because he cannot assure the power and means to live well, which he hath present, without the acquisition of more.

Plausibly, as Hobbes suggests, when a surplus of power is achieved, there may be no compelling reasons to cease the search. And although the marginal utility of more power decreases for those with a power advantage, decision-makers may still see no reason to stop the pursuit, even while acknowledging that the next increment of power contributes negligibly to the security interest. Analogously, those profiting from financial investments see no reason to abstain from further investment, despite the fact that the additional wealth generated by it has no effect on their personal well-being whatsoever. Decision-makers may plausibly adopt the same mentality with respect to power.

Moreover, the revisionist decision may appear more intelligible when connected to the ultimate desire for absolute security or hegemony. The psychological satisfaction of any power distribution, however favorable, pales in comparison with the psychological satisfaction of supremacy. So if power superiority can be obtained at acceptable costs, the target of complete assurance renders the maximizing decisions understandable.

So despite the apparent psychological anomaly of the never-waning appetite for power prescribed by this mechanism, it is a known behavioral regularity and also conceivable in terms of individual-level psychology and judgment.

That said, since individual insensitivity to marginal gains appears unable to exhaust the possible action tendencies of rational decision-makers in anarchy, one may wonder whether mechanism 5a has a twin mechanism exhibiting a different causal pattern. By denying that increments of power diminish in value at some point, a contrary mechanism indeed suggests itself. Call it mechanism 5b, power preservation. It may read as follows:

> 5b: Based on situational awareness, decision-makers seize opportunities to *preserve* the power of their state when the marginal returns of power amassment are either insignificant or fail to outweigh the costs.

This mechanism would be more akin to Waltz' (1979: 126) supposition that the "first concern of states is not to maximize power but to maintain their position in the system". Rather, Waltz (2008: 57) argues, than upsetting the status quo, "sensible statesmen try to have an appropriate amount of it [power]". Decision-makers in this account clearly place a somewhat lower value on security and accept that to "balance" an opponent suffices (cf. Waltz 1979: 129). They are, again citing Wolfers' anticipation of this mechanism (1962: 92), content with "the maintenance, protection, or defense of the existing distribution of values".

Snyder (2002), without relating it explicitly to a mechanistic-centered research strategy, hints at these twin mechanisms in his review of Mearsheimer's book, suggesting "a potential for integrating offensive and defensive realist theory" (ibid.: 173). As both Offensive and Defensive Realists locate the source of causation in the international structure,

> the two theories could work in tandem – the one chiefly explaining the security behaviour of status quo powers, the other the behaviour of revisionist states. A given state might be oriented offensively in some situations and defensively in other; the two theories would alternate in explaining its behaviour.
>
> (Ibid.: 158)

Snyder's integrative attempt at paying heed to the insights of the two theories could be fulfilled by the mechanistic perspective enunciated here. It is a known characteristic of mechanisms that they often come in contrary pairs, and it appears as if the two realist theories implies two distinctive micro-level mechanisms under influence of which decision-makers may act. Depending on circumstances, they may conceivably conform to either mechanism 5a or mechanism 5b. Therefore, both mechanisms ought to be included in the catalogue.

One may reasonably object that unless the triggering conditions eliciting either 5a or 5b are identified, the pair of mechanisms is useless for explanatory purposes, because any attempt at prediction breaks down. Admittedly, even after several hundred years of political history, we still do not know which conditions will elicit 5a or 5b. What we do know, however, is that one mechanism of the pair is often realized thereby excluding a huge amount of causal alternatives. Besides, when we know the outcome, we may, after the fact, suspect we know something about why it was brought about.

However, there is one complicating factor that needs to be addressed. It cannot be ruled out that decision-makers are mindful of the likely effects of policies conforming to either mechanism 5a or 5b. If so, their decisions might not be prompted by any set of triggering conditions, but rather result from *calculated consideration*. On the face of it, it is plausible that decision-makers would see sound reasons to act consistent with both mechanisms, especially in light of the different signals policies conforming to either mechanism would send. Whenever interests collide between actors, there are, on the one hand, objective reasons not to display restraint, as it can spur an opponent to press for concessions. By acting consonant with mechanism 5a, one reduces the likelihood of being perceived as weak as it sends a clear signal of resolve. The chance of any policymaker, no matter of what predisposition, versed in international politics failing to grasp this point is negligible. After all, it is the cornerstone of deterrence.

However, there is a flip-side to the deterrence argument, whose persuasiveness would also be evident to rational decision-makers operating under anarchical conditions, often referred to as the spiral model. The crux of the spiral model is that display of resolve, i.e., actions consonant with mechanism 5a, while plausibly precluding perceptions of weakness, also gives opponents stronger incentives to step up defiance. Since evidence of resolve and power maximization possibly triggers a concurrent need for more protection on the part of others, it may prod others to respond in kind, resulting in conflict escalation. Therefore, policymakers would, on the other hand, also find objective reasons to act consonant with mechanism 5b, as this would send more conciliatory signals and accordingly promise to avoid a spiraling conflict that might reduce the overall level of security.

Since deterrence arguments and spiral model considerations are closely linked, even suggesting different outcomes from the very same act, one would think that calculating policymakers look upon this as a strategic quandary (Jervis 1976: 58–76). Two extreme options are available corresponding respectively to mechanism 5a and 5b. On the one hand, by choosing to act in accordance with mechanism 5a one would show resolve and display strength while hoping to deter. On the other hand, by acting in accordance with mechanism 5b one would show restraint and display conciliation hoping to avoid conflict spirals. Since both options at the same time are potentially advantageous and perilous, calculating decision-makers would come to realize that decisions in accordance with neither of the mechanisms may offer the most viable solution. Rather, policymakers may defy both extreme options and strive for a more balanced strategic alternative, suggested by mechanism 5c:

> 5c: Based on situational awareness and mindfulness of the likely signals of policies consonant with mechanisms 5a and 5b, decision-makers seize opportunities to show resolve, advance forcefully and display strength *within reasonable limits* hoping to deter conflict without sparking any.

On the plausible supposition that decision-makers are sensitive to the above quandary and attempt to strike a balance between policies conforming to mechanisms 5a and 5b, we have identified a *reason mechanism*, suggesting that foreign conduct comes about as a result of a considerate attempt to find a middle way between power maximization and power preservation. Acting under the influence of this mechanism, decision-makers amass power within reasonable limits.

Mechanism 6: The primacy of military means

Among the range of strategic options, decision-makers rely heavily on the *military instrument* as they pursue confrontational policies.

Given the decision to pursue power, decision-makers still have a range of options. But what means and strategies are most apt to realize the goal of relative advantage vis-à-vis others? Presumably, all means available to a state of presumptive importance to the power competition, such as culture, economy, diplomacy and military, would be mobilized to the production of intended security effects. Yet acting under the influence of this mechanism, policymakers will come to expect the utility of military force to be superior to all other means. Military projections would be considered an appropriate and legitimate instrument of statecraft as long as they contribute to the amassment of power and benefit the national security interest.

As argued by Thomas Schelling (1966: Chapter 1), military capacity improves a state's position in interaction and bargaining situations, instances of so-called "diplomacy of violence". As the decision-makers will utilize the military capacity to its highest potential, they will not fail to appreciate its non-use dimension. Accordingly, the threat of military coercion will be used strategically both to enhance the bargaining power vis-à-vis rivals and to deter them from contemplating military attack.

But although decision-makers are bent on power amassment by military means, they are not "mindless aggressors" (Mearsheimer 2001: 37). On occasion, they "decide that the perceived costs of offense are too high and do not justify the expected benefits.... Nor do states start arms races that are unlikely to improve their overall position". In short, "a state has to know its limitations to survive in the international system" (ibid.). Since it is not always clear whether military efforts will pay off, decision-makers will be called to make rational judgments. They only opt to alter the balance of power "if they think it can be done at a reasonable price" (ibid.: 2).

Yet, considerations of reasonableness are liable to be contested, not least because different means appear apt to maximize power. On the one hand, building arms and acting in a militarily confrontational manner promises to increase power, as it cultivates a strategic deterrent and potentially increases relative influence over rivals. On the other, the benefits of military procurement and offensives may not always outweigh the costs if such actions trigger avoidable hostility on the part of others, if they cause an unnecessary arms race or if the offensives fail to achieve the intended security effects. That both militarily confrontational and diplomatically conciliatory policies appear apt to maximize power thus creates a strategic quandary.

Although it is reasonable to impute sensitivity about this quandary to decision-makers, this mechanism entails that they ultimately place principal confidence in the military instrument. Given the irresolvable uncertainty about other states' intentions, decision-makers will, on consideration, typically refuse conciliatory, non-military strategies as the risk of being exploited will loom too large. Acting under the influence of this mechanism, decision-makers rely instead on confrontational power amassment through military means, even though rational cost sensitivity and considerations of reasonableness confine the initiatives that will be carried out.

This mechanism adds little detail and plausibility to the proposition to this effect put forth by realist theory. One may intuitively wonder why other non-violent means of conflict resolution, such as argument and persuasion, have a less prominent place among individual state leaders when they hold the promise of resolving disputes at a much lower cost. A general presumption to the effect that individuals resort to violence when their interests collide is dubious.

The individual-level plausibility of this mechanism derives from the inevitable apprehension on the part of the decision-makers that the *potential* for violence ultimately makes the conflicting interests in international politics a matter of life and death. Throughout history decision-makers have therefore come to view military ascendancy as the means by which they can most appropriately match the stakes. As long as the threat of violence, however marginal, lingers, there is a plausible chance that decision-makers will attach a special utility to military capability; it is the only instrument that can be utilized for coercion with full *reliability* and prevention of oneself from being coerced. Therefore, "[m]ilitary power ... promise[s] great benefits", as Robert Art (2003: 4) writes, "Were this not the case, states would disarm".

Mechanism 7: Self-help thinking

Apprehensive about the conditions under which they live, self-help reasoning and thinking hold sway over the policymakers.

This mechanism ensures that decision-makers in the absence of a supranational authority principally rely on the capabilities of their own state. "The reason is simple: it pays to be selfish in a self-help world" (Mearsheimer 2001: 33). Leaders decline to subordinate their autonomy to other states and institutions and refuse to rely on others in the pursuit of their own security interest. In short, "states cannot depend on others for their own survival" (ibid.: 33). Although cooperation sometimes occurs, the competitiveness of state interaction ensures that decision-makers ultimately are dedicated unilateralists embodying "patriotic instincts" (Osgood 1953: 9).

Acting under the influence of this mechanism, decision-makers will never let down their guard as they engage other states. "Each state tends to see itself as vulnerable and alone, and therefore it provides for its own survival" (Mearsheimer 2001: 33). This will be observed as unwillingness to let foreign actors impinge on their priorities, especially in security matters. They will not "subordinate their interest to the interest of other states, or to the interest of the so-called international community" (ibid.: 33).

This mechanism inhibits both the constraining capacity of international rules and norms and of committed cooperation. If an international institution sets up rules and develops customs to constrain its members, they will only be observed under this mechanism as long as abiding by them sits well with self-interested power considerations. Beneficial outcomes are more important than abiding to rules; in cases where national security interests collide with institutional interests, the former hold sway. It follows that decision-makers are insensitive to disapproval or of other sanctions such as implicit or explicit ostracism from others, if their self-interested duties cause them to disobey rules and norms of appropriate conduct. The psychological reaction of shame, in short, is extinguished as a regulating force under this mechanism.

Moreover, self-help thinking thwarts international cooperation. Considerations about relative gains and fear of cheating are the two principal obstacles to cooperation and inhibit realization of common goals. As decision-makers enter international venues, they keep a wary eye on the likely distribution of benefits since they are all competitors. They will be reluctant to endorse common polices unless they are assured the outcome tilts the balance of power in their own favor and, out of fear, will refuse cooperation attempts by their counterparts to cheat on or exploit agreements in order to maximize their own advantage.

The individual-level plausibility of the self-help mechanism is strong, but debatable. On the one hand, the mental disposition to be solely concerned with own welfare is frequently observed, so frequently that it arguably would be imprudent of decision-makers of state A to act on the assumption that other actors, whose behavior matters to state A's well-being, do not act out of self-interest. And acting on the presumption that others are rational egoists forecloses the option of transferring the procurement of security interest to others.

On the other hand, as Keohane (1984) demonstrates, even interaction between egoistic individuals can result in trust, and there is much to gain from it, not least since it renders costly preparations necessary in its absence superfluous. The prospective long-term benefits of showing confidence in others may exceed the risk of being cheated on. In short, "Realism's pessimism about welfare-increasing cooperation is exaggerated" (ibid.: 29). To the extent this holds true, the self-help mechanism loses plausibility.

Despite Keohane's suggestion, the mechanism of self-help is a defendable proposal. Conditions of scarce resources, conflicting interests, and the fact that decision-makers act as trustees of their state in strategic interaction, suggests they will hesitate considerably before embarking on policies that potentially forgo their self-interest. Both the insistence of complete independence and the worry that one might be taken advantage of are intelligible and do not seem to require any psychological effort on the part of decision-makers in order to shape their thinking, even if an extreme attitude to this effect appears implausible.

Mechanism 8: Precautionary action

On matters of national security, decision-makers invoke worst-case scenarios and appeal to precautionary arguments owing to an aversion to the risk of acting on too sanguine threat assessments.[7]

In anarchy, the stakes are high. At the same time, irresolvable uncertainty surrounds the decision-making situation. These two factors encourage a cognitive inclination on the part of the decision-makers to value a good margin of safety in security matters. Accordingly, when they forge a response to the uncertain security situation they prefer to err on the side of caution. In effect, they take care to do too much, rather than too little, in the pursuit of the national security interest. They prefer to prepare for threats that eventually turn out to be spurious, rather than failing to prepare for threats that turn out to be real. Since sanguinity implies risks of forgoing national security interests, arguments for precautionary action prevail in security deliberations and are successively followed by precautionary action. As Boot and Wheeler (2008: 37) write, in the realist world "the way to cope with existential uncertainty at the level of interpretation is to impose operational certainty at the level of response". Operational certainty makes decision-makers faced with risks apt to put precaution first, as the worst consequence of inaction, i.e., putting survival at risk, is unacceptable.

The allure of precautionary reasoning follows from the pessimistic estimates states make about the condition in which they live. States, we are told, "regard each other with suspicion, and they worry that war might be in the offing". Consequently, they are inclined to "anticipate danger" (Mearsheimer 2001: 32) and "eliminate any possibility of a challenge" (ibid.: 35).

Precautionary arguments are apposite to pessimists coping with circumstances where signs of danger are inconclusive and an undesired event might occur. Such situations presumably arise with some frequency in the international system inasmuch as signals can often be subject to diverging evaluations. In the absence of an optimal choice, precautionary choices ensure greater weight is given to the prerequisites of security than other considerations, such as resource frugality. At the core of such arguments, imperfect information is seen as insufficient reason for suspending action as inaction might be even costlier (Sunstein

2005). As inaction potentially puts the national security at risk, and since states are excessively reluctant to take such risks, precautionary reasons push themselves forward.

An agent of a precautionary bent is compelled to reflect on possible, but uncertain, *scenarios*. Decision-makers, says Mearsheimer (2001), direct special attention to the worst-case scenario. He often alludes to the worst case in his book to drive home his arguments (cf. ibid.: 142). As Layne (2006: 126) writes, "according to Mearsheimer, regional hegemons do worry – and they should. Strategically, they are always thinking about worst case scenarios". Faced with uncertainty, the policymakers identify the worst cases among various possibilities, and embark on action likely to ensure the worst outcome is the least bad. If the worst case is extremely unlikely, this thinking would not make sense, but under the international system war is always in the offing.

Under sway of this mechanism decision-makers favor policies aimed at purging uncertain threats to achieve a good margin of safety, even when such policies are costly. This extreme caution derives from the mandate never to put the national security interest in jeopardy. The mechanism suggests, as Stephen Brooks (1997) has pointed out, that decision-makers "are conditioned by the mere possibility – and not the probability – of conflict.... [T]he mere possibility of conflict induces a high degree of caution, given the extreme potential costs of neglecting to be defensively vigilant" (ibid.: 448). Accordingly, this mechanism imputes to agents a distinct rational judgment which departs from the more intuitively sound, agnostic evaluations of threats. Although precautionary action would be unreasonable in many walks of life (cf. Runciman 2006: 58), the suggestion can stand in light of the anarchical conditions.

Mechanism 9: Timing

Considerations about *timing* may cause decision-makers to postpone power-maximizing initiatives for a more propitious moment owing to their rational disposition.

This mechanism suggests decision-makers pay particular heed to considerations about timing in their cost/benefit analysis. Decisions aimed at amassing power may be deferred if the situational circumstances are inappropriate or there is reason to think that the circumstances will change for the better in the course of time. "The trick for a sophisticated power maximizer is to figure out when to raise and when to fold" (Mearsheimer 2001: 40). Various situational factors are likely to inform considerations of timing: If, say, the decision-makers know an unpopular dictator of state Y, possessing strategic territory, is about to die, they might well defer immediate plans of conquest because waiting until the dictator passed away would present a more propitious moment for invasion. The chaos in the wake of the dictator's demise would presumably provide for a more promising moment for a successful war. Conceivably, other arguments, say considerations about weather conditions, ("let us wait till the winter is over"), could be an argument to the same effect.

62 *Assumptions and theory*

This mechanism amounts to a qualifier to the tendency of expansion, since it tempers the suggestion that decision-makers jump at any opportunity to change the balance of power in their own favor. The mechanism thereby reduces the overall determinacy of the framework. On the other hand, it alerts us to arguments that potentially direct policymakers to abstain from maximizing initiatives.

Questions of timing are sometimes contested because uncertainty surrounds the decision-making situation. The point at which threats become imminent is ultimately a judgment call and two rational minds may judge the urgency of the situation differently. It is for example debatable if an observation, say mobilization, amounts to evidence of a prelude to attack or coercive diplomacy. Since individual judgment may differ about the most propitious moment to attack, considerations of timing will presumably sometimes call for a postponement.

Mechanism 10: Geography

Considerations of *geography*, in particular the existence of water between states, cause states to temper maximizing initiatives, owing to the rational presumption that power projection across oceans is difficult.

This mechanism alerts us to another consideration to which rational decision-makers pay heed in their cost/benefit analyses. According to this mechanism, the immutable influence of geographical constraints impedes the maximizing tendency. The prospect of having to project military power across long distances of water will tame expansive ambitions. "The principal impediment to world domination is the difficulty of projecting power across the world's oceans onto the territory of a rival great power" (Mearsheimer 2001: 41). Generally, leaders will be reluctant to launch amphibious attempts to conquer territory.

Interestingly, this logic appears to relieve states from some of their fears concerning geographically distant states. As they know how difficult it is to project power into a state on the far side of an ocean, offensive actions by adversaries, they will infer, will be unlikely. This inference will presumably reduce their worry (cf. Layne 2006: 126). However, it is unclear whether this mechanism holds stronger sway than other mechanisms pulling in the opposite direction, for example the liability of precautionary thinking. Even so, considerations about geography, i.e., the "stopping power of water", are able to temper decision-makers' maximizing efforts. Realizing geography is a considerable obstacle to other states' maximizing initiatives may make decision-makers more complacent. The mechanism is intuitively sound. Considering the material barriers to actions is a staple and suggesting otherwise would make a travesty of sound reason.

Mechanism 11: Power distribution and deterrence

Awareness of the power distribution in the international system, i.e., the balance of power, may encourage decision-makers to temper maximizing initiatives.

This mechanism alerts us to a third consideration of the cost/benefit analysis likely to temper decision-makers' maximizing initiatives. Considerations of balance of power sometimes suggest attempts to expand are rash in light of potential retribution: "Every state wants to be the king of the hill, but not every state has the wherewithal to compete for that lofty position, much less achieve it" (Mearsheimer 2001: 37). This is tantamount to saying that rational calculations about the expected costs can deter decision-makers from otherwise attractive initiatives. Actions that would otherwise appear attractive will lose some of their allure when the counterpart's wherewithal is taken into consideration. Consequently, when the "perceived costs of offense are too high and do not justify the expected benefits" (ibid.: 37) decision-makers will defer offensive action. This follows from rational cost sensitivity.

The overall power distribution or polarity of the system may also hold decision-makers back from prescribing expansive initiatives. After reviewing the power distribution of a system, leaders might sometimes conclude that the relative power of their state will not be promoted by offensive engagement. If, for example, two states on one continent are competing against each other for hegemony, decision-makers on a different continent may conclude that their relative power in the system benefits most by non-interference. They expand only when opportunities arise, when the benefits in terms of power outweigh the costs.

This mechanism is strong with respect to psychological plausibility because fear of retribution and consequential disadvantageous outcomes would be as strong as the fear of other states succeeding in actions initiated by themselves. This follows from the disposition to calculate chances of success.

Mechanism 12: Regional hegemony

When states achieve regional hegemony, i.e., dominate a distinct geographical area, they will attempt to prevent other states in other parts of the world from duplicating their feat. That apart, however, their maximizing propensity is tempered and the revisionist tendency extinguished.

This mechanism applies only to regional hegemons. It therefore follows that the incentive to maximize power wanes as regional hegemony is achieved. The mechanism is arguably incompatible with the general tendency to amass power and it patently stands in opposition to mechanism 5a. All the same, it rests on the reasonable presumption that individuals observe arguments of decreasing marginal utility suggested by mechanism 5b.

Importantly, decision-makers of a regional hegemon will not stay completely aloof, but strive to prevent other states from dominating their region and from enjoying the luxury of being less concerned with security. However, this does not justify further expansion. Rather, decision-makers in a position of regional hegemony will operate as offshore balancers, taking appropriate measures to frustrate attempts by distant great powers to achieve regional hegemony. As Mearsheimer (2001: 42) says, "the ideal situation for any great power is to be the only regional hegemon in the world. That state would be a status quo power".

3.3 Conclusion

On consideration, realism begets a repertoire of twelve distinct mechanisms under which decision-makers presumably formulate security policy. What are the advantages of a mechanistic rendering of decision-making?

In the first place, Mechanistic Realism shows how the repercussions of anarchy ultimately reside in the minds of those who cope with the circumstances; it therefore avoids overly abstract analysis without basis in individual decision-making or the minds of the decision-makers. As all the invoked mechanisms have *subjective* applicability, our attention is directed to how state behavior results from the motivation, emotions, assessments and judgments of individual decision-makers. Consequently, the critique that realist analysis only acknowledges *objective* threat assessments and *material* factors decoupled from individual judgment (cf. Little 2007: 11 for an exposition of this point) breaks down. If these mechanisms agree with observations of individual decision-making they enhance our understanding of the processes responsible for observed state behavior.

In the second place, Mechanistic Realism exhibits how anarchy as a systemic condition standardizes decision-making and suggests why some mental patterns recur across individuals with putatively different psychological inclinations. By aspiring to account for all the causally relevant features inside the black box, the derived mechanisms account for how anarchy extinguishes diverging idiosyncratic temperamental or philosophical predispositions on the part of decision-makers. When given executive power, all relevant instigators of their thinking are presumably derived from the systemically induced mechanisms: the above elaboration adds plausibility to this contention. Whether it can resist empirical testing, remains to be seen, but the presumption is indeed bold. Moreover, the result of opening up the theory's black-box statements in terms of the increased transparency and detail makes it easier to establish empirically whether the invoked mechanisms are responsible for the choices made.

In the third place, by splitting the theory into distinct pieces, explanatory significance can be ascribed to some of the posited mechanisms and the relevance of others reasonably doubted. In effect, insights can be drawn from realism without having to vouch for the validity of the entire theory. Contrary observations do not necessarily require discarding every piece of it and instead of regarding the derived mechanisms as generally valid, they can be viewed as "sometimes true", i.e., with *limited applicability* (Hernes 1998: 74). Limited applicability makes the contribution to universal theory building modest. Yet those mechanisms supported by evidence can reasonably claim a place in the toolbox of building blocks in foreign policy explanations.

Whenever evidence at odds with the mechanisms is discovered, no *fundamental* problem should arise because fidelity to the comprehensiveness of the theory is forsaken from the outset. Evidence of additional mechanisms would simply suggest the mechanisms in the catalogue are insufficient to account for the findings inside the units. Insofar as other factors influence state behavior, it obviously complicates foreign policy analysis, but does not render the realist mechanisms irrelevant, obsolete or worthy to be discarded; it only means the repertoire is incomplete.[8] Giving attention to a specified set of mechanisms may even alert us to a need for closely related and/or completely diverging mechanisms to account for observations departing from what these mechanisms lead us to expect. And having to expand the toolbox does not imply having to extend it indefinitely as the diversity of foreign policy consideration does not appear limitless.

In the fourth place, decomposing realism reduces the significance of some of its weaknesses. A justified criticism of the original theory finds its "metaphysical commitment to the state that is prior to scientific analysis and falsification" (Wight 2006: 94) difficult to square with the emergence of new actors in the international system. Rosecrance (2002: 161) formulates the critique thus:

> The emergence of terrorism as a major factor in international politics is particularly inconsistent with Mearsheimer's theory: his "tragedy of great power politics" refers only to the threat that powers pose to each other, not to a threat from below that can undermine them all.

Undoubtedly, Offensive Realism ignores non-state actors. In an interview Mearsheimer (2004) acknowledges that "there is no place in the theory for non-state actors like Al-Qaida". If non-state actors shape international politics, excluding them from our theories is unwarranted. If anything, 9/11 revealed the capacity of non-state actors to shape events in the international system and, some would argue, therefore impugns the validity of realism altogether.

However, this criticism has far less sting when leveled at Mechanistic Realism as it neither purports to be an all-inclusive theory applicable to every relevant actor in the international system nor sees states as the only relevant actors in the international system. The catalogue aspires to delineate mental mechanisms shaping foreign policy decision-making inside states. While one would expect other mechanisms to describe non-state actors' behavior more accurately, it is easy to conceive of worse theoretical starting points than Mechanistic Realism even for these actors.

A related charge leveled at realism criticizes the theory for not paying heed to terrorism as a method of political violence. Since terrorist methods and threats are presumably of a different nature from threats from nation states, realist theories, one could argue, are obsolete or at least confined to interstate relations. "From a structural realist perspective – and this represents an obvious weakness of the approach – terrorism is of limited significance" (Dueck 2006: 153).

This critique is not without merit. Nothing in realist theory suggests terrorism would disturb the general pattern of state behavior. From this, using realism to understand the US response to 9/11 is fundamentally inappropriate to many, since elimination of terrorism presumably was the main target of the response. Yet Mechanistic Realism is more flexible on this score. In principle, it is agnostic when it comes to types of threats. The mechanisms in the catalogue are, contrary

66 *Assumptions and theory*

to other versions of realism, applicable to any case in which politicians grapple with how to conduct security policy regardless of the type of threat they experience. Whether the source of the fear is state armament or terrorism, these mechanisms are expected to shape foreign policy choice.

Finally, Mechanistic Realism leaves less room for creative and ingenious interpretation. It is relatively explicit about the dominating motives, the ways in which fear comes about, the kind of reasoning one would expect, and the decisive psychological inclinations. While indeterminate in the sense of not pulling in the same direction, the catalogue of mechanisms surely eliminates huge amounts of causal precursors. Verifiable presence of different motives, reasons and inclinations would seriously question the explanatory power of the mechanisms in the catalogue and suggest a need to add more.

Part II
The empirical merit of Mechanistic Realism

4 The explanatory power of Mechanistic Realism

The insufficient degree to which realist scholars have engaged the micro-level evidence does not mean that the US response to 9/11 has escaped scholarly analysis. Quite to the contrary, the research attention that has been brought to bear in the case of US response to 9/11 has been remarkable. It almost amounts to a paradox. George W. Bush, who is often depicted as a short-witted man, on the basis of which one would expect easily comprehensible policies, has triggered a monumental interest from the scholarly community. Surprisingly, the bulk of the numerous contributions have converged on an inadequately justified consensus suggesting that the US response to 9/11 was primarily the work of a neo-conservative clique. In fact, the view that the ideology of a domestic interest group, loosely referred to as the neo-conservatives, swayed the deliberations within the Bush administration has been accepted as the most persuasive account of the US response to 9/11.

In order to pave the way for the empirical validation of Mechanistic Realism I shall in this chapter very briefly review the standard interpretation of the Bush administration's response to 9/11 and suggest five reasons why it is inadequate. Then I shall offer my interpretation of the available data, and demonstrate that evidence of the Bush administration's post-9/11 policymaking process can be subsumed under, and hence be explained by, the mechanisms posited by Mechanistic Realism.

Inspection of the data suggests a good fit for several of the mechanisms described in Chapter 3 with data from the black box. Some of the mechanisms have clearly swayed the decision-makers, even if their relative causal impact is hard to assess. Despite incomplete evidence, the innumerable potential causal factors, the unprecedented features of the situation, the unknowns of global terrorism and eloquent talk of "revolutionary change" (Schlesinger Jr. 2004: 21) and "foreign policy revolution" (Daalder and Lindsay 2005), Mechanistic Realism can safely be said to enrich our understanding of this case. Not all rival explanations are dispelled, but some are rendered less credible in light of the exploration undertaken in the following pages. Peremptory dismissal of the validity of these mechanisms has no justification and those declaring realist insights obsolete will struggle to ward off the inferences presented here.

Nonetheless, three provisos must be made. First, the data exhibit *nuances* in the mental operations after 9/11. Insignificant changes in the circumstances might conceivably have led to different decisions. For example, uncertainty did not foster fear in every case (mechanism 3), and individuals opting for expansionist policies (mechanism 5) stood opposed to individuals opting for a more confined attempt at preserving power (mechanism 5b). Moreover, the mechanisms in the catalogue that presumably tame power-amassing endeavors, ("timing", "geography", "power distribution" and "regional hegemony"), seem to have been far weaker impediments than one would expect.

Secondly, although the following exploration reveals that Mechanistic Realism can account for important features of the Bush administration's response, it does not exhaust the factors in play. To adequately account for all relevant precursors to the response, the explanatory toolbox must be expanded. The influence of causal factors unrelated to realist insight draws out the significant *limits* to Mechanistic Realism, which I shall record but not dwell on at length in this chapter. In the next chapter, I discuss more thoroughly how idealism shaped the decisions; read without these qualifications, this chapter leaves a correct, but nonetheless too one-sided an impression.

Third, the epistemological difficulty of identifying the causal precursors to the US response to 9/11 calls for explanatory modesty. Even with the support of evidence and conclusions of other scholars, it is worth emphasizing the limited confidence which surrounds many of these inferences. All of them are therefore subjected to withdrawal or correction upon the emergence of new information.

4.1 Neo-conservatism and the US response to 9/11

While the scientific rigor of the analysis concluding that Bush's foreign policy was dictated by a group of ideologues varies, the core argument of what can be referred to as the *neo-conservative thesis* is remarkably unison. Halper and Clarke's (2004) book, *America Alone. The Neo-conservatives and the Global Order*, is arguably one of the most authoritative statements of the kind. Their book, measured by the frequency of references to it, is a natural starting point for considerations of the impact of ideology on the Bush administration. According to them, neo-conservative ideology was solely responsible for US policies after 9/11, despite having a negligible relation to the material circumstances facing the US at the time and the fact that the neo-conservatives were insensible to the true US national security interest. Allegedly the group "substituted 'ideology' for 'interest'" (ibid.: 5) and US conduct was accordingly nothing but an "operational roll-out of the neo-conservative template" (ibid.: 205).

> [T]he nation was not provided a policy that responded directly to the crisis at hand. Instead, the neo-conservatives succeeded in having their preexisting ideological agenda adopted – one that leaves the nation more dangerously exposed to terrorism and brings numerous deleterious consequences.... Hijack may be a harsh word, but there is no better description for what occurred.
>
> (Ibid.: 139)

Furthermore:

> The paper trail [i.e., evidence] is unambiguous. Minds were already made up. A preexisting ideological agenda was taken off the shelf, dusted off, and relabeled as the response to terror.
>
> (Ibid.: 4)

Furthermore:

> Iraq was ... the arena in which to demonstrate the crucial tenets of neo-conservative doctrine: military pre-emption, regime change, the merits of exporting democracy, and a vision of American power that is "fully engaged and never apologetic".
>
> (Ibid.: 206)

Halper and Clarke acknowledge that the neo-conservatives valued security, but insist the protection of the state was forgone in order to fulfill unrelated objectives. Instead of responding strategically to protect the state, the primary goal of the decision-makers, Halper and Clarke argue, was to use US military power to create a new global order (ibid.: 156–157).

In Halper and Clarke's account, the causally efficacious post-9/11 beliefs can be distilled into a "few simplistic slogans" (ibid.: 5): (1) a good versus evil mentality, (2) a belief in military force as the first, not the last option of foreign policy and (3) a primary focus on the Middle East as the theatre of US interest (ibid.: 11). These ideas subsequently informed the policy: "It was like attracting a line of railroad cars to a locomotive of which they [the neo-conservatives] were the secret drivers" (ibid.: 203).

These ideological beliefs, we are told, had evolved long before the terror attacks and Halper and Clarke, drawing on several studies of the same tenor, recount the milestones of its genealogy and point to views of the important idea suppliers. Much attention is given to a drafted strategy document, known as the *Defense Planning Guidance* (DPG), from 1992, in which several tenets of neo-conservative ideology were put on paper. Only a draft was leaked to the press, and as some of the ideas came under criticism, the official version of the strategy document revised the most provocative elements. Importantly, however, the content of the draft

> line[s] up closely with the principle put forth in the 2002 NSS ... [and] detailed the nature and scope of threats faced by the United States in 1992 in a manner consistent with the September 17, 2002, NSS.
>
> (Ibid.: 145–146)

> In sum, the doctrine laid out in NSS was exactly what Bush had warned against in his campaign speeches and debates – but it was entirely consistent with the approach advocated by the neo-conservatives for over a decade.
>
> (Ibid.: 143)

"In a stroke of opportunistic daring" the ideas put on paper in 1992, that had "little or nothing to do with combating terror", became premises for US foreign policy after 9/11 (ibid.: 4). The most important premise was the belief that military use of force to overthrow rough states was an apt remedy to defend US security.

Since it was difficult for the neo-conservatives to defend publicly that the US should put the interest and aspirations of a small policy clique before the national interest, the group was forced to manipulate the political process in order to get their pre-existing agenda accepted (ibid.: 203). Through "discursive manipulation" (ibid.: 206–208) they succeeded "to fashion a 'political discourse' that hard-wired the public mind" (ibid.: 202) to accept their political program. By deliberate manipulation of the facts and "artful presentation" they managed to create "an entirely new reality" (ibid.: 203) allowing them to translate a preconceived ideology into foreign policy even if it "rested on a series of flawed principles" (ibid.: 2). The policies, in short, were no rational "response to the unfolding emergency" (ibid.: 34), but brought about because they correlated with the preconceived ideological template.

Indications contrary to this thesis owe to the finesse of the misrepresentation staged by the administration. For example, observations suggesting that the threat from grand-scale terrorism caused the decision-makers to experience fear, the prime motive imputed to states by realism, are only available due to the artful way in which the neo-conservatives constructed a "synthetic neurosis" on the part of the public (ibid.: 203). The fear displayed, for example in Colin Powell's UN speech in which he argued that Iraq was a threat to US security, was fictive, but had to be nurtured because "building a climate of fear" (ibid.: 208) was expedient: "Fear for terrorism provided the necessary glue to meld otherwise uncorroborated statements, assumptions, predictions and ideas into a case for war" (ibid.: 209).

By assuming ideology was all that mattered for the US response, the neo-conservative thesis renders it futile to ponder the impact of different explanatory variables, including the suggestion on which Mechanistic Realism rests, namely that more permanent features of the international system and rational adaption to those circumstances shaped the response. If Halper and Clarke are correct in seeing the US response to 9/11 as purely ideologically driven, Mechanistic Realism has nothing whatsoever to contribute in terms of explanation.

However, on closer inspection it is rash to embrace the neo-conservative thesis. I shall make five short comments to explain why reservations are appropriate. In the first place, the thesis *lacks prima facie credibility*. Although Halper and Clarke offer empirical justification, the thesis as a whole relies too heavily on contrivance to be considered the best truth candidate available. In itself, this would be an insufficient rebuttal, but insofar as the explanation defies immediate appeal and strains our imagination, subsequent affirmation is more difficult to achieve. By contrast, when observers well versed in neo-conservative ideology write that there "is practically none [observations] in support of the aides-as-architect theses". (Barnes 2006: 61) it immediately sounds more plausible, since neither of the highest-ranking decision-makers, (Bush, Cheney, Rice, Rumsfeld or Powell), were steeped in neo-conservative ideology prior to 9/11, while the most frequently invoked neo-conservatives (Pearl, Krauthammer and Podhores), stood outside government. For sure, Paul Wolfowitz was both a member of the administration and, according to some, a neo-conservative. Yet if he alone swayed the policies according to the neo-conservative thesis, one has to impute to him magical skills.

In the second place, the thesis *is empirically weak*. It is weak because accepting the thesis requires dismissing much contrary evidence. Imperceptibly, Halper and Clarke assume all members of the administration invested a colossal amount of energy in fabricating a deceptive paper trial. It is especially hard to disbelieve all the indications of genuine fear from this period and instead subscribe to the notion that these indications were artfully concocted. Since this is a crux of their argument, the paucity of evidence on this score is unfortunate. Considering Halper and Clarke's accusation of the administration of hoodwinking, they must expect their readers to guard with equal care against signs of hoodwinking on their part. Since the available data clearly are not as "unambiguous" as they claim, the thesis fails any reasonable objectivity test.

In addition, the conclusions themselves rest on empirically questionable extrapolations. There is no smoking gun capable of dispelling all doubt about whether a deliberate deception took place, something like a non-disclosed document delineating a strategy for misleading the public in order to pursue goals unrelated to the threats facing the US. In the absence of same, Halper and Clarke are understandably puzzled by aspects of the administration's efforts to promote the merits of an Iraq war. In retrospect, it is easy to find instances where the certainty of official statements went beyond what the existing evidence warranted (Prados 2004). There are also reports that members of the administration instigated efforts to corroborate that Hussein constituted a threat, while failing to appoint devil's advocates challenging the consensus view, something that has been taken as evidence of a desire to deceive (cf. Suskind 2007: 123–124). But from such puzzlement to insist that all efforts to explain publicly the rationale for war were part of a deliberate deception campaign is a large and dubious inferential leap. Without exploring more thoroughly whether the flaws in accuracy, those in Powell's UN speech, for instance, were down to a misreading of the evidence in good faith, the suspicion remains unsubstantiated, especially since several explanations of misplaced judgment that do not rest on conspiracy are available. And even if the message presented to the public was "polished" to muster support, the administration may still genuinely have believed the unpolished version.

In the third place, the neo-conservative thesis *relies on a questionable post hoc ergo propter hoc argument*. The thesis says a pre-existing agenda was "taken off the shelf" and implemented after 9/11. Certainly some neo-conservatives involved in the administration's deliberations after 9/11 had written a strategy paper in 1992 which on some measures resembles the NSS 2002. But that arguments made in 1992 pertaining to how the US ought to behave internationally would have been replicated ten years later does not in itself warrant any causal inference. That one occurrence precedes another occurrence is in itself no reason to believe the first *caused* the second.

Indeed, it is reasonable to call attention to the fact that some arguments resurfaced. As Gordon and Trainor (2007: 72) write, the "development of the preemption strategy had an instructive history". Its instructiveness has a limit, however. Insofar as the 2002 strategy was written by different people (who interestingly dispute any connection to the 1992 document), the same arguments could evidently be hatched and considered sound even if the DPG had not been written. Ultimately, it is questionable to use an apparent replication as evidence in support of a hypothesis in which the ideas spelled out in the 1992 document had a proximate causal role in shaping Bush's policies in the wake of 9/11.

Similarly, many neo-conservatives had advocated military regime change in Iraq long before 9/11 – take the open letters to President Clinton (the 1998 PNAC letter, signed by Rumsfeld and Wolfowitz). This argument was stated several times as well, which on the face of it corroborates the view of the war as resting on ideological grounds unrelated to the war on terror. But again, when some of the same individuals brought up the advisability of regime change in Iraq after 9/11, whether their advocacy was in thrall to previously held preferences as opposed to recent assessments of the new circumstances is hard to know. That arguments are repeated perhaps indicates ideologically guided preference formation, but it is unwarranted to invoke arguments for regime change in Iraq put forward *before* 9/11 as evidence for claiming that the policy of regime change in Iraq *after* 9/11 was an "operational roll out of the neo-conservative template".

It would be especially questionable in light of dramatic reappraisal most neo-conservatives report having subjected their thinking to after 9/11. Their reasons for regime change altered profoundly when they realized that international terrorists, who had demonstrated on 9/11 their ability to bring about large-scale civilian killing, could cooperate with states equipped with weapons of mass destruction (WMD). Although conceivable, whether their previous advocacy for regime change impinged on their new-found judgment is unclear. In addition, absent former advocacy for regime change in Iraq, one would expect their concern that terrorists could conspire with rogue states to have come to the fore. After all, many arrived at this position without having advocated regime change previously. But the survival of the old argument does not mean it was causally necessary.

Fourth, the thesis *takes too lightly the problem of spuriousness*. Although several decisions made by the Bush administration echo neo-conservative tenets, the ideological tenets themselves could still have been (by-)products of the material conditions, and therefore owed their causal significance to structural pressures highlighted by realism. To the extent that neo-conservative beliefs have their foundations in non-ideational factors they are, at any rate, not purely ideational because their causal powers will be contingent on other material factors. The claim, for example, that the "ideology ... purposefully places the United States on a war footing" (Halper and Clarke 2004: 4), appears insufficiently alert to the possibility that other variables or reasons could have placed the US on a war footing after 9/11 even without the ideological influence of the neo-conservatives.

Similarly, invoking a neo-conservative idea, such as belief in the utility of unilateralism, as an explanatory variable implies that one is able to show that this idea arose "with some range of autonomy from preexisting objective conditions" (Parsons 2007: 110). If the invoked idea in a causal analysis follows predictably or is a natural response to the systemic conditions, as appears to be the case with unilateralism, the ideational elements add little to the explanation. That the Bush administration frequently observed that the US was by far the most powerful country in the international system is a clear indication of their environmental awareness. It makes it probable that some of the tenets of the neoconservative ideology were closely linked to non-ideational factors, such as the distribution of power in the system. If so, the autonomous causal impact of the neoconservative ideas breaks down.

Fifth, the thesis *is explanatory only in a limited sense*. It dispels the oddity of some of Bush's priorities by evidencing their conformity with beliefs and patterns of thinking to which the neo-conservatives had long adhered, but fails to identify the mechanisms by which these beliefs and thinking patterns caught on in the first place. Consequently, the explanation elicits new and equally perplexing puzzles that remain unanswered.

Contending that the US went to war with Iraq because there was a consensus in the administration about an ideology that favored war with Iraq is tantamount to contending that they wanted to go to war because that was what they wanted. It raises other questions as well. Why was there a consensus within the administration about this proposal? Why exactly did this ideology catch on, when the US policy community offers a rich flora of ideologies? And if the Iraq war was caused by an ideology that elevated the Middle East to the pivot of US interests, one would want an account explaining why and how the use of military force as the "first option" in relation with distant countries merged into an ideology. The neo-conservative thesis does not quell these puzzles, but leaves us in limbo. Further inquiry would probably reveal several alluring *reasons* of a neoconservative bent under the given circumstances. But if the prevalence of ideology boils down to provision of alluring reasons, the argument that a pre-existing agenda, unrelated to the present circumstances was implemented, breaks down.

4.2 Mechanistic Realism and the US response to 9/11

Taken together, these five deficiencies seriously impugn the neo-conservative thesis. The rest of this chapter outlines an alternative interpretation based on Mechanistic Realism. It fares much better.

Mechanism 1: The primacy of security

The preponderance of evidence of the decision-makers' intent suggests security as the highest-ranking goal in the hierarchy. This should come as no surprise. As

Stephen Biddle (2005: 4) notes, the "freedom and safety of the American people have always been the country's primary national interest"; suggesting that the desire for security, without inspection, can be taken as the primary precursor to actions in the aftermath of 9/11 as well. Although observations to the opposite effect would have been perplexing, a selection of corroborating observations deserves mention.

Following 9/11, Bush immediately gave less priority to domestic issues, directing all his attention to security matters: "I'm necessarily spending more time on war-related issues and on homeland security related issues, and that's just the reality of it", he admitted (in Daalder and Lindsey 2005: 85). Among the tasks ascribed to the President, nothing appears to have preoccupied Bush as much as the security of the state.

In his first public remarks after 9/11, Bush (2001a) listed as his first and fundamental priority the defense of the state. The country's "sense of safety and security has been threatened [by] evil, despicable acts of terror". He depicted the US as a defensively oriented state wanting "peace and security in the world", which was now "moved" to fight "the war against terrorism". The public display of security concerns pervaded the thinking behind closed doors as well. Bob Woodward (2003: 31) reports Bush's first comment to his cabinet after the attacks: "This is the time for self-defense".

This preoccupation was repeated ad infinitum the following year. In his 2002 State of the Union Address, Bush (in Halper and Clark 2004: 140) reiterated the determination of the US to "do what is necessary to ensure our nation's security". Illustratively, the opening statement of the National Security Strategy from 2002 reads: "Defending our nation against its enemies is the first and fundamental commitment of the Federal Government" (NSS 2002: iv).[1] In his memoir, Bush (2010) explains how every controversial decision he made must be understood in light of the fact that he "had vowed to do what was necessary to protect the country.... My most solemn duty, the calling of my presidency, was to protect America" (ibid.: 224, 155). This chimes with the view of Bush's Vice President, Dick Cheney (2011: 369), "[t]he president and I were determined to do all we could to prevent another attack.... The security of our nation and of our friends and allies required that we act".

Other members of the administration adhered to the same order of priorities. The Secretary of Defense, Donald Rumsfeld and his Deputy Secretary, Paul Wolfowitz (Rumsfeld and Wolfowitz 2001), testifying before the Senate on December 12, 2001, made the following remarks:

> We have no greater responsibility as a nation, than to stop these terrorists – to find them, root them out, and prevent them from murdering more of our citizens.... But those who are responsible for our national defense must not lose sight of the fact that these are *not* normal times. We have been attacked. We are at war. And we must take the steps necessary to defend our people, and protect them from further harm.... We will ... ensure that the American people can once again live their lives in freedom and without fear.

It is difficult to escape the sense of national security being at heart of the administration's concerns. The suggestion that the national interest was defined purely in terms of security is corroborated in interviews. Condoleezza Rice, the President's National Security Advisor, indicated to Nicholas Lemann (2002) what she considered to be *the* national interest: "[O]pposing terrorism and preventing the accumulation of weapons of mass destruction in the hands of irresponsible states now define the national interest" (ibid.: 3).

Moreover, an internal Pentagon memorandum, reportedly intended as a conceptual elaboration of the forthcoming security policy and circulated within the administration (quoted in Feith 2008: 296), demonstrates acknowledgement that all higher-order values ultimately depend on sovereignty: "Our key political values – democratic self-government and protection of individual rights – can be safeguarded only if the US remains a sovereign state". In sum, the suggestion that the security of the state was *the* most important impetus of the policies pursued is well supported by the evidence.[2]

Despite this, several analysts dispute whether the administration's priorities were as clear as the above observations indicate. Rather than taking the observations as evidence of a principal preoccupation with security, Stephen Holmes (2007: 306) avers that "the Administration's response to 9/11 was controlled by hidden agendas". What appear to be security concerns are, on inspection, better viewed as pretexts for other goals, such as to "expand the executive power and weaken Congressional oversight", "field test ... [the] theory that in modern warfare speed is more important that mass", "overcome the legacy of Vietnam", "improve the security of Israel", and "the need to have troops in the region to protect the world's oil supply" (ibid.).

According to Holmes, hidden agendas shaped consequential decisions, such as the decision to attack Iraq, quite decisively. "That such political ambitions and hidden agendas played a role in motivating the Iraq war cannot be reasonably disputed" (ibid.). If Holmes is right, national security considerations held significantly less sway over policy formulation than it would appear, and did not rank highest in the hierarchy of goals. If correct, mechanism 1 tells us less about the intent behind the US response than first meets the eye.

Although implying coordination and fraud of conspiratorial proportions, suggesting that hidden agendas rather than security concerns motivated the decisions after 9/11 also challenges the validity of mechanism 1. The most prevalent argument of this nature is that realization of idealist goals adhered to by ideologues within and outside the administration trumped security concerns.

There are statements by Bush to support this suggestion. The most intimate moment in an interview long before the Iraq war suggests that *idealist sentiments* were an important precursor to Bush's actions. "I thought he might jump up he became so emotional as he spoke", Woodward (2003: 340) notes, as Bush struggles to drive home his point:

> It is visceral. Maybe it's my religion, maybe it's my – but I feel passionate about this.... There is a human condition that we must worry about. As we

think through Iraq, we may or may not attack. I have no idea, yet. But it will be for the objective of making the world more peaceful.

(Ibid.: 340)

The desirability of democratization in the Middle East was frequently aired publicly too. In February, not long before the war, Bush (in Mann 2004: 351) voiced his aspirations openly:

> A new regime in Iraq would serve as a dramatic and inspiring example of freedom for other nations in the region. It is presumptuous and insulting to suggest that a whole region of the world or the one-fifth of humanity that is Muslim is somehow untouched by the most basic aspirations of life.

Condoleezza Rice (in Pfiffner 2004: 9) also underscored the importance of moral consideration in making the case for war:

> This is an evil man who, left to his own devices, will wreak havoc again on his own population, his neighbors and, if he gets weapons of mass destruction and the means to deliver them, on all of us. *There is a very powerful moral case for regime change.* We certainly do not have the luxury of doing nothing. [My italics]

While public displays of idealism can be written off as cynical attempts at disguising narrow interests behind sentiments of morality, reports from within the administration defy such suspicions. In his memoir, Bush's former Press Secretary, Scott McClellan (2008a), who worked in the White House as the policies were forged, aspires to show how non-security considerations prevailed, and how Bush's democratic mission made him stray from national security concerns.

> For Bush, removing the "grave and gathering" danger that Iraq supposedly posed was primarily a means for achieving the far more grandiose objective of reshaping the Middle East as a region of peaceful democracies.... [W]hat drove Bush toward military confrontation more than anything else was an ambitious and idealistic post-9/11 vision of transforming the Middle East through the spread of freedom.

(Ibid.: xiii and 128–129)

If US foreign conduct was shaped by individuals or interest groups who aspired to democratize other countries more than maintaining the security interests of the US, it shows how factors unaccounted for by Mechanistic Realism can sway a state's international conduct. If correct, the prospects of finding regularities in decision-makers' priority-setting are bleaker than Mechanistic Realism suggests. That several analysts invoke the causal impact of missionary idealism inspires confidence in its relevance and reminds us not to take Biddle's presumption lightly. Indeed, McClellan's testimony combined with Bush's intimate revelations and several researchers' allegations that an idealist agenda trumped security considerations deserve careful scrutiny and I shall have more to say about the impact of *idealism* in the next chapter.

All the same, there is a paucity of empirical evidence to say that concerns other than security ranked highest in the hierarchy of goals. Without dismissing the suggestion entirely, the conclusion is hard to embrace wholeheartedly as it would mean a significant bulk of evidence to the opposite effect was a concoction and members of the administration spent a considerable amount of their time producing deceptive documents to conceal their real intentions (for future historians). In light of all the evidence to the contrary, it would be rash to interpret, for example, Hussein's ousting as primarily motivated by a desire to see a democratic government in place in a distant region.

Even McClellan acknowledges his failure to realize the impact of idealism at the time when it supposedly triggered action. This calls for skepticism towards his judgment. That he has no other documentation than memories of personal conversations adds to the empirical weakness. In a TV interview, June 2, 2008, McClellan (2008b) provided some insights into the empirical basis for his claims.

> In terms of coercive democracy, I absolutely think that that was the driving motivation of – and I know that – or believe that because I have been to the meetings with the president when I was press secretary. And he talked so passionately about spreading freedom, and that Iraq would be the – Iraq and Afghanistan would be the linchpin for really the broader Middle East becoming a democratic region.

Reports of passionate conversations several years after the decision was made are insufficient to inspire confidence in democracy-building as the war's primary motivation. It undercuts McClellan's argument in which he mentions other influential members of the administration who did not share Bush's idealist aspirations. "As for Dick Cheney and Donald Rumsfeld, my sense is that they were mainly interested in eliminating a threat to regional and global peace and greater economic security" (McClellan 2008a: 130). Those motives square better with mechanism 1.

Other first-hand accounts reject McClellan's claims as well. Douglas Feith (2008: 234), who was personally sympathetic to the idea of encouraging democracy (cf. Boyle 2004: 97), contradicts McClellan:

> I do not doubt that President Bush meant what he said when he spoke high-mindedly of his policies and the unselfish, humanitarian benefits he hoped to achieve. But to my knowledge ... he [Bush] never argued, in public or private, that the United States should go to war in order to spread democracy. While he was willing to conclude that the United States might have to go to war in self-defense, I never heard him say that we should do so simply or primarily to help a pro-democracy movement oust a dictator.

Unlike McClellan, Feith attempts to corroborate his claim by disclosing internal documents produced at the time in an appendix to his book (Feith 2008: 531–565). One attachment is a letter from Rice to all the executives, dated October 29, 2002, which outlines the goals, objectives and strategy related to Iraq. She writes: "Such a document was very useful in explaining our policy in Afghanistan" (ibid.: 541); she hopes this document can serve the same purpose for Iraq.

Only the eighth, and final, bullet point under the headline "goals" mentions democracy: "Encourage the building of democratic institutions". If promotion of democracy was the administration's primary goal, one would have expected to find it more prominently displayed in such a letter, not subordinate to the four top priorities, i.e., an Iraq that (1) "Does not threaten its neighbors", (2) "Renounces support for, and sponsorship of, international terrorism", (3) "Continues to be a single unitary state", (4) "Is free of weapons of mass destruction, their means of delivery, and associated programs" (ibid.: 542).

In addition, a more binding choice of words would have been appropriate; "encourage" is hardly the verb to portray a formidable commitment. One can cling to the argument that all the other goals are invoked to rig the real motive or persuade internal skeptics of the democratic agenda, in which case Rice's initial comment on the document's purpose to explain the policy must be utterly untruthful. Indeed, all other indications that democracy promotion did not rank highest in the hierarchy of goals, including observations referred to earlier in the paragraph, must be viewed as contrivances. It is simply too hard to believe. Even Bush (2010: 253) is frustrated and puzzled by attempts to launch allegations and theories that question his order of priorities: "Those theories are false. I was sending our troops into combat to protect the American people".

In light of such considerations it would be rash to conclude that idealist sentiments trumped the principal preoccupation with security. Rather, the order of priorities actually chimes with mechanism 1. The next chapter will qualify this conclusion, but not change it.

Mechanism 2: Observations and fear

There is ample evidence of the fear felt by decision-makers faced with their adversaries' capability to inflict harm, corroborating mechanism 2. According to Suskind (2007: 122), "deep inside the administration, and at the uppermost levels of security clearance, the fires of fear raged". Reports from CIA Director George Tenet (2007), probably the person in closest contact with the threatening signals, confirm this. His memoir is pervaded by suggestions of a recurring causal path running from observations to fear:

> But you simply could not sit where I did and read what passed across my desk on a daily basis and be anything other than scared to death about what happened (ibid.: 99).... Always there was palpable fear in the room that the United States was about to be hit again – either here or our interests abroad

(ibid.: 230–231) ... we would try to get a handle on the flood of information about terrorism pouring in from around the world. Virtually every day you would hear something about a possible impending threat that would scare you to death (ibid.: 230). Few understand the palpable sense of uncertainty and even fear that gripped those in the storm's centre in the immediate aftermath of 9/11.

(Ibid.: 236–237)

Likewise Rice (in Daalder and Destler 2009: 269) told a *New York Times* reporter how the constant exposure to information about impending threats[3]

had a powerful effect on Bush's state of mind and her own. She felt she was constantly on edge, in a state of paranoia, but rational paranoia, as even old threats – and Iraq would soon be one – took on new meaning.

Cheney (2011: 368–369) recounts how the accumulative intelligence estimates were reasons for consternation: "After 9/11 no American president could responsibly ignore the steady stream of reporting we were getting about the threat posed by Saddam Hussein.... We could not ignore the threat or wish it away".

Some advisors are less candid and appear reluctant to admit to being fearful. On inspection, it is hard to ignore that fear lurked in their minds as well. Consider for example what Philip Zelikow (2007), the principal author of the National Security Strategy 2002, answered when asked to talk about the extent to which fear of being attacked informed the arguments of the National Security Strategy:

The reasons don't fit under such a neat label. States do like to be able to defend themselves against catastrophic attack. Thus the practical question is: How best to do that?

He then referred to an article called "Offensive Military Options" (Zelikow 1993), in which he discusses how states should cope with proliferation of nuclear weapons:

[T]here are some states, in some circumstances, whose development, acquisition, or deployment of nuclear weapons could endanger the vital interests of the United States (ibid.: 162) ... [suggesting that] political norms should support the use of force to contain the danger presented by those countries which have been branded as nuclear outlaws by the international community.

(Ibid.: 191)

Despite Zelikow's evasiveness and insistence that fear is "too neat" a label, it is difficult to make sense of his argument without invoking fear. Zelikow prefers the practical question of "how" to defend. But if states "do like to defend themselves" (Zelikow 2007) and "norms should support the use of force" (Zelikow

1993: 191) in some specified circumstances, and he grapples with how best to defend the US against catastrophic attacks, it must be because he *fears* a situation in which these attempts fail. Arguably, Zelikow's evasiveness can be dispelled by analyzing the substance of his argument, which suggests that even his reasoning was conducted under the influence of fear.

When asked how 9/11 affected the strategic thinking of the administration, Zelikow (2007) said that "the event had had a profound impact. In 2001, all the top officials who reflected on the 9/11 experiences took away some strong suggestive inferences for the way one thought about policy". Other events had shaped the thinking too.

> But the issues [how to keep America safe in the face of terrorism and WMD] were not new from 9/11. The revelations after the 1991 war with Hussein about the extent of Iraq's nuclear program also caused quite a bit of reflection.... The document [NSS 2002] was influenced most strongly by the experience with Iraq in 1990–1991 and the UNSCOM discoveries and by the 9/11 attacks (coming after the [USS] *Cole*, after 1998 bombings, after the Millennium alert, etc.)
>
> (email interview)

A common feature of all these observations is they are taken as evidence of the adversaries' capability to defy US security interests. The "experience with Iraq" refers to the 1990 invasion of Kuwait, the "UNSCOM discoveries" to Hussein's weapons programs, and the other invoked episodes to "successful" terror attacks. Insofar as evidence of a counterpart's capability to inflict harm informed what "one thought about policy", it validates mechanism 2.

Members of the administration also took 9/11 as evidence, not only of a capability, but also of an intention to inflict *mass casualties*. That interpretation differed from the common view under which the primary purpose of terror is to inflict psychological distress.[4] According to Feith (2008: 214), 9/11 refuted that approximation as it "was not an act of political theatre".

> [O]ne had to presume that terrorists would have been glad to kill all thirty thousand people who worked at the World Trade Center, and even multiples of that number.... This was why keeping weapons of mass destruction out of the hands of terrorists became, suddenly and inevitably, a far more pressing and higher-order concern than it had been before.
>
> (Feith 2008: 214)

The administration's worry that terrorists wanted WMD was not built on speculation, but material intelligence. In late November 2001, Great Britain claimed to have evidence that al-Qaeda wanted WMD (Woodward 2004: 46). This was the beginning of the intelligence operation that later uncovered a proliferation network headed by Abdul Qadeer Kahn, who sold nuclear secrets to perhaps a dozen countries (Gat 2006: 643). Tenet (2007) devotes much of his attention to this matter. This concern loomed larger than any other, he writes. "One mushroom cloud would change history. My deepest fear is that this is exactly what they [the terrorists] intend" (Tenet 2007: 280).

> What we discovered stunned us all. The threats were real. Our intelligence confirmed that most senior leaders of al-Qa'ida are still singularly focused on acquiring WMD (ibid.: 259).... Moreover, we established beyond reasonable doubt that that al-Qa'ida had clear intent to acquire chemical, biological, and radiological/nuclear weapons, to possess not as a deterrent but to cause mass casualties.
>
> (Ibid.: 260)

According to Woodward (2004: 47), this particular type of "intelligence had a dramatic impact on Bush. He did not want to underreact.... The fear never went away". Illustratively, in an address to the United Nations, Bush (in Dueck 2006: 156) enunciated that "our greatest fear is that terrorists will find a shortcut to their mad ambitions when an outlaw regime supplies them with the technologies to kill on a massive scale".

The anthrax incident, occurring in October 2001 (Daalder and Lindsay 2005: 117) and killing five, was taken as confirmation of hostility on the part of adversaries, even though the perpetrators of this episode were never identified. It added credence to descriptions of the likely devastating consequences of WMD attacks. According to McClellan (2008: 108), the anthrax event had "an enormous impact on President Bush's mind-set". After sixteen confirmed cases and many false alarms, "the fear permeating the country was real" (ibid.: 109); the "influence of the anthrax attacks on policymaking within the Bush White House shouldn't be underestimated ... I know President Bush's thinking was deeply affected by the anthrax attacks" (ibid.: 111).

It is also worth noting the deliberate lowering of the threshold of evidence needed to instill fear. In effect the receptors with which the US measured threats appear to have been deliberately recalibrated to be more sensitive. "[T]he standards of proof [of threats]", says Cheney (in Woodward 2004: 30), "would have to be lowered – smoking gun, irrefutable evidence would not have to be required for the United States to act to defend itself". In practice one would think that heightened sensitivity would result in more signals being considered reasonable ground for concern.

Several analysts believe the fear was "genuine" and "weighed heavily on Bush" (Dueck 2006: 156). Jervis appears confident that members of the administration "revealed their *true fears* when they talked about the possibility that he [Hussein] could use WMD against the United States and its allies" (Jervis 2003b: 373, my italics). Suggestions to the opposite effect would imply an impressive act of political theatre. Yet many have seriously disputed whether the administration's fear was genuine. Invocations of fear were nothing but a false pretext to mobilize support for goals unrelated to the threats. Gurtov's (2006) view is representative on this score.

> [T]op policymakers under Bush substituted their own politically motivated judgments for the findings and uncertainties of the professionals who were charged with providing and assessing intelligence.
>
> (Ibid.: 67)

According to Thomas Powers (2010: 8), after analyzing what he considers deliberate misuse of intelligence about Iraq, "no claim of imminent danger could be described as intellectually honest". Indeed, it is possible to agree that the threats were publicly presented as more urgent than the intelligence warranted and to doubt that fear ultimately was the prime impetus of the Iraq war. Nevertheless, in light of the evidence presented above it would be unwarranted to deny how some of the observations that the administration took as evidence of threats also created a sense of fear. There is simply too much evidence for the ability of mechanism 2 to capture a mental operation that occurred frequently within the Bush administration, even if the evidence is insufficient to dispel suspicions that fear was not the administration's primary or only motivating force.

Mechanism 3: Uncertainty and fear

Examination of the evidence from within the administration suggests uncertainty contributed to foster fear among the decision-makers, corresponding to the mental operation encapsulated by mechanism 3. The frequency of observations to this effect indicates a recurring phenomenon. Consider five episodes lending the mechanism micro-level credence.

(1) Daalder and Lindsay (2005) describe Bush's reception of daily intelligence briefings with the CIA Director, George Tenet. Often, as Tenet (2007: 234) also writes in his memoirs, the content of the briefings was uncertain, "tiny threads". In October 2001, he placed Iraq at the top of the list of states hostile enough to supply terrorists with WMD.

> Even though the available intelligence constituted what one knowledgeable source called an "incomplete mosaic" of fact, inference and potentially false leads, Tenet's briefing "sent the president through the roof."
>
> (Daalder and Lindsay 2005: 118)

The noteworthy feature here is how extremely alarmed Bush became ("sent through the roof") despite the efforts of the intelligence community to disparage the quality of the information on which the briefing was based and the uncertainty surrounding the report.

(2) Reflecting back to the time period after 9/11 Tenet (2007: 342) quotes and subscribes to what an intelligence officer once told him:

> Intelligence is central to the Bush administration.... And then after 9/11, the first attack on American soil of any magnitude in sixty years, they were in fear. In fairness to them, people do not understand how goddamn dangerous

we thought it was. *The absence of solid information on additional threats was terrifying*. (my italics)

It is hard to escape the congruence indicated by this account between a mental micro-process and mechanism 3. Reporting that the "absence of solid information was terrifying" dovetails with "uncertainty fosters fear".

(3) Another episode is described by Suskind (2007: 70). A Pakistani nuclear scientist had been interrogated by the CIA. He revealed that he had discussed "the global struggle against the imperialist" with bin Laden. They talked about "nuclear logistics", including "various nuclear bomb designs". The scientist had, among other things, told bin Laden how costly and difficult it was to enrich uranium, after which bin Laden supposedly interrupted him: "What if you already have the enriched uranium?" Information of this conversation was passed to the Vice President: "Was it a question or a statement? That was not clear. Either way, the clarification of these specifics fuelled Cheney's darkest fears" (ibid.: 70). Again, not knowing enough to fit every bit of intelligence into a larger picture appears to have had a disturbing rather than a soothing effect.

(4) Consider Cheney's much-discussed and often-quoted statement in a *Meet the Press* interview in which he alluded to possible cooperation between terrorists and Iraq:

> The Czechs alleged that Mohammed Atta, the lead attacker, met in Prague with a senior Iraqi intelligence official five months before the attack, but we've never been able to develop anymore of that yet either in terms of confirming it or discrediting it. We just don't know.
>
> (Quoted in Feith 2008: 590)

Cheney's statement is usually taken to imply the "administration was ... convinced that there was a connection between the terrorists and the Iraq government in the form of a meeting in April 2001 in the Czech Republic between Mohamed Atta ... and an Iraq diplomat" (Pfiffner 2004: 10). But Cheney is not categorical in this instance. Rather than "convinced", Cheney's state of mind appears to have been uncertain. While the statement is commonly argued to be "little more than a scam to fool the public" (Holmes 2007: 305), Cheney's uncertainty may plausibly have been an expression of actual worry. Read without conspiratorial suspicions, the lack of convincing evidence disconfirming the existence of the connection would seem to have caused fear rather than complacency.

(5) Consider finally the differing interpretations of a report issued by the International Atomic Energy Agency (IAEA) containing satellite photos of industrial buildings being rebuilt in Iraq. The agency spokeswoman, Melissa Fleming (in Prados 2004: 25) responded calmly to the report:

> Construction of a building is one thing. Restarting a nuclear program is another. We have a lot of commercial satellite imagery that there has been

construction at cites that were formerly nuclear. But what that means we don't know.

In contrast, Bush (in ibid.) immediately sensed alarm at the report: "I don't know what more evidence we need". The contrast is illuminating as it suggests that individuals in different roles drew different conclusions from similar observations. Here we have an instance where there is scope for judgment. Whereas an observer without executive power reacts calmly, Bush appears to have become fearful. The comparison adds confidence to the existence of a causal pattern running from uncertainty to fear on the part of decision-makers vested with responsibility for a country's security.

What these five examples suggest is corroborated by observations pertaining to Iraq. Here too, lack of specific, convincing information regarding Hussein's capabilities and intentions appears to have had a worrying, rather than a calming effect. Illustratively, in a speech October 7, 2002, Bush (in Moens 2004: 183) rhetorically asks how close Hussein was to having nuclear weapons and answers: "Well, we don't know exactly, and that's the problem". In other words, uncertainty was itself reason enough to worry.

Uncertainty also worried other members of the administration:

> At [the] heart of the US problem with Iraq was uncertainty. Even if new inspections occurred, we would not learn for sure what was happening with Iraq's WMD programs and stockpiles.
>
> (Feith 2008: 302–303)

According to George Tenet (2007: 328), "[i]t was never a question of known imminent threat; it was about an unwillingness to risk surprise". He was constantly "haunted by the possibility that there was more going on than we could detect" (ibid.: 316). Faced with limited information of uncertain quality, one reasonable expectation is cautious conclusions or suspension of belief. Reportedly "the intelligence we heard ... every night, were just tiny threads. They had to be woven into tapestry before we could make sense of what we were seeing" (ibid.: 234). Yet in spite of having only "tiny threads", both Feith and Tenet were alarmed.

Likewise, Cheney does not suspend belief confronted with uncertainty. In September 2002, he (in Daalder and Lindsay 2005: 157) admitted, "We don't have all the evidence. We have 10 percent, 20 percent, 30 percent. We don't know much". But despite acknowledging the scant evidence he concludes unequivocally, "We know we have part of the picture. And that part of the picture tells us that he [Saddam Hussein] is, in fact, actively and aggressively seeking to acquire nuclear weapons" (in Daalder and Lindsay 2005: 157). When not knowing much, Cheney appears pessimistic, concludes dismally, and becomes fearful rather than complacent.

In her memoir, also Condoleezza Rice's (2011) account of her psychological reactions to uncertainty dovetail with mechanism 3. She recounts the "uncertainties about the precise state of Saddam's weapons of mass destruction" and explains how the available data led different intelligence agencies to arrive at alternative predictions regarding when Iraq would acquire a nuclear device. Yet Rice elaborates on why she as a policymaker would not want "to take the risk of accepting" anything but the most threatening assessment, "particularly after 9/11 and the specter of WMD terrorism" (ibid.: 169).

Although the bulk of the post-9/11 evidence can be subsumed under mechanism 3, the empirical material does not support a hypothesis that uncertainty inevitably leads to fear. The US view of great power relations during the same period, not least its relations with Russia, reveals a contrary tendency where uncertain signals can also lead to complacency. The National Security Strategy of 2002 (page v) contains the following passage:

> Today, the international community has the best chance since the rise of the nation-state in the seventeenth century to build a world where great powers compete in peace instead of continually prepare for war. Today the world's great powers find themselves on the same side – united by the common dangers of terrorist violence and chaos.

In a lecture given on April 29, Condoleezza Rice (2002: 6) expanded on the idea of great power rivalry deferred indefinitely owing to common commitment to international order:

> After the end of Cold War ... we may well be on [the] cusp of an era in which the world will not be bedeviled by great power rivalries ... September 11th and its aftermath illuminated a fundamental divide between the forces of chaos and those of order. And all the world's great powers clearly see themselves as falling on the same side of this divide.

Only about a month after 9/11, Colin Powell (2001: 6) attested to the same sentiment arguing that, "the prospects for international cooperation across a broad range of issues has [sic] never been brighter". However, even if all states saw terrorism as a threat and as a reason to pursue a common cause, downplaying conflicts of interest and potential for rivalry is incompatible with mechanism 3, as uncertainty still surrounds the situation.

A concrete example illustrates the inadequacy of mechanism 3. Having stated "the United States and Russia are no longer strategic adversaries", the NSS 2002 highlights the Moscow Treaty on Strategic Reductions. "[It] is emblematic of this new reality and reflects a critical change in Russian thinking that promises to lead to long-term relations with ... the United States". According to Woodward (2003: 326–327), Bush "desperately wanted a signed treaty with the Russians to reduce strategic nuclear weapons". Even faced with Rumsfeld's opposition to the deal (Rumsfeld had asked suspiciously, more in accordance with mechanism 3, "What difference would a piece of paper make?" (ibid.: 327)), Bush signed the treaty on May 24, 2002.

Whether Russia complies with the agreement is, despite high-flown rhetorics about the competition for peace, ultimately fraught with uncertainty. Fear would thus be expected following mechanism 3. Although concerns were voiced (e.g., "We are attentive to the possible renewal of old patterns of great power competitions" (NSS 2002: 26)), Bush appears confident that complacent amity was an appropriate sentiment in US relations with Russia, even in such sensitive matters as arms reductions. "[R]ecent developments have encouraged our hope that a truly global consensus about basic principles is slowly taking shape" (NSS 2002: 26). That uncertainty on this matter was optimistically interpreted, resulted in complacency, and did not create a sense of fear, is at odds with how anyone under the influence of mechanism 3 would react. It may suggest that mechanism 3 has a twin mechanism, mechanism 3b, whereby uncertainty instead of fostering fear fosters complacency.

Interestingly, Waltz (1979) has previously hinted at a mechanism at par with mechanism 3b, capable of accommodating the above observation. Strong states facing uncertainty could "hold back until the ambiguity of events is resolved without fearing that the moment for effective action will be lost" (ibid.: 195). This amounts to a competing model of how states react to uncertainty and resonates with Jervis's (2003b: 371) presumption that decision-makers "generally hesitate to take strong actions in the face of such uncertainty ... they are predisposed to postpone, to await further developments and information". In these accounts, rather than instilling fear, uncertainty can elicit composed optimism.

Although clearly evident in relations with Russia, mechanism 3b is unable to explain why uncertainty about future terrorism and the status of Iraq's capabilities and intentions caused fear. Yet the fact that it operated in relation with other great powers was significant as it allowed the US to undertake measures in the war on terror that otherwise would have inconceivable. Had the US had stronger concerns about great power rivalry, say a presumption to the effect that a great power would come to the support of Iraq in the case of a US attack, it would have reduced US options.

The fact that two reaction patterns follow from uncertainty even within the same individual and in the same time period, makes it difficult to predict how states will react to uncertainty. It demonstrates how pairs of mechanisms capture more empirical complexity than universal propositions and that parsimonious determinacy is sometimes at odds with validity. It also illustrates how seemingly incompatible theoretical proposals can be interpreted in terms of different mechanisms able to explain outcomes after the fact. After all, it is reasonable to include even mechanism 3b in the mechanistic toolbox.

Although positing two different causal paths precludes predictions, it is worth noting the different epistemological circumstances surrounding the uncertainty pertaining to the possibility that terrorists might acquire WMDs from Iraq and that surrounding future Russian hostility, as it might say something about the conditions for the activation of either mechanism. Uncertainty as to whether terrorists had operative plans, the range of their intentions and the strength of the support they could muster from other states seems to have contributed to fearfulness because rational computation of these matters is extremely complicated. As the National Strategy to Combating Terrorism (NSCT 2003: 16) says,

> The shadowy nature of terrorist organizations precludes an easy analysis of their capabilities and intent. The classic net assessment of the enemy based on the number of tanks, airplanes and ships does not apply to non-state actors.

Uncertainty resulting from this fact is what led Rumsfeld (2002: 23) to conclude that the US now has to "prepare for the unknown, uncertain, the unseen and the unexpected". In comparison, the evidence of Russian intent, while also fraught with uncertainty, is still easier to distill and manage. Unexpectedly, perhaps, the triggering of mechanism 3 appears more likely in cases of uncertain terrorist threat than in cases of uncertain great power rivalry.

Mechanism 4: Counter-wishful thinking and fear

Typically, information shapes beliefs with inescapable force. When the Bush administration learned something of the threat of Iraq – the inability, say, of the IAEA inspector ElBaradei (2003) to identify WMD in Iraq despite his best efforts, saying for example on February 14 that "we have to date found no evidence of ongoing prohibited nuclear or nuclear-related activities in Iraq" – they would probably find it impossible to consciously repress that knowledge. This follows from their rational disposition. Yet some of the evidence from this period indicates that members of the administration somehow came to fear terrorists equipped with WMDs from Iraq despite information and arguments giving little reason for disquiet. They often arrived at strong judgments with a conspicuously sinister slant but based on limited evidence. As Hans Blix has noted (in Moens 2004: 188): "I think they [members of the Bush administration] were inclined to put exclamation marks where there should have been question marks". This calls for an explanation.

The most prominent explanation offered in the literature invokes spurious motives. The administration, it is claimed, deliberately rigged their interpretations to make the threat of nuclear terrorism appear more urgent than they knew it was in order to justify a war they wanted for spurious reasons. Gurtov (2006: 67) writes: "The evidence concerning policymaking on Iraq under George W. Bush strongly suggests outright efforts to deceive the US public, Congress, and the world community". Prados (2004: 17) adds that,

> President Bush and his cohorts crafted a litany of largely baseless charges about Iraq, then repeated, escalated, and rearranged those charges in places and times calculated to contribute to their goal of opening the way to an unprovoked war.

Allegations of tortuous motives are hard to discard. Yet those liable to doubt the influence of political fraud will welcome explanations not invoking it exactly for that reason. Although explanations implying policymakers acted in good faith will strain credulity in the eyes of Gurtov and Prados, it is worth considering whether the mechanism of counter-wishful thinking can explain why many of the administration's judgments went in a worst-case direction. Although the suggestion is empirically weak, it is far from baseless.

It seems that information from Iraq, including Hussein's failure to comply with the UN's demands for transparency, left a *"genuine ambiguity* about the status of Iraq's WMD programs" (Litwak 2007: 164, my italics). The phrase "genuine ambiguity" captures the different opinions held by reasonable individuals regarding the Iraqi threat. The evidence of the existence, magnitude, quality and level of sophistication of the weapons, as well as the likelihood that Iraq would hand them over to terrorists, was open to reasonable disagreement.

Jervis writes that while "the preponderance of evidence indicated that Iraq had WMD, it was not sufficient to prove it beyond reasonable doubt" (Jervis 2006a: 14). Hans Blix, the person who presided over the UN weapons inspection in Iraq, noted that his

> reports did not lend themselves to categorical conclusions.... At the time, no one – the UN inspectors and myself included – could *guarantee* that Iraq was without any weapons of mass destruction.
>
> (Ibid.: 264, 256)

Blix thought the evidence warranted a cautious conclusion about Iraq's possession of limited amounts of WMD: "the inspectors ... had searched all over Iraq for a number of years without finding any traces" (Blix 2004: 256). Even though Iraq had not complied fully with the inspectors, nothing undeclared had yet been discovered (Blix in Moens 2004: 189).

But despite careful inspection, this ambiguity cannot be detected in Bush's thinking. He appears to have been systematically more attentive to and put more weight on information that imparted danger. As he evaluated the Iraqi threat he inflated alarming information and ignored what would on the surface have been evidence in his interest (i.e., lack of Iraqi weapons). Illustratively, in a speech Bush gave in Cincinnati on October 7, 2002 (in Litwak 2007: 146) he offered a profoundly sinister interpretation:

> Understanding the threats of our time, knowing the designs and deceptions of the Iraqi regime, we have every reason to assume the worst, and we have an urgent duty to prevent the worst from occurring.

Later, before the UN General Assembly Bush (in Ritchie and Rogers 2007: 96) said:

> The history, the logic and the facts lead to one conclusion: Saddam Hussein's regime is a grave and gathering danger. To suggest otherwise is to hope against the evidences. To assume this regime's good faith is to bet the lives of millions and the peace of the world in a reckless gamble.

In both these instances Bush ignores ambiguity and endorses the grimmest interpretation available. As Litwak points out, and as Blix's memoirs testify, not only "one conclusion" was conceivable. Many reports "certainly known to the US Department of State, Department of Defense and CIA" which "were based on visits to sites, interviews and close examination of records from Iraq" (Blix 2004: 256, 261) had not discovered WMD activity. The judgment of Hussein as *not* presenting "a grave and gathering danger" was indeed questionable given the fact that the intelligence estimates developed by the CIA and other agencies were alarming, often couched in a confident and preemptory tone (Braut-Hegghammer and Riste 2005: 87). It could not be excluded that the threat was real, but doubting the seriousness of it was not necessarily "to hope *against* the evidence" or a commit a "reckless gamble".

That Bush's judgment was confidently sinister is even more baffling in light of his surprise at one point over the paucity of evidence giving reason for alarm. The CIA reportedly failed to make a convincing case of the Iraqi threat in a presentation before Bush.

> I've been told all this intelligence about having WMD and this is the best we've got?... I don't think this is quite – it's not something that Joe Public would understand or would gain a lot of confidence from.
> (Woodward 2003: 249)

This more than suggests Bush must have sensed the evidence on which he based his sinister judgment was thin. Yet that did not instill reservations. Likewise, Powell reportedly found it difficult to stitch together a convincing UN briefing because the evidence was thinner than he expected. According to Jervis (2006a: 13–14) he "spent several days closely querying intelligence officials about the information" and exercised "due diligence", indicating that the analytical procedures, while not necessarily the raw data, were flawless. But even meticulous engagement with the ambiguous data did not lead Powell to doubt the main conclusions of his presentation. On the contrary, he places little emphasis on the limited knowledge on which his conclusions were based in his UN presentation. His inferences are explicit, not tentative, and doubts and reservations do not surface. Prados (2004) finds no less than thirty-five instances of Powell misleading the UN, a staggering number considering the level of certainty he demanded of information to be used in his UN speech.

Mechanism 4 posits a mental readiness to believe what one fears. One possible explanation of the sinister judgment about the status of Iraqi WMD programs and the possibility that Iraq would deliver these weapons to terrorists is that the decision-makers were led to believe what they feared. The mechanism would have been less suggestive were it not for the fact that the administration's interpretations of ambiguous data on several occasions were believable, but systematically sinister. Faced with ambiguity they consistently erred on the alarmist side.[5]

Because many of these instances involved publicity, they cannot be used to dismiss the suspicion that the interpretations were deliberately rigged. However, an *internal* presentation, dated September 12, 2002 (CFA 2002), illustrates just how prevalent the mood of excessive pessimism regarding Iraq was and incentives for hoodwinking the audience presumably less pressing. The first two pages highlight the "serious and growing threat to the US":

> We are rightfully concerned about the failures – intelligence and policy – that made 9/11 possible.... We have more information now about what Iraq might do than we had last year about [what] al Qaida might do. Implication: we have to be willing to "connect the dots" now – can't wait for the "smoking gun"... we have to make use of many types of evidence – specific intelligence items are only part of the story. Also have to look at history, including actual use of CW [chemical weapons]. We have to assess the strength of Iraq's motivation to acquire WMD. In addition, Iraq is very good at denial and deception – as we learned after the Gulf War. We were surprised at how many WMD-related facilities we hadn't known about. We must take this into account in assessing the intelligence evidence that we have available. Experience tells us that what we have found is only a small part of what actually is there.
>
> (CFA 2002)

These few lines contain several indications of the counter-wishful reading I believe was made of the situation. First, there seems to be an injunction to "connect the dots" (i.e., *apparent* threats are *real* threats) even if there are too few dots for an integrated opinion about the matter. Second, inferring that knowledge about what Iraq "might do" warrants preventive action without knowing the *probability* of Iraq doing it, arguably requires a sinister slant of mind since ignoring probabilities possibly exaggerates apparent threats. Third, indicating a need to supplement observational evidence with inferential deduction is to invite worst-case speculation to impinge on judgments. Fourth, the description is narrowly attentive to incidents of alarm (for example previous use of chemical weapons) but ignores Hussein's limited options after the containment regime was put in place after 1991 and that he had not seriously threatened US security interests since that time. Fifth, the document reveals a clear presumption to the effect that all information from Hussein is by definition deceptive. Sixth, the document discloses a liability to inflate the seriousness of what is actually known, implying that the sinister information available is in effect only the tip of the iceberg. Overall, writing and subscribing to these few lines requires a pessimistic inclination. It is not the only possible explanation, but it is still plausible that the ominous verdict found in this document owes to counter-wishful thinking.

Situations of rational indeterminacy after 9/11 were not confined to evaluations of ambiguous threats. In questions of security policy, conflicting but equally persuasive causal logics sometimes made reasonable people disagree. As in the case of the ambiguous evidence, when several causal logics made sense, the Bush administration expected the least fortuitous causal route to prevail. Consider an example regarding the utility of deterrence.

Toppling Hussein was thought of as a bulwark against two eventualities. In the first place to prevent terror attacks with WMD supplied by Iraq. In the second place to prevent a WMD-armed Iraq from initiating war in the region, in which case the barrier of US intervention would be higher. The first eventuality rested on the assumption that Hussein would be reckless enough to impart WMD to terrorists. The second eventuality was premised on a view of Hussein as a cost-insensitive risk-taker who, armed with WMD, was prepared to gamble on being able to expand with impunity.

While both assumptions were defendable, neither was beyond reasonable dispute. At the time, many believed that the transfer of WMD to terrorists and use for expansionist endeavors in the region could be deterred. Mearsheimer and Walt (2003: 52), for example, maintained:

> One problem with this argument [that Saddam Hussein is not deterrable]: It is almost certainly wrong.... In fact, the historical record shows that the United States can contain Iraq effectively – even if Saddam has nuclear weapons – just as it contained the Soviet Union during the Cold War.[6]

The Bush administration, on its side, saw it differently. In the recently quoted internal presentation, both deterrence and containment were discussed, but found less promising than "preemptive action". In relation to containment it was argued that you "Can't contain when Iraq could use terrorists to deliver WMD". Deterrence was dismissed on several considerations: the "possibility of unattributable, and hence, undeterrable WMD attacks", that "Saddam has a history of recklessness", and "If Iraq obtained nuclear weapons, it might believe that it could safely engage in conventional aggression" (CFA 2002).

The administration's rejection of deterrence is counter-wishful in two respects. In the first place, of two plausible causal paths, the Bush administration expected the least fortuitous one to prevail, suggesting the necessity of war. In the second place, the arguments given for rejecting deterrence had a sinister slant and begged qualification.

First, while terror attacks do sometimes occur without clues to suggest who is accountable (think of the anthrax incident in the US), in which case retaliation lacks a target, leaders of WMD countries run a great risk of being held accountable if *their* weapons are used in a terror attack. That risk plausibly deters them from providing weapons to terrorists. Additionally, it is unclear what Iraq would gain by providing WMD to terrorists.

Second, while recklessness on Hussein's part cannot be excluded, he would hardly be totally insensitive to the personal costs and the risk of being toppled. That he was reckless enough to use chemical weapons against Iran does not entail a willingness to use such weapons against a more deterring state with a formidable retaliatory capacity, such as the US.

Third, while a nuclear deterrent would doubtless inhibit some states from countering a conventional Iraqi attack, it is far from clear that it would deter the US. After all, before the 1991 Gulf War the US defended the sovereignty of

Kuwait despite Hussein's WMD capability. In sum, even the causal logic adhered to by the administration inflated the likelihood of a counter-wishful outcome. Mechanism 4 may suggest why.

As noted in Chapter 3, counter-wishful thinking is almost as baffling as the observations it aspires to explain and making sense of the baffling fact that the Bush administration systematically subscribed to sinister conclusions by invoking the mechanism is in some sense only to restate the puzzle. Yet there are some reports suggesting that what appears as counter-wishful thinking did not happen behind the decision-makers' back, but rather resulted from deliberate attempts to offset what was suspected to be wishful thinking.

Consider how Rice (in Daalder and Destler 2009: 282) accounts for why the sinister interpretations of the information typically prevailed:

> As a student of this business [i.e., international politics] I know that intelligence estimates almost always underestimate capabilities. They rarely overestimate capabilities.

George Tenet (2007: 330) also suggested that correction influenced his overall assessment of the status of Iraqi WMD:

> In many ways, we were prisoners of our own history.... Inevitably, the judgments were influenced by our underestimation of Iraq's progress on nuclear weapons in the late 1980s and early 1990s – a mistake no one wanted to repeat.

For Feith (2008: 64), compensation was justified given "the errors the US intelligence community had made in recent decades.... So we were particularly skeptical about intelligence products". These reports are revealing insofar as Rice, Tenet and Feith seem deliberately to overcompensate for the possibility of underestimating threats. What appears as counter-wishful thinking may have been a product of a deliberate attempt to prevent wishful thinking from distorting the threat assessment. But the effort to prevent wishful thinking (i.e., believing wrongly that there are no weapons when they in fact exist), it seems, led to another distortion (i.e., believing wrongly that there were weapons when they in fact did not exist). Possibly, in attempting to avoid believing what they hoped was the case, they instead began to believe what they feared. If so, the phenomenon is rendered less baffling.

To sum up, one reason for exploring alternative accounts of how the Bush administration arrived at an alarmist threat perception is to counter suggestions of political fraud. The mechanism of counter-wishful thinking explains the sinister judgments of the administration without recourse to suspicious premises by suggesting that decision-makers came to believe what they feared. The causal importance of this mechanism, while not beyond dispute, still has sufficient evidential backing to justify its inclusion in the explanatory toolbox. The statements indicating overcorrection as responsible for directing the administration's judgments towards a worst-case scenario, while *making sense* of what otherwise seems a strange mechanism, can hardly account for every observation subsumed under mechanism 4.

Mechanism 5: (a) Power maximizing, (b) Power preservation and (c) Power amassment within reasonable limits

Mechanism 5a posits that a neutral desire for security breeds expansionism, mechanism 5b suggests that desire for security triggers power-preserving behavior, whereas mechanism 5c suggests that considerate decision-makers amass power within reasonable limits. Which of these precepts squares with observations? Overall, mechanism 5a appears truer to the facts. According to Renshon (2007: 15), one tenet of Bush's strategic thinking was exactly "the judgment that when it comes to catastrophic terrorism, the best defense is a good offense", suggesting that the offensive initiatives pursued were a corollary of the administration's desire to forestall new terror attacks.

Zbigniew Brzezinski (2007) reaches the same conclusion. After asserting "enough is known already to permit a broad recapitulation of how Bush's response to 9/11 emerged and took shape" (ibid.: 140), he concludes, "[a]mong members of the foreign policy team, an overwhelming consensus naturally favored a muscular response" (ibid.: 141). Although muscularity is a vague term, Brzezinski's main message is that the idea to go on the offense took hold of the decision-makers after 9/11.

Less allegorically, Dunn (2003: 286) maintains that the administration endorsed "a policy approach that is resistant to an acceptance of the status quo and prepared to take risks in the belief that it can achieve better results". This concurs with Jervis (2003b), who, after discussing various facets of the impact of US hegemony on the policies, sums it up:

> All this means that under the Bush doctrine the United States is not a status quo power. Its motives may not be selfish, but the combination of power, fear and perceived opportunity leads it to seek to reshape the world.... In a process akin to the deep security dilemma, in order to protect itself, the United States is impelled to act in a way that will increase, or at least bring to the surface, conflict with others. Even if the prevailing situation is satisfactory, it cannot be maintained by purely defensive measures.
>
> (Ibid.: 383)

Apart from the cryptic reference to unselfish motives, Jervis's brief account is consonant with mechanism 5a. In fact, his conclusion that purely defensive motives impel maximizing behavior captures its essence.

Allegations to the effect that the administration was bent on changing the status quo by initiating offensive policies come as no surprise given that this intent was underscored on numerous occasions. Considering the dubious legitimacy of offensive initiatives in international politics, one would expect more reticence on this score, but contrary to that expectation, Bush frequently argued for offensive actions in the pursuit of the national security interest.

> Yet the war on terror will not be won on the defensive. We must take the battle to the enemy, disrupt his plans and confront the worst threats before they emerge. In the world we have entered the only path to safety is the path of action. And this nation will act.
>
> (Bush 2002a)

In similar vein, "In the face of today's new threats, the only way to pursue peace is to pursue those who threaten it" (Bush in Sammon 2002: 234). Such statements are without difficulty subsumed under mechanism 5a.

Reports by individuals well placed to come to grips with Bush's thinking, find the offensive stance presented to the public to reflect his genuine position. In May 2002, Rice (quoted in Ritchie and Rogers 2007: 85) underscored Bush's dissatisfaction with a defensive approach to security. "[T]he president felt that it is extremely important to make clear that the status quo is not acceptable with this [Iraqi] regime". Another insider, Douglas Feith, confirms the impression that Bush favored offensive polices:

> The President shared our determination to make this a global war of initiative, one that broke with the standard, backward-looking retaliatory posture the United States has taken in the past against terrorist enemies.
>
> (Feith 2008: 84)

Bush's determination on this score harmonized with the recommendations of the Secretary of Defense. In a memorandum handed Bush, Rumsfeld argued that,

> [V]ictory in the war on terrorism would require geopolitical changes substantial enough to cause every regime supporting terrorism to worry about its vulnerability. If the war does not significantly change the world's political map, the US will not achieve its aim.
>
> (Ibid.: 82)

As these testimonies appear to show, the idea of cementing the status quo was viewed with discontent, allowing a revisionist posture to prevail.

Interestingly, the idea of going on the offensive occurred immediately after 9/11. After acknowledging the necessity for self-defense, Bush immediately advised his closest advisors of the prospects presented by the situation: "This is a great opportunity" (Woodward 2003: 32), he reportedly said. "I will seize the opportunity to achieve big goals" (Woodward 2003: 282, 339). In light of the dismal circumstances in the wake of the attack, this is, on the face of it, an awkward if not misplaced statement, whose oddity is dispelled by subsuming it under mechanisms 5a.

In fact, most reports from the deliberations among the top officials suggest that most members of the cabinet saw "opportunities" for power expansion despite the perilous situation. A confrontational campaign aimed at increasing US power was soon presented as the most viable strategic option. This was, it was argued, an occasion to shape the environment and thereby prevent further attacks. "Forget about 'exit strategies'", wrote Rumsfeld (2002) only days after 9/11, "we're looking at a sustained engagement that carries no deadlines".

According to Rice (in Woodward 2003: 282),

> The country could sit on its unparalleled power and dispense it in small doses, or it could make big strategic power plays that would fundamentally alter the balance of power. Bush planted himself in the visionary camp.

Bromwich (2008: 28) takes the administration's early emphasis on opportunities not as a sign of hyperbolic positivism, but as clear evidence of an underlying expansive intent.

> Imaginative leadership, the President was saying, must do far more than respond to the attack, or attend to the needs of self-preservation. Better to use the opportunity to "go massive", as Rumsfeld noted on September 11.

If the motives Bromwich imputes to Bush and his advisors are correct, it seems they were indeed acting under the sway of mechanism 5a. That the administration's impulse in the wake of an attack was not confined to punishing the perpetrators, but included seizing the moment to pursue larger goals squares well with mechanism 5a and the expectation that leaders seize opportunities to alter the distribution of power in their favor.

In light of the attention Mechanistic Realism pays to the limited scope of choice under anarchic conditions, it is worth noting that the decision-makers report that the situation was indeed determinative. Presumably, the terrorist threat compelled an assertive strategy:

> We felt *compelled* to choose a more ambitious strategic goal – to prevent further attacks that would kill Americans and compromise our security.... A hostile power may be able to inflict such massive damage that no adequate compensation would be possible. These considerations lead *inevitably* to a doctrine of anticipatory self-defense.
>
> (Feith 2008: 67, 296, my italics)

Even commentators argue that an offensive response was inevitable. According to Renshon (2007), the offensive stance followed inescapably from the circumstances:

> Instead, strategic evaluation of the nature of the threat led to the prominence of the offensive in the Bush Doctrine.... In fact, it is not just that the situation favors the offensive, but rather that it requires the offensive.
>
> (Ibid.: 218)

Also, the NSS 2002 alludes to necessity: the "overlap between states that sponsor terror and those that pursue WMD *compels* us to action" (my italics). Yet the suggestion that the reaction was invariably in favor of offensive initiatives that forced themselves upon the decision-makers lacks proper nuance, as evidence of intra-administrational debate abounds. Arguments in favor of a limited response were also mooted, resonating better with mechanism 5b. Wolfowitz (2003: 6) reports open discussions on this matter within the administration. A crux of the controversy was "whether we should have this larger strategic objective which is getting governments out of the business of supporting terrorism, or whether we should simply go after bin Laden and al-Qaida". Feith (2008: 51) reports:

> Here we came back to the distinction between punishment and prevention. Rumsfeld, Wolfowitz and I all thought that US military action should aim chiefly to disrupt those who might be plotting the next big attack against us. Of great concern was a terrorist attack using biological or nuclear weapons. We needed action that would affect the terrorist network as extensively as possible.

Clearly, limited responses were advocated. Colin Powell initially argued for a tough but restrained retributive response focused on Afghanistan: "If there are [other] states and regimes, nations that support terrorism, we hope to persuade them that it is in their interest to stop doing that" (in Mann 2004: 302). To his understanding, 9/11 did not necessitate a renewed confrontation with Iraq as there was more to gain by accommodation (Ritchie and Rogers 2007: 73). Members of the military seem to have agreed that a narrowly scoped campaign was appropriate. Gen Jack Keane's (in Ricks 2006: 33) statement is symptomatic: "the United States should put aside the Iraq question and keep its eye on the ball". Presumably, the "ball" was the terrorists responsible for the terror attack.

There seems, in other words, to have been two types of thinking around, differing on the preferred size of the strategic objective. The different prescriptions do not seem to be caused by different threat perceptions. Rather, an identical perception of danger and the same desire for national security seem to have elicited expansionist (mechanism 5a) or tempered responses (mechanism 5b). This suggests that neither power expansion nor power preservation was inevitable. Insofar as defensive arguments can be recognized in the internal debates alongside offensive ones, there appear to be two coexisting causal patterns in play corresponding to competing and contrary versions of mechanisms 5a and 5b.

As elaborated on in Chapter 3, this dualism is typically presented as a contest between competing realist theories. Waltz (2008: 79), representing the defensive wing, "see[s] power as a possibly useful means with states running risks if they have too little or too much of it.... Power is a possibly useful means, and sensible statesmen try to have *an appropriate amount* of it" (my italics). Following Waltz, the structurally induced incentive to acquire more power is tempered because excessive strength can be self-defeating, prompting other states to coordinate military opposition, thereby triggering mechanism 5b.

Mearsheimer (2001), in contrast, representing the offensive wing, argues that the incentive for states to amass power never ends as long as the system remains anarchic. He acknowledges that "systemic factors constrain aggression, especially balancing by threatening states.... But defensive realists exaggerate those restraining forces" (ibid.: 39). Consequently, there is reason to expect unremitting efforts to maximize power, as it is impossible to determine what an "appropriate" amount would be. More is therefore always better, and mechanism 5a suggests itself.

These observations support the view presented in Chapter 3 that this theoretical debate could be recast in the language of mechanisms. Instead of insisting that one of these causal patterns always prevails, a more integrative interpretation would be to view mechanisms 5a and 5b as equally plausible mechanisms, each being triggered under different circumstances. When the outcome is known, we can assume we know something about which mechanism caused it, but it is difficult to know in advance which of the causal paths will be activated. The value of this integrated view is that both mechanisms appear to be in play, even if the preponderance of observations in this present case can be subsumed under the mechanism positing that decision-makers pursue security through maximizing initiatives. But other conditions could arguably have caused the moderate arguments, which interestingly surfaced, to prevail.

Despite the fact that power-maximizing and power-preserving arguments were invoked, there is hardly any evidence available to support the suggestion of mechanism 5c, namely that the administration struggled with the quandary of amassing power within reasonable limits. According to the data, the Bush administration seemed in effect to ignore this quandary and set far more store by considerations underlying deterrence arguments.

Consider some examples. On September 17, 2001, discussing what to do about the regime in Afghanistan, Bush (in Woodward 2003: 98) said, "Let's hit 'em hard. We want to signal that this is a change from the past. We want to cause other countries like Syria and Iran to change their views". Underlying the desire to signal a change from the past was Bush's contempt for Clinton's limited response to earlier terror attacks. Reportedly, bin Laden once suggested that Clinton's withdrawal from Somalia after "only" eighteen soldiers had been killed, reinforced his perception of the US as a weak "paper tiger". The Bush administration believed "the root cause of such a perception lay in the weak and irresolute American response to terrorist attacks, primarily in the Middle East since the 1980s" (Tunç 2005: 8). Their frequent analogies to Munich and the way they rejected "the false comfort of appeasement" to bolster the argument that the only way to deal with an aggressor is early and decisive use of force, further supports the point (cf. Record 2004: Chapter 6).

Woodward (2003: 38) comments that Bush believed that the US response to previous terror attacks "had been so weak as to be provocative, a virtual invitation to hit the United States again" and quotes Bush saying,

> I do believe there is the image of America out there that we are so materialistic, that we're almost hedonistic, that we don't have values, and that when

struck, we wouldn't fight back. It was clear that bin Laden felt emboldened and didn't feel threatened by the United States.

(Ibid.: 38–39)

Lemann (2003) reinforces the significance of this belief and even suggests it was the "real reason" for the Iraq war. He quotes Bush: "We have learned that terrorist attacks are not caused by the use of strength. They are invited by the perception of weakness". Then Lemann asks, "If you believe this, as Bush seems to do with every fiber of his being, how could you in good conscience not go to war in the region from which the worst terrorism emanates?" The utility of adding preventive war as a central component to the National Security Strategy, while often presented as an alternative to deterrence, is closely related to the utility of signaling strength:

> [The] idea of pre-emption is to deter states not from using weapons of mass destruction but from acquiring them in the first place.... Overthrowing Saddam because of his refusal to relinquish these weapons would be a clear demonstration to other tyrants that attempting to acquire WMD is a losing proposition.
>
> (Krauthammer quoted in Colucci 2008: 145–146)

Furthermore, inside reports on the deliberations suggest one reason for the Iraq war was to advertise, through the demonstration of US resolve, that challenging the US would never pay off, and, on the contrary, provoke forceful US counteraction. Suskind (2007) reports:

> The primary impetus for invading Iraq, according to those attending NSC briefings on the Gulf in this period, was to make an example of Hussein, to create a demonstration model to guide the behavior of anyone with the temerity to acquire destructive weapons or, in any way, flout the authority of the United States.... More specifically, the theory was that the United States – with a forceful action against Hussein – would change the rules of geopolitical analysis and action for countless other countries ... Saddam was simply a demonstration model to show the new resolve of the United States and its postmodern rules of international behavior.
>
> (Ibid.: 123, 214)

In response to reservations about the war, Bush simply replied, "Sometimes the show of force by one side can really clarify things" (ibid.: 233) and Iraq would be a "game changer" (ibid.: 214).

Rumsfeld, in particular, flagged the need for demonstration before the war. Gordon and Trainor (2007) sum his argument up:

> The United States needed to do more to demonstrate that there were serious consequences for mounting an attack on the US and to show it would not

suffer unsavory governments that were affiliated with terrorists. There was no flowery talk of inculcating democracy in the heart of the Middle East. Rumsfeld was advocating a demonstration of American power.

(Ibid.: 21)

Record (2004) similarly maintains that concern with strategic reputation loomed large.

Another general undeclared war aim in 2003 was the Bush administration's felt need to demonstrate America's will and capacity to use force decisively.... By demonstrating the credibility of American power, an invasion and occupation of Iraq, the Bush administration believed, would strengthen deterrence by putting other actual and aspiring rough states on notice that the United States meant business.

(Ibid.: 68)

In short, it is impossible to deny that the administration viewed power maximizing as apt precisely because it would communicate a clear signal of US resolve. The belief is spelled out in NSS 2002 (NSS 2002: 30), with noteworthy frankness: "our forces will be strong enough to dissuade potential adversaries from pursuing a military buildup in hopes of surpassing, or equaling, the power of the United States". Revealing a desire to maintain primacy beyond challenge and to dissuade all competition indicates that this belief loomed large. It is not that the emergence of the deterrence argument itself is a mystery. Clearly, the US would be expected to consider maximizing policies capable of boosting perceptions of American resolve. Hoping that the Iraq war would change the calculations of adversaries and the enormous costs would dissuade them from defying the US aggressively, falls within the bounds of what mechanism 5a promises.

However, attentiveness to the possibility of one's own actions provoking more mistrust and intensifying the conflict they are intended to prevent was conspicuously absent. To the extent that terrorist resentment of the US was motivated by US involvement in the Middle East, starting a war in the region would predictably add grist to the mill of resentment. Yet there is hardly any indication that the administration did give such spiral model consideration its due. The Bush administration did not visibly struggle to identify the "reasonable limits". Insofar as the forceful policies were not balanced against the likelihood of the initiatives increasing the incentive for other defiant actors to step up their defiance, mechanism 5c is devoid of explanatory power in this case.

Mechanism 6: The primacy of military means

Although the range of available means to pursue the national security interest is wide, the data suggest that the Bush administration, while flexible, set primary store by the military instrument, an observation made comprehensible by invoking mechanism 6.

That said, Bush did not have military tunnel vision. He was clear from the beginning that the US "will use all our resources to conquer this enemy" (Bush 2001b). Indeed, non-military means were enunciated as vital in the conflict: "every means of our diplomacy, every tool of intelligence, every instrument of law enforcement, every financial influence" (Bush 2001e). It was throughout emphasized that the struggle against the terrorists was "different from any other war in our history. It will be fought on many fronts against a particularly elusive enemy over an extended period of time" (NSS 2002: 5). Time and again it was iterated that the commitment would require the use of all "all tools in our arsenal" and that "[w]e will not triumph solely or even primarily through military might" (NSCT 2003: 1). An internal Pentagon Memo from Rumsfeld October 3, 2001 (quoted in Feith 2008: 84–86), confirms the view that all means in the US repertoire had to be utilized (Rumsfeld Memo October 3, 2001). It also exhibits skepticism about the "war" label as it simplified the multidimensional aspect of the conflict and risked overemphasizing the role of the military (Feith 2008: 87).

Yet the prevailing view within the administration was that military power had special utility. Tellingly, the terrorist attacks were instantly interpreted as war. The day after 9/11, Bush told the press that the attacks "were more than acts of terror. They were acts of war" (Bush 2001b: 1). Calling them war was by no means preordained; indeed it was unprecedented. Nevertheless, Bush (in Feith 2008: 12) immediately informed the administration that "We believe we are at war and we'll fight it as such. I want us to have the mindset of fighting and winning a war" and requested military options right away (ibid.). Other statements from the early aftermath of the attack indicate that Bush instantly began to contemplate a military response: "Our military is powerful and it's prepared" (Bush 2001a). In an interview Bush recalled his gut reactions when he was first told that the Twin Towers were attacked. "I made up my mind at that moment that we were going to war" (Woodward 2003: 15). On September 15, having collected his initial thoughts, he announced that he was planning a "broad and sustained campaign to secure our country and eradicate the evil of terrorism" (Bush 2001c). Later the same day he told "everybody who wears uniform: get ready" (Bush 2001d). In his memoirs, Bush (2010: 154) recalls that "[p]utting America on a war footing was one of the most important decisions of my precedency".

Soon after 9/11 Bush asked Congress to authorize the "use of United States Armed Forces against those responsible for the recent attacks launched against the United States" (quoted in Ritchie and Rogers 2006: 208). The language in the authorization bill leaves no doubt that use of military force was in the offing. It unequivocally authorizes Bush to

> use all necessary and appropriate force against those nations, organizations, or persons he [the President] determines planned, authorized, committed, or aided the terrorist attacks that occurred on 11 September 2001, or harbored such organizations or persons, in order to prevent acts of international terrorism against the United States.
>
> (Ibid.: 208–209)

On any measure, this was a wide authority to use the military. Less than a month later the war in Afghanistan began. Seventy-two days after 9/11, Bush instructed Rumsfeld to draft a new war plan for Iraq (Woodward 2004). While no decision was made to implement it, the instruction to start preparations speaks to the importance of the military instrument.

In a lecture addressing the topic "The war on terrorism and the Bush administration's foreign policy", Rice (2002: 3) revealed that, unlike those who believed war was obsolete in the post-Cold War era, she viewed military force as key:

> We see that wars of consequence are not mere relics of a bygone era.... And when we were attacked on September 11th, it reinforced one of the rediscovered truths about today's world: Robust military power matters in international politics and in security.

It is difficult to conceive of a way to advocate more clearly the crucial importance of military power to achieve US security goals. This view is also evidenced in various strategy documents from the period. The NSCWMD (2002: 2, 3) reads:

> The possession and increased likelihood of use of WMD by hostile states and terrorists are realities of the contemporary security environment. It is therefore critical that the US military and the appropriate civilian agencies be prepared to deter and defend against the full range of possible WMD employment scenarios.... The United States will continue to make clear that it reserves the right to respond with overwhelming force – including through resort to all our options – to the use of WMD against the United States, our forces abroad, and friends and allies.

The importance of the military is further demonstrated by the ambition stated in the NSS 2002 that US military forces will be strong enough to dissuade potential adversaries from pursuing a military buildup in the hope of surpassing, or equaling, the power of the United States (quoted in Walt 2005: 43). Notably, this document also elaborated the rationale of preventive war, generally seen as a controversial strategic innovation.

The conclusion that military power held a unique position among members of the administration pervades the analysis of the administration. Korb and Conley (2009: 235) maintain that Bush "defined power almost exclusively as hard power and consequently relied heavily on the military to carry out his policies, to the exclusion of other tools of statecraft". Halper and Clarke (2004: 144) aver that "[u]nderlying Bush's foreign policy is the assumption that the use of military force to overthrow noncooperative governments in troubled areas, if that can be accomplished, is the remedy for terrorism and tyranny". In the same fashion, Arthur Schlesinger Jr. (2004: 21) claims that the "essence of our new strategy is military: to strike a potential enemy, unilaterally if necessary, before he has a chance to strike us", even suggesting that the Bush administration thought of war as more expedient than previously: "War, traditionally a matter of last resort, becomes a matter of presidential choice".

Although the importance of the military instruments appears undisputed, the reasons for using the military extensively call for further scrutiny. The noteworthy thing in the internal deliberations was the emphasis put by the decision-makers on the importance of *demonstrating* military power. They considered military action strategically sound, not only as it realized measurable goals, but also because it communicated overwhelming strength. Since appeasing policies were believed to forfeit respect, cultivating the impression of military boldness was considered important. David Frum's (2003: 170) views represent the thinking.

> [T]he United States should recognize that although it cannot expect to be loved, it can enforce respect – and the surest way to forfeit this respect is to seem overeager to please. Western attempts to ingratiate ourselves were interpreted in the Muslim world as signs of weakness and fear, not of friendship and goodwill.

At the root of the administration's thinking was the view that different types of international actions elicited fundamentally different perceptions of US power. Negotiations, diplomacy, obedience to international law, compromise and accommodation, aiming to reassure potential rivals, were believed to foster impressions of weakness while displays of military force were believed to elicit awe. Members of the administration took 9/11 as evidence that previous policies of the first category had sent wrong signals to US enemies. Because previous terror attacks had not been met with a formidable response, especially during Clinton's presidency, the US had presumably nurtured a reputation for weakness, encouraging the terrorist to strike again. Consequently, there was now a strategic danger in a non-military response, since it would reinforce the impression of weakness and invite new attacks. According to Feith (2008: 65) there was

> broad agreement that a less-than-impressive response to 9/11 might embolden the terrorists to strike again. The United States had to find a way to demonstrate a break with our past practice and establish that we were willing to go to war to protect ourselves and our freedom.[7]

The most obvious way to make sense of the weight put on a demonstrative response is to interpret it as a policy aimed at nurturing credibility to increase deterrence. Jeffrey Record (2008: 76) maintains that Bush wanted

> to demonstrate the credibility of American power and to strengthen deterrence by putting other actual and aspiring rough states on notice that defying the United States invited military destruction.

The argument that demonstration of strength deters enemies and strengthens security coincides with the rational ways of utilizing the military under mechanism

6. Interpreted in that light, the sole purpose of military power displays, signaling strength, was to achieve security ends. Tunç (2005) frames it as a "major rationale of the administration for the Iraq war ... the US had to put itself at risk because it had failed to demonstrate its will and determination to confront its adversaries", and his evidence inspires confidence in his claim that the establishment of higher credibility was indeed important to the administration.

Despite documenting the purely strategic approach of the decision-makers to the issue, Tunç nonetheless terms it a "psychological rationale for war". There may have been more "psychology" involved in the decision to use the military than first meets the eye, however. The strategic soundness of policies nurturing deterrence, as Morgenthau (1968: 69) notes, "makes it easy to conclude that the policy of prestige is not important and does not deserve systematic discussion". But in this case, the intensity with which the Bush administration believed in the utility of demonstration makes one wonder if they had departed from a strict power analysis in their deliberations. Given their lack of trust in deterrence (deterrence was obsolete in the era of terrorists, they frequently argued), why deterring initiatives loomed so large is baffling. Based on what is known it is at least reasonable to ask if the allurement of the military instrument had something to do with a psychological need for prestige as well.

Holmes (2007: 312–313), after acknowledging that "it cannot be proved", suggests that the administration was humiliated by the fact that terrorists had attacked the US on their watch. "The thought that America, including Washington D.C., had become indefensible was psychologically intolerable.... [T]he need to knock over something, visibly and dramatically ... may actually have provided a potent reason, in some agitated minds, for invading Iraq". If so, the administration's accentuation of the military instrument has a more complex impetus than mechanism 6 suggests.

It is obviously difficult to demonstrate whether psychological needs for prestige contributed to the ascent of military polices, especially as strategic interests favor the same initiatives. But alertness to the possibility that such factors were involved seems at least warranted. While its relative causal impact is difficult to measure, that does not speak for its complete absence. And if a motivational hybrid underlay the administration's thinking about the utility of military power, it suggests a nuance not taken into account by Mechanistic Realism.

All the same, we must guard against overstating the importance of this non-instrumental factor. The administration would hardly root for a costly battle for the sake of looking tough, especially if it failed to produce other intended effects. Considerations of prestige are probably not sufficient to instigate military action, but may contribute to their allure. It does not undercut the validity of mechanism 6, but introduces a note of caution.

Mechanism 7: Self-help thinking

Under mechanism 7, decision-makers acting on behalf of their state are considered self-reliant in their pursuit for security. Hardly any analyst of the

Bush administration fails to note the prevalence of self-help thinking within the administration. A typical observation reads: "[T]he Bush administration has made the clear strategic decision to pursue US political and security interests by preserving its sovereign freedom of action and policy autonomy" (Monten 2007: 119). Although Renshon (2007: 9–12) documents convincingly how the numerous judgments to this effect were more normative and patronizing than descriptive and analytical, the imputation of self-help reasoning cannot solely be ascribed to a derogatory bias, as there is a solid amount of data supporting it.

Stephen Walt (2005) does not jump to normatively laden conclusions. After analyzing the world's power distribution after the Cold War, he acknowledges that all three US Presidents in this period have taken unilateral advantage of the fact that the US was by far the most powerful state in the system. But on inspection, Walt finds Bush comparatively

> more skeptical of existing international institutions – including America's Cold War alliances – and far more willing to "go it alone" in foreign affairs.... Bush's basic goals were not radically different from those of his predecessors, but his willingness to use US muscle to achieve them – and to act alone – was new, and startling.... [And] September 11 reinforced Bush's unilateralist inclinations...
>
> (Walt 2005: 31, 58)

In Walt's account, Bush's policies correspond with expectations of mechanism 7.

That self-help thinking held sway within the administration is substantiated by an involved decision-maker, Greg Newbold (2006), the Director of Operations for the Joint Staff in the Pentagon from 2000–2002. In an interview (Newbold 2007), said he regretted the complete disregard of the administration for collective international norms.

> International norms are a very good argument, but were largely ignored. Numbers of people in the administration, notably Rumsfeld, were dismissive about the UN. Additionally, they thought that coalition war fighting was a bankrupt proposition: that coalitions cannot fight. They thought that negotiations and international authorities were of marginal significance. It is fair to say that at this particular moment of time, international norms represented no restraint on the people in charge. I hope and believe that that exemplifies an exception in the history of American foreign policy.

Daalder and Lindsay (2005) largely reach the same conclusions. According to them, Bush's primary reliance on US capacities came at the expense of multilateral venues: "[Bush] relied on the unilateral exercise of American power rather than on international law and institutions to get his way" (ibid.: 2).

This argument, although frequently invoked, begs two qualifications. First, contrasting the exercise of "US power" with "international law and institutions" overlooks the achievement of the US in shaping the international laws to which it adheres and how it dominates the institutions of which it is a member (Walt 2005: 36–37). As Dueck (2004: 519) writes, the "international institutions that shape political and economic affairs in the world today were largely created by the United States, to serve American interests, as they continue to do". It is therefore inaccurate to view institutional venues as clear-cut alternatives to US power inasmuch as they can be viewed as an extension of, not an alternative to, it.

Second, speaking of institutions as alternative venues for achieving own goals trivializes the existence of collective action problems. Unilateral action, that is, without the endorsement of international institutions or allies, need not be a state's first order of preference, but may become the only viable path because a shared goal is not sufficient to initiate action in a group where no member wants to shoulder the costs.

The second qualification is important, because the administration did not reject cooperation unconditionally, but endorsed it in principle. They understood the potential utility of cooperation and wanted its benefits. In the NSS 2002 (NSS 2002: vi, 6) we read how

> Alliances and multilateral institutions can multiply the strength of freedom-loving nations. The United States is committed to lasting institutions like the United Nations, the World Trade Organization, the Organization of American States and NATO as well as other long standing alliances.... The United States will constantly strive to enlist the support of the international community.

Formulations like these are often dismissed as shallow rhetoric. But as Alexander (2007: 54) demonstrates, on several policy matters the administration has "been consistently multilateral". One prominent example is police and intelligence capability-sharing (Waltz 2008: 246). Gaddis (2004) even maintains that "cooperation among the great powers ... [was an] innovation in the Bush strategy". So while unilateralism on occasions held sway, it is difficult to argue whether the administration rejected out of hand the potential benefits of cooperation.

Even so, the administration understood that cooperation has limits and sometimes viewed it necessary to act without allied consent. They were unwilling to tailor their own preferences to those of others but willing to initiate action despite allied resistance. In crucial policy matters after 9/11 the administration "did not bend its policy to meet others' preferences" (Jervis 2003b: 374). They were "beholden to the notion that international cooperation is desirable in and of itself" (Alexander 2007: 53) and they would, in their own words, "not hesitate to act alone if necessary" (NSS 2002: 6). If unilateral actions are defined as those that "do not involve adjustments in policy preferences" (Monten 2007: 121), they are clearly what the US set in motion.

Closer examination of the evidence reveals three components to the administration's self-help thinking. First, considerations related to collective action problems were clearly on display and go some way to explaining the unilateralist stance. The realization of some US preferences implied procuring public goods. Feith (2008: 90) notes how

> The war on terrorism would benefit all free and open societies, and we believed our democratic friends would be willing to contribute forces and other resources to the effort.... We had a practical interest, moreover, in spreading the burden.

Of course, the administration understood that some undertakings required the US to take the initiative, since the totality of the political will was insufficient to instigate actions fulfilling goals that were of greater importance to the US than to most other states. Regime change in Iraq is an apt example of the intensity of Bush's preference to oust Hussein relative to that of other state leaders. It was therefore clear to Bush that regime change in Iraq ultimately depended on US willingness to initiate it, follow it through and shoulder the costs. In a message to the UN General Assembly Bush (quoted in Ritchie and Rogers 2007: 94) said, "if the United Nations Security Council won't deal with the problem, the United States and some of our friends will".[8]

Kagan (2003) has famously argued that a state's goals are a function of its military capabilities. Accordingly, different attitudes towards regime change in Iraq should reflect military asymmetries.[9] Without accepting Kagan's argument in full, it does call attention to another dimension of the collective action problem that faced Bush. It was beyond the capacity of most other states to do anything about Iraq. Only US military superiority made action a feasible proposition. As an advisor to the British Prime Minister, Tony Blair, told Woodward (2004: 177), "Iraq is an American question. It is not a British question. And it couldn't be anybody else's because no one else had the capability. We couldn't have invaded Iraq".

For other states, military, economic, legal and normative constraints doubtless excluded war with Iraq from the opportunity set. Besides, as Jervis (2003a: 85) observes, "Europe faces obvious incentives to free ride in such situations". So although there is no necessary association between power preponderance and unilateralism (Oudenaren 2004), in practice, the leading power is sometimes the only one capable, making unilateralism hard to escape.[10]

Second, unwillingness to forgo political autonomy and worries about the ineffectiveness of multilateral execution were among the considerations that led the US to operate self-reliantly. Constraints on autonomy were unwelcomed.

> [W]ars can benefit from coalition of willing, to be sure, but they should not be fought by committee. The mission must determine the coalition, the coalition must not determine the mission, or else the mission will be dumbed down to the lowest common denominator.
> (Rumsfeld 2002: 31)

Rumsfeld's remarks suggest the US will pick the coalition partners it prefers. Those who accept US objectives and want to commit to the efforts are free to do so, but the least willing will neither have veto power, nor any expectations of constraining US actions. That the US interest in contributions was restricted is illustrated by the initial rejection of NATO support in Afghanistan. When NATO decided to categorize the 9/11 attacks as an attack on the entire alliance, the initial US response was to decline the offer, presumably out of concern for autonomy and efficiency (Korb and Conley 2009: 241). "Despite the campaign speeches about the importance of alliances, it was, in their view, far better to have few or no allies than to make a deal that would constrain America's freedom of action overseas" (Mann 2004: 363).[11]

The reluctance to forgo autonomy was revealed by Bush, too, particularly when US preferences were in discord with international norms. In those instances Bush made it clear that no international body would make him suspend action in security matters (Ritchie and Rogers 2007: 112). He was (in Monten 2007: 122) adamant that the US did not need a "permission slip to defend the security of [our] country". Illustratively, in a discussion with reporters on whether the US could launch a war against Iraq without the consent of the United Nations, Bush (2002c) said:

> I can't imagine an elected member of the United States Senate or House of Representatives saying, "I think I'm going to wait for the United Nations to make a decision". It seems to me that if you're representing the United States, you ought to be making a decision on what's best for the United States. If I were running for office, I'm not sure how I'd explain to the American people: "Say, vote for me, and, oh, by the way, on matters of national security, I think I'm going to wait for somebody else to act".

Refusal to let international laws, norms and customs – such as requiring the Security Council's authorization before taking military action – stand in the way of realizing US preferences confirms the cogency of mechanism 7.[12]

It is worth mentioning, however, that tepid relations with the UN did not imply the administration was totally dismissive of binding international constraints. But the institutional constraints were, in the view of the administration, not structured according to the needs of the times. This, for example, was how the UN charter argued in favor of prohibiting everything but war in self-defense, something that precluded a legal mandate for preventive wars. Instead of totally ignoring this legal constraint the administration argued that it had to be revised or reinterpreted in order to be pertinent to the new circumstances and the threat from terrorism:

> For centuries, international law recognized that nations need not suffer an attack before they can lawfully take action to defend themselves against forces that present an imminent danger of attack. Legal scholars and international jurists often conditioned the legitimacy of preemption on the existence of an imminent threat – most often a visible mobilization of armies,

navies, and air forces preparing to attack. We must adapt the concept of imminent threat to the capabilities and objectives of today's danger.

(NSS 2002: 15)

Waltz (2002: 348) sees this argument as a subtle form of unilateralism: "America's attempt to make its own international rules ... is an extreme example of unilateralism". Institutional arrangements unable to address present US challenges were easily overruled. Typically, when the UN did not mandate war with Iraq, it did not prevent its initiation, strongly suggesting that self-help reasoning trumped institutional commitments.

The administration's take on UN constraints brings considerations of relative gains to the fore, and they appear to have been the third impulse behind US unilateralism post-9/11. The question of relative gains is simple: if benefits are distributed, who benefits most? Obedience to a supranational regime implies a transfer of autonomy from those who establish it. It is debatable who benefits most from transferring their autonomy. On the one hand, supranational regimes may leave the mightiest worse off since great powers tend to be the only actors likely to consider acting in defiance of the established rules. This, at any rate, is the argument of those who hold institutions as expedient tools of the weaker states and counterproductive for the powerful (Kagan 2003).[13] If correct, the US is the short-term loser from submitting to international constraints on the use of military force.

On the other hand, arguments to the opposite effect have merit too. Monten (2007: 127–128) argues that great powers benefit in the long run from international regimes as they contribute to order and predictability. In exchange for forgoing autonomy, great powers gain stability to the effect of prolonging their period of preponderance. By "'locking in' its power advantages through a favorable order a leading state makes an investment in the long-term preservation of its position" (ibid.: 128). Accordingly, by abiding by international laws, the US can preserve a stable international order. If the price for stability is limited to forgoing autonomy on occasion, multilateralism may pay off in the long run by conserving a system that works to a state's own advantage.[14]

These opposing arguments put the US in a dilemma relating to relative gains. On the one hand, there were immediate benefits (measured as higher autonomy) attached to not accepting multilateral constraints. For example, obedience to the norm of state sovereignty would preclude terror prevention inside other states. On the other hand, there were potential long-term benefits of complying with the rules as it might cement an order that worked to US advantage.

The Bush administration was aware of the dilemma. A passage from an internal Pentagon memorandum (quoted in Feith 2008: 296) says, "US government leaders also understand that anticipatory self-defense appears to introduce a certain instability and unpredictability into the international system".[15] Yet in the situation after 9/11, the prospective long-term benefits of an institutional order did not exert powerful constraints on the US. Rather, situational autonomy weighed heavier (Monten 2007: 127). Due to considerations of relative gain, the

US ultimately defied international constraints, an observation that can be subsumed under mechanism 7.

Mechanism 8: Precautionary action

Mechanism 8 posits that decision-makers, worried about the merest likelihood that the worst will happen, take meticulous care to do too much, rather than too little in the pursuit of the national security interest. While acting under the influence of this mechanism can be extremely costly, arguments used by members of the administration lend credence to the mechanism. The paramount argument seems to have reflected the possibility that terrorists could acquire WMD; this possibility evoked excessive caution on the part of the administration.

A first observation notes the importance Bush attaches to the task of weighing risks. To Woodward (2003: 343) he reports,

> I'm the kind of person that wants to make sure that all risk is assessed. But a president is constantly analyzing, making decisions based upon risks, particularly in war – risk taken relative to what can be achieved.

Without clearly revealing an attitude towards risks, Bush is evidently aware of risk evaluation and its critical place in his decision-making. Feith (2008: 229) provides further information about how a typical risk assessment proceeded within the administration. Examination of "intelligence and other information" resulted in a grid that arrayed the problems and available options. "The grid summarized the pros and cons of each action for each problem state, noting where persuasion might work and where compulsion might be necessary" (ibid.: 229). On some occasions, it appears, strategic quandaries emerged.

> The Bush Administration found it difficult in its early months to agree on a course of action toward Saddam Hussein's regime.... War would be risky; no one could know in advance the duration or cost of such conflict. But leaving Saddam in power would be risky, too. Reasonable people differed then, and differ now, on whether war was the right choice.
> (Feith 2008: 213, 224)

There seems, in other words, to be reasonable disagreement about how risk should be assessed, including the risk posed by Iraq.

If mechanism 8 shapes choice, decision-makers would favor the low-risk alternative when faced with a difficult choice. Of two options – "persuasion" or "compulsion" – with approximately identical, but uncertain expected utilities, a precautionary agent would not be indifferent but favor the option whose negative consequences were better than the negative consequences of the other option. If a war with Iraq went badly, the US would predictably lose soldiers, waste money and create instability in the region. If persuasion failed, WMD might be used against the US. The former would be the less bad of the two potential negatives.

We know this was the option the administration eventually settled on. Mechanism 8 suggests why.

Inside accounts inspire confidence in claims that precautionary reasoning of this type held sway within the administration. One particular illustration stands out. It involves the Vice President, who allegedly became "a self-appointed special examiner of worst-case scenarios" (Woodward 2004: 237). During an intelligence briefing, Cheney asked whether the CIA thought al-Qaeda had a nuclear weapon. CIA's most senior WMD terrorism analyst replied (in Tenet 2007: 264), "Sir, if I were to give you a traditional analytical assessment of the al-Qaeda nuclear program, I would say they probably do not. But I can't assure you".[16] Absolute assurances could not be given. Cheney allegedly responded, "If there's one percent chance that they do [get WMD], you have to pursue it as if it were true" (ibid.: 264).

Suskind (2007) reveals other details of this meeting. He quotes Cheney saying at first somewhat hesitatingly,

> We have to deal with this new type of threat in a way we haven't yet defined. With a low probability, high-impact event like this ... I'm frankly not sure how we engage. We have to look at it in a completely different way.
> (Ibid.: 62)

After receiving more information, Cheney offered the memorable passage, "If there's a one percent chance that Pakistani scientists are helping al-Qaeda build or develop a nuclear weapon, we have to treat it as certainty in terms of our response" (ibid.: 62). Suskind (2007) extrapolates much from this single incident, taking it to imply the establishment of a so-called *One percent doctrine*. Presumably it gave expression to a new thrust in US policy: "If there is one percent chance of such an act occurring [transfer of WMD to terrorists], we must act as if it's a certainty" (ibid.: 65). Although it is probably misplaced to equate the principle with an operational doctrine, Suskind's reporting makes it hard not to construe Cheney's attitude as one of extreme intolerance to uncertainty about the possibility that terrorists could acquire WMD and his conclusions are clearly of a precautionary kind.

When Tenet remarks on Cheney's position, he shares Cheney's excessive worry, arriving at an equally radical idea:

> There was no question in my mind that he [Cheney] was absolutely right to insist that when it came to discussing weapons of mass destruction in the hands of terrorists, conventional risk assessments no longer applied; we must rule out any possibility of terrorists succeeding in their quest to obtain such weapons. We could not afford to be surprised.
> (Tenet 2007: 265)[17]

On consideration, Cheney and Tenet probably did not subscribe to the One percent doctrine in a literal sense simply because it would have been impossible to use it consistently to guide action. It is more pertinent to interpret the statements as reflecting an extremely cautious mindset (see Jervis 2010: 203). Complacency was simply not an option because the worst-case consequences of an uncertain eventuality were on a different scale. As Tenet notes, "this was an issue about which we could not afford to be wrong" (Tenet 2007: 259). Therefore they appear willing to dilute the standards of proof needed in order to justify countermeasures. This is in accordance with Rumsfeld's (in Heng 2006: 128) view that "absolute proof cannot be a precondition for action".

In more general terms, the necessity of precaution was highlighted by NSS 2002. One crucial paragraph deserves to be quoted.

> Given the goals of rough states and terrorists, the United States can no longer rely on a reactive posture as we have in the past. The inability to deter a potential attacker, the immediacy of today's threats, and the magnitude of potential harm that could be caused by our adversaries' choice of weapons, do not permit that option. We cannot let our enemies strike first [...]. The United States has long maintained the option of preemptive actions to counter a sufficient threat to our national security. The greater the threat, the greater is the risk of inaction – and the more compelling the case for taking anticipatory action to defend ourselves, even if uncertainty remains as to the time and place of the enemy's attack. To forestall or prevent such hostile acts by our adversaries, the United States will, if necessary, act preemptively.
>
> (NSS 2002: 15)

The precautionary underpinning of this excerpt is clear. Inconclusive information about threats from agents that cannot be deterred, justifies anticipatory measures. When the potential costs of inaction are unacceptable, prevention is called for even if future peril is shrouded in uncertainty.

The Iraq war was defended in terms like these and the war is frequently referred to as an operational rollout of the argument in the security strategy. Despite uncertainty about the Iraqi threat, the Bush administration preferred a good margin of safety. "The stakes were too high to trust the dictator's word against the weight of the evidence.... The lesson of 9/11 was that if we waited for a danger to fully materialize, we would have waited too long" (Bush 2010: 229). That the threat was not beyond dispute was insufficient to defer action. Cheney (in Woodward 2003: 347) suggested that the worst-case consequences of omission prompted preventive action.

> If he [Hussein] attacked the United States or anyone with the weapons of mass destruction available to him – especially on a large scale – the world would never forgive them for inaction and giving in to the impulse to engage in semantic debates in U.N. resolutions.

Moreover, premised on the assumption that Iraq at one point in the future would acquire WMD, it was argued that it was better to prevent this eventuality sooner rather than later, especially because the sanguine threat estimates could be wrong.

> If we're wrong and we had four of five or six years before he [Hussein] posed a nuclear threat, then we just went early. If anyone willing to wait is wrong, then we wake up in two or three years, and Saddam has a nuclear weapon and is brandishing it in the most volatile region in the world. So which of those chances do you want to take?
> (Rice in Woodward 2003: 350)

Again this exemplifies a preference for doing too much, rather than too little in the pursuit of the national security interest. While the relative importance of the precautionary arguments for attacking Iraq will remain moot, it is hard to find arguments against subsuming this aspect of the administration's thinking under mechanism 8.

Mechanisms 9–12: Timing, geography, power distribution and deterrence and regional hegemony

None of the four mechanisms suggesting how "systemic factors constrain aggression" (Mearsheimer 2001: 39) appears to have played a decisive role in taming US foreign policy after 9/11. That is not to say such considerations were not invoked within the administration, but they appear to have had negligible impact.

There were timing issues, but rather than restraining offensive initiatives, they appear to spur them on. In the case of Iraq, evidence suggests it was considered important to start the war before the summer, owing to the summer heat in Iraq. Again, rather than restraining offensive thinking, this view accelerated war preparations (Braut-Hegghammer and Riste 2005: 106). In addition, according to (Daalder and Lindsay 2005: 13), Cheney's argument that there is "no question but what [*sic*] it is going to be cheaper and less costly to do now than it will be to wait a year or two years or three years until he's developed even more deadly weapons, perhaps nuclear weapons", prevailed.

Geography, not least the stopping power of water, did not seem to present a formidable barrier, to the war in either Afghanistan or Iraq. In the latter case, however, one geographical concern did loom pretty large; when Turkey refused to let US launch attacks on Iraq from its territory, the US was left with Kuwait as a base. However, this constraint did not temper the desire to attack, it only made the operational logistics more challenging and the endeavor more risky (Gordon and Trainor 2007: 81).

With respect to power distribution and deterrence, four comments can be made. First, Afghanistan and Iraq lacked the support of powerful states, which made it easier for the US to effect regime change. This was taken into consideration. Second, the fact that other states in the region, such as Iran, could become relatively more powerful as a result of war with two of its neighboring states did not appear to have been a major concern. Third, the prospect of costs and opportunity costs, i.e., the likely drain on US resources of fighting wars, and weakening of its overall position in the system, were contemplated, but not acted upon. When Powell (in Woodward 2003: 346) raised the issue saying, "War could trigger all kinds of unanticipated and unintended consequences", Cheney simply replied that that was "Not the issue". Fourth, I have come across no evidence of concern that the war would create fear in other states to the effect of spurring the formation of a countervailing coalition against the US. The risk of setting off arms races, giving other states incentives to get WMD to prevent US from attacking them or to obstruct US interests does not appear to have been taken into consideration. Rather, it seems, the Bush administration believed that a determined willingness to use military power would cause less defiance on the part of others (cf. Woodward 2003: 340–342).

Finally, the fact that the US enjoyed regional hegemony did not appear to have tempered their maximizing propensity. Rather, it was argued, the opportunities of the power imbalance had to be seized (Layne 2006).

4.3 Conclusion

In the Introduction I pointed out that the truth candidacy of realism was contested, but that neither the invalidity claims nor validity claims were based on a detailed analysis of whether the thinking of the individuals responsible for US conduct conformed to mechanisms implied by realist theory. This chapter contributes to advancing that debate.

On the one hand, it has demonstrated how important aspects of the Bush administration's thinking, evidenced in internal deliberations, official pronouncements and interviews, validate several mechanisms included in Mechanistic Realism. Observations considered significant by most observers can be subsumed under, and thereby explained by, more general causal patterns derived from realism. Their aptitude for being true is hard to dispute based on this review.

The evidence suggesting that security ranked highest in the US hierarchy of priorities was, on consideration, stronger than the evidence suggesting a different order of priorities. Exposure to threatening signals evidently fostered fear. So did the uncertainty with respect to future terror attacks. Although empirically weak, the phenomenon of counter-wishful thinking suggested why some judgments on the administration's part went in a sinister direction and a strategy for maximizing power was preferred to one aiming to preserve the status quo. Military means were considered pivotal in this pursuit along with self-help reasoning, resulting from collective action problems, unwillingness to forgo autonomy and consideration of relative gains. The administration's desire to achieve a good margin of safety in security matters suggests that precautionary reasoning had causal impact.

On the other hand, there are enough observations to the contrary to suspend an ultimate validating judgment. First, the fact that presumably constraining mechanisms did not temper expansive efforts goes against expectations. That realist scholars despised the administration's policy could plausibly be attributed to the fact that these restraining considerations were not heeded. Second, the review above, which added detail to the mental operations, suggests the existence of related mechanisms. Both the fact that uncertainty did not universally foster fear and the fact that more restrained strategic responses were mooted take the sting out of the determination of the mechanisms in the catalogue. Third, insofar as doubt lingers with respect to the impact of additional factors on decision-making, there is a call for further scrutiny. Not least the impact of idealism, hinted at above, requires a more careful investigation.

On the whole, although a final answer to all the puzzles pertaining to the administration's response cannot be offered here, the first eight mechanisms do receive considerable support from the available evidence, and we are therefore justified in trusting Mechanistic Realism in capturing several of the underlying mental operations affecting decision-makers as they formulate foreign policy. If incomplete, Mechanistic Realism does help dispel some of the puzzles regarding the US response to 9/11.

5 Idealism

In Chapter 4 I vented five critical objections to the neo-conservative thesis and I vouched for the conclusion that national security concerns ranked highest in the US hierarchy of goals. Yet I also made observations that could be taken as evidence of idealist motives. In particular, I put forward, evaluated and finally found unpersuasive the suggestion that a desire to democratize the Middle East was a sufficient instigator of the Iraq war. The unreliable quality of the evidence to this effect (remember McClellan's backward deduction from conversations with Bush years after the decision), and the implausibility that so much evidence suggesting that security concerns ranked highest among the priorities was concoction, led me to conclude that idealist motives, while present, were at best second-rank and would, absent security concerns, have been an insufficient instigator of the war.[1]

That conclusion is hard to dismiss. Marvin Zonis (2007) agrees:

> Absent as a major motivating factor for Hussein's ouster was the desire to bring democracy to the Iraqi people. But that became an ever more powerful explanation offered by the President as the primary motives [security] proved illusory.
>
> (Ibid.: 236)

Even if Zonis is correct and idealism was not a "major motivating factor" and was only eventually presented as the primary purpose of the war when the publically presented security rationale was undermined by the fact that no WMD were found in Iraq and no solid links between Hussein and al-Qaeda were established, idealism might still have been a *minor* factor. Even factors of lower rank might have been causally efficacious. In fact, examination of the evidence and proposed idealist explanations suggest that Mechanistic Realism leaves out considerations that were evidently present. While presence does not imply causal impact, it does indicate that the mechanistic catalogue is possibly incomplete. Most analysts of the subject, at any rate, find it difficult to defend the view that Bush acted under the influence of no other considerations but purely selfish security concerns. The amount of evidence supporting the notion that idealism impacted the policy is so overwhelming that it prompts further scrutiny.

118 *The empirical merit of Mechanistic Realism*

Jervis (2003b: 386), for example, whose analysis is wedded to structural variables and security motives, finds the Iraq "war hard to understand if the only objective was to disarm Saddam". However, "as part of a larger project [of democracy promotion], the war makes more sense". Even if Jervis is correct and the Iraq war "makes more sense" when the desire to democratize the Middle East is included among the variables, the variety of conclusions offered about the significance of idealism is, as I will soon demonstrate, nonetheless perplexing and anything but easy to make sense of.

I have no pretention to finally settle the question about the impact of idealism or to bring perfect sense to this matter. This chapter should however temper our understanding of the idealist "factor", major or minor, and how it operated. Analysis of the statements by members of the administration and careful reading of scholarly attempts at coming to terms with the role of idealism suggest that it would be helpful to distinguish between six distinct categories: (1) anti-idealism, (2) pure idealism, (3) weak idealism, (4) over-determining idealism, (5) idealism induced by security in abundance, and (6) impure idealism.

These six positions amount to an analytic scheme and bring more clarity to how idealism influenced the Bush administration, without providing an epistemologically satisfying answer to the questions of how much basis there ultimately is for an idealist explanation. However, sorting the various positions on idealism this way demonstrates that the role of idealism in this case was more complicated than most of the loose idealist arguments suggest. It impairs our understanding if we lump everything together into one vague causal contributor under the idealist label, just as it impairs our understanding if we fail to take into account the presence and potential impact of idealist motives at all.

5.1 Anti-idealism

The first and fundamental barrier to a successful idealist explanation is to deflect the total rejection of idealism, namely the idea that all indications of idealism are just a rhetorical device, which is the *anti-idealist thesis*. Although not explicitly stated, Mechanistic Realism's is wedded to this thesis. If the anti-idealist thesis is correct, there is no basis for idealist explanations whatsoever. Anti-idealism is frequently invoked by IR scholars, and although an extreme position resting on a sinister anthropology, the barrier is not as easy to overcome as it might seem. On closer scrutiny it appears that several analysts who invoke idealism as a causally efficacious variable, argue that these policies were pursued only to advance the long-term self-interest of the US. And as I shall demonstrate, this may, in fact, be an imperceptible endorsement of anti-idealism.

The anti-idealist thesis calls for suspicion whenever an idealist principle or an unselfish motive surfaces as the reason for a state decision, as the idea implies that the sole purpose of such declarations is to disguise self-interested motives. Morgenthau (1968) adhered to anti-idealism, suspecting all signs of other-regard in international politics to be concealed attempts at power amassment:

> It is the very nature of politics to compel the actor on the political scene to use ideologies in order to disguise the immediate goal of his action. The immediate goal of political action is power, and political power is power over the minds and actions of men.
>
> (Ibid.: 85)

Mearsheimer (2001) is less categorical, allowing idealism limited scope when states enjoy security in abundance. As a crude rule, however, he subscribes to anti-idealism, arguing that policymakers adjust their rhetoric in order to hoodwink publics who often dislike power-political reasoning. Analysts are therefore well advised not to take idealist declarations at face value, since they rarely reflect the reasoning behind closed doors.

> Because Americans dislike realpolitik, the public discourse about foreign policy in the United States is usually couched in the language of liberalism. Hence pronouncements of the policy elites are heavily flavored with optimism and moralism.... Behind closed doors, however, the elites who make national security policy speak mostly the language of power, not that of principle, and the United States acts in the international system according to the dictates of realism.
>
> (Ibid.: 25)

Although hard to misunderstand, there is some confusion with respect to anti-idealism and it must be clarified. First, anti-idealism implies no moral nihilism, but is compatible with the view that states cherish ideals and ethical doctrines, such as liberalism or communism. All the anti-idealist thesis says is that such doctrines have negligible impact on foreign policy. On some occasions, however, ethical doctrines coincide with the national interest, in which case there is no conflict between the pursuit of power and the pursuit of ideals, "non-security goals sometimes compliment the hunt for relative power" (ibid.: 46). Mearsheimer (ibid.: 26) illustrates the point by alluding to US policy toward fascism during the Second World War and communism in the Cold War, policies that in both instances were solely dictated by power-political concerns. That the pursuit was presented in a liberal wrapping and consistent with idealist principles, cherished in the US, was a welcomed, but incidental bonus that does not thereof lend idealist explanations credit. Although it *appeared* that the US acted on idealist motives, they only coincided with power logic, and did not contribute causally.

Second, as it is often difficult to establish beyond reasonable doubt whether idealist rhetoric reflects genuine idealism, or, on a more fundamental level, self-interest, it raises the question of what our analytical *presumption* should be in situations of hermeneutic ambiguity: Should doubt speak to the advantage or disadvantage of a decision-maker invoking idealist motives? The anti-idealist thesis offers a clear injunction in such instances – absent extremely strong evidence to the contrary and in all cases of doubt, self-interested motives ought to be imputed to foreign policy decision-makers. When passing judgment on the motive behind foreign conduct, anti-idealists go along with Bentham's dictum (in Elster 2007: 108): "the most contrived assumption to the shame of having suspected that the behaviour of a public person might have a laudable motive".[2]

While certainly a defendable position considering the pervasiveness of selfishness throughout the history of international relations, the presumption runs the risk of reducing decision-makers to cynical skeletons, a reduction that does injustice to the vagaries of human motivation observed elsewhere. Yet even those uncomfortable with an (overly) pessimistic anti-idealist presumption would probably agree in demanding a heavier burden of proof from those who impute idealist motives to Bush, than from those who impute self-interested motives to him, even if this demand is indebted to a debatable, sinister anthropology.

Several analysts, often of a neo-Marxist persuasion, have invoked anti-idealism to explain Bush policies. They view virtually all appeals to idealism by the administration as cynical window dressing and accuse the administration's public revelations of masking underlying imperialist ambitions and corporate interests. Consider the position of Noam Chomsky (2007: 6), who sees a "deep hatred of democracy on the part of western elites" pervading all the rhetoric about the promotion of democracy and freedom.

> I'm sure that these issues [control of oil in the Middle East] are discussed in internal planning. It's inconceivable that they can't think of this. But it's out of public discussion, it's not in the media, it's not in the journals, it's not in the Baker–Hamilton report. And I think you can understand the reason. To bring up these issues would open the question why the United States and Britain invaded. And that question is taboo.

More qualified, Michael Klare (2003) rejects the veracity of all official reasons for ousting Hussein, not least Bush's idealist desire to promote democracy. Although acknowledging that some of the reasons offered are indeed "powerful motives for war" (ibid.: 130), they are still not what is driving the policies, Klare avers. With few exceptions, the official pronouncements conceal the real motives, which are "all related to the pursuit of oil and the preservation of America's status as the paramount power" (ibid.: 132). Accordingly, what gives itself out as idealism is bogus.

One problem with Klare's anti-idealism, is that it smacks of concoction. Obviously it is the nature of arguments about hidden motives that evidence is hard to provide and in order to subscribe to Klare's account one has to accept his inference that since dependency on oil is the "Achilles' heel of American power" (ibid.: 132), all US foreign conduct necessarily seeks to keep oil-rich countries under US control. The functionalist flavor of that inference makes it dubious. Having identified a US need for oil does not warrant the inference that every action is motivated out of this need. Additionally, the inference is questionable in light of evidence to the contrary (cf. Mearsheimer and Walt 2007: 253–255). In surmising that Bush's arguments were tortuous, Klare's inference deserves the very same verdict. Ultimately, he makes Bush's "cunning too cunning" (Montaigne in Elster 2007: 65). Yet refusing to accept conspiratorial and functionalist anti-idealism does not discard the thesis as it does not follow that idealism is never used for disguising purposes.

Consider for example an episode testifying to Bush's use of idealism as masquerade. In the leaked conversation between Bush (2007) and Spanish President Aznar, one of the issues under discussion was the advantage of getting a UN resolution sanctioning the Iraq war. A UN mandate would predictably make the war appear, if not ethically justified, at least more appropriate, given the authority of the Security Council under Article 7 in the UN Charter to approve military action, even in the absence of a military first strike. A UN mandate would have provided a legal basis for the war that arguably would have made it easier to present it as a noble endeavor to enforce the policies of the UN and would have enhanced the perception of legitimacy in those quarters of the world which regard the UN as a normative guarantor in international affairs.

The transcript reveals that Bush's desire for a UN mandate is guided by considerations of expediency, not of principle. He makes it clear to his Spanish colleague that the "time has come to get rid of him [Hussein]. That's it.... If anyone vetoes, we'll go". That appears to suggest that a UN mandate is nothing but a helpful idealist mask for a decision already made as the principal question of international legality was not in itself important enough to suspend action, and failure to get a UN mandate appears insufficient to have swayed Bush's determination to achieve regime change in Iraq.

Still, Bush (ibid.) is adamant that he prefers a new resolution, presumably to increase the legitimacy of the war.

> I made a decision to go to the Security Council. In spite of disagreements within my administration, I told my people that we should work with our friends. It would be wonderful to have a second resolution.

He assures Aznar, for whom a UN mandate appears more crucial, that he will make a serious effort to conceal that the opinion and vote of the Security Council have no impact on his decision: "I'll try from now on to use a rhetoric that's as subtle as can be while we're seeking approval of the resolution". They also discuss how the resolution can "be tailored" in order to get it passed. One suggestion, of which Bush approves, is to exclude "all means necessary" from the formulation, which is the UN euphemism for war. Bush, not knowing that his words will eventually reach the public, makes it simple: "I don't care much about the content [of the resolution]". What is of importance is that something gets passed.

Moreover, Bush's discussion of this issue with Colin Powell, often presented as the most sympathetic member of the administration to the UN, reveals that Powell too argued his position on grounds of instrumental utility, not on the back of an idealist principle (Gordon and Trainor 2007: 81). Powell stresses the importance of "some diplomatic cover" and the benefit of having "allies to share the burden". If these were Powell's reasons for a UN resolution it is unwarranted to cite his argument for a UN mandate as anything but a device to foster US interest. If anything, Powell's argument vindicates the anti-idealist thesis.

Even if these examples do not refute that idealism motivated the war, they lend the anti-idealist thesis anecdotal support. Both Bush and Powell wanted to make US policies seem as idealist as possible and gaining the approval of the UNSC (United Nations Security Council) would have been helpful in this respect. While only anecdotal, it would be rash to conclude that these were the only instances of their kind. Rather, the instrumental cynicism underlying such observations ensures that the anti-idealist suspicion lingers.

5.2 Pure idealism

The most profound challenge to the anti-idealist thesis is the idea that national self-interest was not the motive behind Bush policies, but an idealist desire to spread democracy, liberate oppressed people, or similar aspirations of idealist intent. Whenever the motive behind a decision is to fulfill a goal or obtain a value that transcends the selfish state interest, it is *pure idealism*. While many scholars are skeptical about a permanent impact of pure idealism in international politics, it has been suggested that idealist actions may come about "in outbursts of crusading ardour, when the nation temporarily abandons its general scale of priorities and soars into new realms of idealism, including self-sacrifice and altruism" (Osgood 1953: 16).

There is a venerable tradition in the study of US foreign policy premised on the argument that pure idealism is a prevalent instigator of US foreign policy as the state itself was founded in order to be a beacon of liberal freedom in the world. These founding ideas presumably still shape the thinking of US decision-makers and assure that all policies pursued contain an idealist element. Some even suggest that the promotion of democratic values is part and parcel of the US self-interest (Melby 1997: 31). Consequently, one should not be surprised to find US foreign policy swayed by desires to redeem others, as this fulfills the ethical aspirations on which the nation is founded.

Kagan (2008) elaborates:

> Americans had always considered themselves the world's most important nation and its destined leader. "The cause of America is the cause of all mankind", Benjamin Franklin said at the time of the [American] Revolution. The United States was the "locomotive at the head of mankind", Dean Acheson said at the dawn of the Cold War.
>
> (Ibid.: 9)

Anatol Lieven (2004) adds that

> This sense of America not just as an unfulfilled dream or vision, but also as a country with a national mission, is absolutely central to the American

Idealism 123

national identity and also forms the core of the nation's faith in its own "exceptionalism".

(Ibid.: 33)

To the extent that the national mission to spread freedom has been the key driver of US foreign endeavors since its founding, it suggests that pure idealism need not be a temporary leap from the normal, as Osgood's quote suggests, but a motive whose causal impact is undiminished.

Evidence to support the claim that Bush observed a duty to promote freedom in the world can be found from his first inaugural address, in which he argued that "if our country does not lead the cause of freedom, it will not be led" (in Zonis 2007: 231). Yet the intensity of this duty appears to have grown steadily during his presidency, not least in the wake of 9/11. It is set out in a much quoted passage from the opening of NSS 2002 (iv):

> These values are right and true for every person, in every society – and the duty of protecting these values against their enemies is the common calling of freedom-loving people across the globe and across the ages.

The intent of this programmatic statement surfaces again and again: "we sacrifice for the liberty of strangers" (Bush 2003a). Similarly, "America has a greater objective than controlling threats and containing resentment. We will work for a just and peaceful world beyond the war on terror" (Bush 2002a). Consider also how Bush (in Colucci 2008: 155) underscores the greater purpose of US foreign policy:

> America has a much greater purpose than just eliminating threats and containing resentment, because we believe in the dignity and value of every individual. America seeks hope and opportunity for all people in all cultures.

Other evidence to the effect that idealism sparked Bush's decisions can be found in his West Point speech (Bush 2002a), in which his desire to extend the peace by fostering democratization appears to be one of his primary concerns:

> Our nation's cause has always been larger than our nation's defense. We fight, as we always fight, for a just peace – a peace that favors human liberty. We will defend the peace against threats of terrorists and tyrants. We will preserve the peace by building strong relations among the great powers. And we will extend the peace by encouraging free and open societies on every continent.

In one memorable instance Bush appeared determined to get this message across to an interviewer. In connection with a speech he gave describing North Korea, Iraq and Iran as evil states, he accounts for the ethical responsibility to promote freedom throughout the world:

> Let me make sure you understand what I just said about the role of the United States. I believe the United States is the beacon for freedom in the world. And I believe we have a responsibility to promote freedom that is as solemn as the responsibility is to protecting the American people.... And I believe we have a duty to free people. I would hope we wouldn't have to do it militarily, but we have a duty.
>
> (Woodward 2004: 88–89)

Other members of the administration appear on the face of it to be guided by pure idealism as well. Undersecretary of State for Global Affairs, Paula Dobriansky (in Colucci 2008: 154), elaborating in December 2001 on the diplomatic front in the war on terrorism argues:

> At the most fundamental level, our first [goal] is the battle to preserve the very structures of civilization that protect individual liberty and human rights, including democracy and religious freedom ... I am pleased to tell you that this [A]dministration's commitment to human rights, democracy and religious freedom is unshakable.... The promotion of democracy and human rights causes lies at the heart of this Administration's foreign policy.

Interestingly, there is evidence even from closed-door meetings, i.e., a setting where the incentive to misrepresent one's own views is considerably lower, suggesting that Bush's idealism is genuine. During the supposedly confidential conversation with the Spanish Prime Minister Aznar, Bush again underscores that his Iraq policy is "guided by a historic sense of responsibility":

> When some years from now History judges us, I don't want people to ask themselves why Bush, or Aznar or Blair didn't face their responsibilities. In the end, what people want is to enjoy freedom. Not long ago, in Romania, I was reminded of the example of Ceausescu: it took just one woman to call him a liar for the whole repressive system to come down. That's the unstoppable power of freedom.... It annoys me no end to contemplate the insensitivity of the Europeans towards the suffering Saddam Hussein inflicts on the Iraqis.... That defensive attitude is terrible.
>
> (Bush 2007)

One has to wonder why Bush invokes a responsibility to promote freedom and voices his contempt for European compliance with the suffering of the Iraqi people in this instance if it does not reflect his real sentiments. That the argument was not intended for the public makes it harder to dismiss as cunning masquerading and the quote does not lend itself easily to an anti-idealist interpretation. Aznar, after all, had already subscribed to Bush's political course.

It is also noteworthy that individuals close to Bush, who should be well positioned to pronounce on his state of mind, often impute pure idealist motives to him. Condoleezza Rice (2011: 325), for example, is adamant that Bush "had a deep personal belief in the power of liberty and an instinct toward a US foreign policy based on values". Also Fred Barnes, who "was given extensive access to President Bush in order to write his account" (Colucci 2008: 99), divides Bush's foreign policy belief system into ten themes, all of which bring his idealism to the fore:

> America's overriding mission in the world is to champion freedom; democracy is for everyone; America does not bestow democracy, God does; history's ultimate destination is freedom; democracy is the best weapon against terrorism; the pursuit of freedom serves the interest of both realists and idealists; democracy leads to peace among nations; the best place for a revolution for democracy is the Middle East; America and Europe bear blame for the absence of democracy in the Middle East; and the campaign for liberty must be lead by the United States.
> (Barnes 2006: 117–118)

As noted in Chapter 4, Scott McClellan (2008a: 132, xii, 129), Bush's press secretary, was convinced that the "major reason" behind the Iraq war was Bush's "divinely inspired passion" which culminated in the "vision of transforming the Middle East through the spread of freedom". It is hard to believe that Bush was able to construct a deceptive narrative in order to keep a misperception alive on the part of his friends and advisors as such hypocrisy is difficult to sustain over time, especially vis-à-vis individuals with whom Bush had to share plenty of information. McClellan's confident and mono-causal claims inspire confidence in light of his role inside the administration. As a press secretary, one would think he was particularly sensitive to the finer nuances of Bush's motives as it was his task to communicate them to the wider public. Perhaps more than any of the others, McClellan must have kept a wary eye on the difference between confidential motives and motives meant for public consumption. For that reason, his conclusion that the idealist motive is sufficient to account for the Iraq war cannot fail to impress.

Additionally, one has to take seriously that acclaimed analysts of Bush's policies conclude that pure idealism was a precursor to many of his decisions, reflecting his duty to the principles of the US constitution and a desire to fulfill goals that transcended national interests. Although many of these conclusions could, given the quality of the data, have been more cautious, questioning the impact of pure idealism is, in effect, to go against the bulk of the research.

Michael J. Mazarr (2003) writes in the article *George W. Bush, Idealist*, that "the Bush administration's assumptions, doctrines and polices stem generally from a very different world view from that proposed by classical realism" (ibid.: 503). He goes through the tenets of realism and maintains that all members of the administration disagree with virtually all those tenets. He concludes that "much of what Bush and his advisors seem to believe is closer to idealism, in the Reaganesque sense – a belief in the victory of certain value systems and a willingness to place American power and the military might in the service of that trend (ibid.: 521).

Daalder and Lindsay (2005) waver throughout their book with respect to Bush's motives. Sometimes they indicate that pure idealism held sway. After 9/11, we are told, Bush "was reborn as a crusading internationalist who had embraced Woodrow Wilsons's vision of a democratic world and who was willing to use America's military might to make it happen" (ibid.: 78).[3]

In his book *Crusading Realism*, Colucci (2008) concludes that "the most central ideal of the Bush Doctrine is the idea of liberating Iraq for democracy" (ibid.: 188). He surmises that the cornerstone of the Bush Doctrine is "the founding of the nation" and the "belief that policy must follow morality and ethics" (ibid.: 210).

> In speech after speech and discussion after discussion, in public gatherings and classified government meetings, the President and those around him invoked this [the spread of liberty] as the moral reason that they are engaged in the war on terror.
>
> (Ibid.: 213)

Having laid out an extensive number of sources in a balanced way, Colucci's conclusion tilts steeply in an idealist direction. Despite being keenly aware that fear of Hussein's weapons and possible links to terrorists shaped the policymaking process, he still believes that the duty to bring the blessings of democracy to a people on a distant shore on balance gives the most compelling explanation of the policies pursued.[4]

As this selection of findings documents, while far from being established beyond reasonable doubt, it is difficult to discard confidently the notion that pure idealism swayed Bush in the wake of 9/11 and that idealist motives were causally contributing to the decision to wage war on Iraq. The uncertain quality of the data on which the conclusions are based, and all the evidence that impugns those conclusions, still warrant skepticism and, presented as the sole causal contributor, I remain unconvinced. Yet the indications invoked here suggest that dismissing the impact of idealism altogether may lead one to arrive at inaccurate conclusions.

5.3 Weak idealism

Skepticism toward both anti-idealism and pure idealism invites composite arguments that lever idealist motives into explanations otherwise wedded to self-interested motives. One composite suggestion is the idea that national interest was not by itself sufficient to set off important initiatives in the wake of 9/11, such as the Iraq war, but sufficient only in combination with an idealist motive. This suggestion is the *weak idealism thesis*. The idealism is weak in the sense that the idealist motive is, based on the data, taken to be the weaker of the two motives in composite explanation and would not alone have been sufficient to spark the initiatives we set out to explain. Placing ideas in the secondary role does not simply follow from a pre-theoretical bias, giving security reasons a more prominent role, but emerges by weighing empirically the relative importance of the respective motives. Although the empirical basis for saying that the security motive was the stronger of the two is not very strong, I have not come across any author arguing that both motives were in play, who also unconditionally suggests that idealism was primary and security secondary.

Bush occasionally hints at idealism as an additional causal precursor, apart from his duty to keep the US secure. In an interview after the Iraq war began, Woodward (2004) asked Bush how he reacted when Powell articulated, in a meeting between the two before the war, his best case against it. Bush says:

> And my reaction to that is, is that my job is to secure America. And that I also believe that freedom is something people long for. And that if given a chance, the Iraqis over time would seize the moment. My frame of mind is focused on what I told you—the solemn duty to protect America.
>
> (Ibid.: 152)

This mix of security and idealist motives "nonplussed" Woodward. Yet it would not be unreasonable to interpret the "solemn duty to protect America", and the weaker duty to give "freedom a chance" to thrive, as weighing more heavily on Bush than Powell's reservations.

Also on other occasions Bush noted that these two motives, in tandem, pulled him towards war with Iraq: "America's interests in security, and America's belief in liberty, both lead in the same direction: to a free and peaceful Iraq" (Bush 2003b). The relative importance of the two is not as clear in this case, only that they were both required to spark the war.

That idealism was necessary to tip the scales, but of secondary importance and of itself not sufficient to justify embarking on the war, is also suggested by one of Bush's closest advisors, Karl Rove. Described as "the President's alter ego and strategic subconscious" (Suskind 2007: 78), Rove should be in a position to have an informed judgment on this matter. In his memoirs (Rove 2010), he vouches that national security concerns *in combination* with a desire to promote a democratic political culture to the Middle East explain why Bush went to war. And in accordance with the weak idealist thesis, Rove suggests that the former motive was measurably stronger than the latter.

In fact, Rove alludes to three jointly sufficient causes. First, having seen the carnage caused by the terror attacks of 9/11, it became an important priority for Bush to prevent WMD from falling into the hands of terrorists. Bush thought that Hussein was ruthless enough to work with "terror surrogates". Therefore he "believed Iraq represented a deeply dangerous threat" (ibid.: 341), which he, as the ultimate guarantor of US security, had to extinguish. Second, Bush thought that installation of democracy in Iraq would be "a bulwark against Islamic extremism". Democracy would consequently "serve our national security interest by creating civil institutions that would have a stake in defeating Islamic extremists" (ibid.: 341). Third, and this is where the idealist motive is levered in, Bush was of the opinion that the Iraqi people deserved to enjoy the "progress of modernity" and a democratic "political culture" for their own sake and regime change in Iraq would provide an opportunity to realize these goals (ibid.: 341).

"Taken together, these considerations justified the decision to remove Saddam Hussein" (ibid.: 341–342), writes Rove. But he also "doubts" whether the Iraq war would have occurred absent the concern with Hussein's WMD (ibid.: 339). Had Bush (hypothetically) not been convinced that Iraq possessed WMD he "would probably have sought other ways to constrain Saddam" (ibid: 339). This suggests that the first consideration was the weightiest motive of the three. But importantly, the two additional considerations were necessary, but alone not sufficient, to set off the war. "Taken together" they explain it, which implies that the third idealist motive was, however weak, causally efficacious.

Rove's account is suggestive partly because it presents a repertoire of transparent reasons whose added impact explains the decision. Furthermore, it explains why Bush on various occasions invoked a cocktail of diverging reasons and why internal documents include goals that conform to and goals that transcend the US self-interest (cf. Feith 2008: 542).

Rove's account may also indicate that idealism was the factor that solved what some thought of as an indeterminate choice situation. As underscored by Feith (2008: 224), the prudence of war with Iraq was something about which "reasonable people [within the Bush administration] differed". If compelling *security reasons* for and against the war were considered to be equally strong, one may presume that the existence of additional idealist reasons, helped to tip the scale. That, at any rate, is the implication of Rove's argument and the weak idealist thesis.

5.4 Over-determining idealism

A second composite suggestion is the idea that self-interested motives were accompanied by idealist motives, which alone would have been sufficient to set off the policies even in the absence of the self-interested motive. If a self-interested reason sufficient for a decision to be made coincides with an unselfish motive that also would have been sufficient to instigate the same action it is *over-determining idealism*. Like two rocks hitting a window simultaneously, both by themselves sufficiently powerful to break it, US policies, for example toward Iraq, were over-determined in the sense of there being two sufficient conditions for their occurrence.

Before the UN General Assembly Bush (2002b) argued that "Liberty for the Iraqi people is a great moral cause, and a great strategic goal. The people of Iraq deserve it; the security of all nations requires it", implying that two independent, coinciding, and equally strong motives set off the regime change policy. That Bush ascribes the same adjective, "great", to both causes makes them seem perfectly symmetrical. "Great" would also have been an inappropriate adjective if not to suggest that one cause, in the absence of the other, would have been sufficient. This interpretation receives confirmation from other statements to the same effect. Bush (in Colucci 2008: 173) suggests that security interests equal the ethical interests when he argues, "Now as before, we will secure our nation, protect our freedom, and help others to find freedom of their own". When discussing the failure to find WMD in Iraq after the war, Bush (in Woodward 2004: 423) insists that "there is no doubt in my mind that we should have done this. Not only for our own sake, but for the Iraqi citizens". All these statements indicate causal over-determinacy.

This composite conclusion is also reached by several other analysts. According Kagan and Kristol (2004), security interests and idealism were on an equal causal footing, each being a sufficient reason for regime change in Iraq. They argue that "the moral and humanitarian purpose provided a compelling reason for a war to remove Saddam ... [L]iberating the Iraqi people would by itself have been a sufficient reason to remove Saddam" (ibid.: 1). Yet they also direct attention to the consideration that Hussein was a "predator and aggressor" who "sought dominance in his region", possessing weapons and ambition, and "intimidating and destroying anyone who stood in his way". Apparently, "[t]his, too, was a sufficient reason to remove him from power". The conclusion that there were two independent reasons, each sufficient to set off the war, makes it a clear statement of an over-determined idealist thesis, summarized in the subtitle of their article: "The liberation of Iraq was abundantly justified".

Also, according to Mead (2004: 116), the reasons for the Iraq war were twofold. In the first place, he underscores that a "sense of clear and present danger from the possibility that Saddam would share his WMD with al-Qaeda or other terror groups, was the stated, rational argument". Yet "the case for invading Iraq was much stronger than fear of WMD, and it was obvious that these considerations were driving US policy on Iraq as much, or more than, WMD concerns". One of these additional considerations was the "humanitarian dimension". Replacing this "dreadful dictatorship" was a "good deed", according to Mead, as "it was a war to make the world safe for democracy" (ibid.: 117). Iraq could be the first step in a democratization wave across the region. Following Mead, it was "obvious" that such idealist considerations contributed to drive the policy as much as the concern with Iraqi weapons. He thereby adds to the list of authors suggesting that considerations of national security in symmetrical measure to idealist considerations over-determined the policies towards war with Iraq.

5.5 Idealism encouraged by abundance of security

A third composite suggestion is the idea that idealist motives were allowed to influence US foreign policy in the wake of 9/11, even though the pursuit of these motives did not contribute to the pursuit of the national interests, because the national interest was already sufficiently taken care of, sufficiently that is, to allow for the luxury of some idealism on the side. This is how Mearsheimer (2001) regards evidence of idealism in international politics. While idealist actions are anomalous and, if unchecked by power considerations, ultimately self-defeating in anarchy, he does not deny their occasional existence. Rather, he concedes, "states pursue non-security goals as well".

They sometimes promote a particular ideology abroad, as happened when the United States tried to spread democracy around the world.... Great powers also occasionally try to foster human rights around the globe.

(Ibid.: 46)

States can *afford* idealist endeavors when their basic security requirements are fulfilled. Since the US power in the international system after 9/11 was asymmetrically balanced to its own advantage, observing it pursuing non-security goals is less bewildering insofar as the requisite behavior did not conflict directly with balance of power logic.

The premise that the US indulges demands of idealism only when more important interests are met sounds reasonable as it squares with a principle of priority favoring the realization of the most vital needs first (Krasner 1978: 341). However, the argument assumes that there is a constant impulse of idealism only waiting for conditions conducive for its outlet. The source and existence of this constant impulse is not clear and realist scholars do nothing to explain how it enters decision-makers' minds. Even if the psychological origin of idealism had been identified, why idealism should have directed itself outward to other states and not inward to the fulfillment of idealist programs to increase domestic welfare remains unexplained.[5] But as the above paragraphs demonstrate, there is no shortage of statements suggesting the existence of such an idealist impulse.

Moreover, the argument that security in abundance was a prerequisite for the idealist impulse to gain traction is supported by evidence. Bush underscored that the US "enjoys a position of unparalleled military strength and great economic and political influence" (NSS 2002: iv). Instead of using this unrivalled "strength to press for unilateral advantage" the US would attempt to "create a balance of power that favors human freedom". It seems that unparalleled strength and absence of threatening rivals, made the objective situation permissive for other motives to influence the policies, and Bush appears ready to seize the opportunity.

Walt (2005: 54) sees a trend in this direction over the last two decades:

The end of the Cold War facilitated these efforts [democracy promotion] in several ways. The collapse of the Soviet Union removed the main threat to US national security and made it less necessary to tolerate anticommunist dictatorships.

Assuming that desires for other-regarding action, such as giving oppressed people the opportunity to select their own leaders, are more or less constant, the mere fact that the circumstances allowed such action may go some way towards explaining why idealism appears to have shaped US policy in the aftermath of 9/11. As severity of constraints is inversely proportional to the opportunity set, pursuit of idealism was now more viable, according to Walt.

This is also the core argument of Krauthammer (2004). He discusses various policy options open to the US in a situation when it enjoys security in abundance:

"What is a unipolar power to do?" (ibid.: 3), he asks. His answer is to adopt a "targeted, focused and limited" (ibid.: 18) commitment to the proliferation of human freedom, to implant democracy "where it counts", a doctrine he labels "democratic globalism" (ibid.: 16):

> What is unique is our advantage in this struggle, an advantage we did not have during the struggles of the twentieth century.... Hence, the fourth school, democratic globalism. It has, in this decade, rallied the American people to a struggle over values. It seeks to vindicate the American idea by making the spread of democracy, the success of liberty, the ends and means of American foreign policy.
>
> (Ibid.: 18)

Krauthammer sees the wars in Afghanistan and Iraq as the realization of this doctrine. The fact that the United States is a "unipolar power" allows it to pursue policies informed by an idealist vision "to bring a modicum of freedom as an antidote to nihilism" (ibid.: 19). Krauthammer's ideas sit well with the view that security in abundance is a necessary and permissive condition for allowing idealism to influence policy even though it is unclear why certain idealist projects "count" while others do not.

However, the security in abundance thesis is inadequate for explanatory purposes. Observing that the conditions were permissive for idealism to influence US foreign policy is only the first step in a successful idealist explanation. A *desire* to pursue idealist goals must be identified and accounted for too. And neither Walt nor Krauthammer answer why the opportunities offered by unipolarity led to foreign policy idealism. One wonders, why exactly was it pertinent to "vindicate the American idea" in Afghanistan and Iraq?

In addition, despite the evident absence of a superpower conflict, no member of the administration appears to have believed that the US enjoyed security in abundance after 9/11. Being attacked, something that had never happened during the entire Cold War, rather spurred a feeling of vulnerability and security deficiency. That US insecurity loomed large undermines the core premise that this interest was sufficiently taken care of. If it is true that the decision-makers after 9/11 felt that the US was short of security and if it is also true that they pursued idealist policies after the attack, then the causal relationship between security in abundance and idealism breaks down. If anything, it suggests the reverse causal relationship, that idealism is triggered rather by *insecurity* in abundance.

5.6 Impure idealism

Finally, when probing the validity of idealist explanation one has to consider the idea that what on the face of it looks like a policy motivated by idealism, is really a policy motivated by the pursuit of long-term self-interest that sometimes happens to call for policies of the kind that are commonly *associated* with idealism. If a decision is made to foster a goal that transcends the immediate self-interest in the belief that the achievement of this goal eventually will foster a self-interested goal and when the production of the long-term goal is what causally brings about the decision, it is *impure idealism.*

The impure idealist thesis supposes the existence of a long-term perspective as it requires the ability and stamina to defer gratification, that is, deciding to produce an unfavorable (or suboptimal) effect now in order to obtain a favorable effect later (Elster 1983: 71). Think of economic aid given to a country, not for its own sake, but because it cements an alliance. Although the immediate outcome of the aid transcends the self-interest, it is given in the belief that this outcome, in due time, will produce another outcome that clearly benefits the self-interest. When the production of an unselfish effect is only an efficient means to bring about a remote selfish end, the idealism is impure.

Gaddis (2008: 2) interprets US initiatives towards Europe during the Cold War as impure idealism. Opposing Soviet domination of Europe by providing economic aid and security guarantees benefited Western Europe and transcended the immediate US self-interest. The resources invested for the purpose could have been allocated to welfare projects within the US but, according to Gaddis, the US deferred such immediate gratification, and implemented polices that did not "promise immediate results". Instead they rested on the "realistic calculation" that a prosperous and democratic Europe ultimately would benefit US power and security within the international system in the long run. The underlying motive for the unselfish policies was the belief that this would ultimately serve a self-interested purpose.

Rice (in Monten 2005: 147 and in Rice 2011: 326) makes the exact parallel to the aftermath of 9/11:

> America's pursuit of the national interest will create conditions that promote freedom, markets and peace. Its pursuit of national interests after World War II led to a more prosperous and democratic world. This can happen again.

Numerous other statements by Bush suggest that impure idealism instigated US actions after 9/11. Bush argued that democratic regime change in Iraq, while costly, would be worth it because of its likely long-term benefits to US security. Democracy promotion would resemble a financial investment: deferring the immediate gratification of assets disposable today, in order to obtain a higher gratification later. The "investment", democratic regime change in Iraq, was commonly associated with idealism, as it promised eventually to bring stability, peace and rule of law to a brutalized country. However, this outcome was merely a means to attain the distant, but far more important gratification of higher security, which apparently was what instigated the endeavor: "The triumph of democracy and tolerance in Iraq, in Afghanistan and beyond would be a grave setback to international terrorism" (Bush in Record 2008: 82).

Rice (2005) conforms to the impure idealist thesis when she writes, "Supporting the growth of democratic institutions in all nations is not some moralistic flight of fancy; it is the only realistic response to our present challenges". Apparently, there is no "neat line" between US security interests and the democratic ideals on which the nation was built, as democracy promotion benefits the security interest. Consequently, she advocates that the "goal of our statecraft is to help create a world of democratic, well-governed states". In her memoir, Rice (2011:,325) elaborates further on "the place of idealism ... in US foreign policy". Although her idealism seems sincere, there is nothing to suggest that her position amounts to a genuine genuflection to US values. Rather, echoing Krauthammer's (2004: 15) insistence that realist scholars must be thought "that the spread of democracy is not just an end but a means, an indispensable means for securing American interests", she believes that the promotion of US values is an effective tool to foment US interests:

> [T]he freedom agenda was not just a moral or idealistic cause; it was a redefinition of what constituted realism, a change in the way we viewed US interests in the new circumstances forced on us by the attacks of that horrible day [9/11]. We rather quickly arrived at the conclusion that US interests and values could be linked together in a coherent way.
> (Ibid.: 325)

Interpretations of US motives by individuals close to Bush support the view that impure realism was causally efficacious in bringing about the post-9/11 policies, including the Iraq war. Wolfowitz (in Colucci 2008: 96), when asked what he considered the driving motives behind Bush's policies, highlighted two features. First he underscored Bush's commitment to eliminate the threats to the US posed by global terrorism. Second, he viewed Bush's endeavor as a "strategy to encourage the spread of freedom and democracy in the Muslim world as part of an effort to alter the environment in which terrorism and extremism have grown over the last several decades". Wolfowitz, nicknamed the "sunshine warrior" because of his optimism about the ability of the US to be a militant force for a better world, is often said to have brought intellectual weight to the idealist cause within the administration (cf. Keller 2002). Interestingly also, his idealism appears impure.

It is also the view of Charles Krauthammer, a man of some influence situated outside government, that Bush's decisions rested on an indirect strategy:

> [C]learly the Bush Doctrine ... calls for the promotion of democracy globally.... The overall objective is not necessarily democracy per se, but rather an end to global terrorism.... Now the current administration's belief is that a world of democracies is their primary strategy towards achieving that goal.
> (Krauthammer, in Colucci 2008: 105)

As noted earlier, Karl Rove (2010) was of the opinion that idealism was a necessary, but insufficient, motive for the Iraq war. Yet he underscores that Bush's most "critical insight", which made him a "rare" political leader, was his idea that "by promoting freedom, the United States could give millions of Muslims a compelling reason to stand with us in the struggle" (ibid.: 519). Bush apparently understood that democracy provided the best "bulwark against this new tyranny" (ibid.: 519), which is another indication that impure idealism held sway.

Impure idealism is also the intent imputed to Bush by several researchers. Renshon (2007) concludes his analysis of the administration's thinking with the verdict that the idealist content of the policies was impure: The "democratic impulse is hardly altruistic". Rather, Bush believed that "a healthy dose of democracy" is an expedient means to prevent political instability that breeds terrorism directed against the US (ibid.: 20). Zonis (2007: 233), on his side, identifies four self-interested rationales that justified the seemingly unselfish goal to spread democracy: democratic states fight terrorism; democratic states drain the swamp from which terrorists are recruited; democracies are stable and peaceful; and democracies foster trade and prosperity.

According to him Gaddis (2002: 2), "the Bush administration, unlike several of its predecessors, sees no contradiction between power and principle. In this sense it is thoroughly Wilsonian". Jervis (2003b: 366) interprets Gaddis to mean that democracy promotion was "at the heart of the doctrine". However, this interpretation misleads, as Gaddis adamantly maintains that democracy promotion is absolutely not at the heart of the doctrine, that is, not the underlying motive, but simply a proper means to bring about security. There is no contradiction between power and principle because democracy promotion is "right on target" in confronting the new threats to US security (Gaddis 2002: 4). In effect,

> There is a compelling *realistic reason* now to complete the *idealistic task* Woodrow Wilson began more than eight decades ago: the world must be made safe for democracy, because otherwise democracy will not be safe in the world.
>
> (Ibid.: 4, my italics)

Tunç (2005: 9) similarly argues: "This was idealism not for its own sake, but was closely linked to a strategic imperative of reducing terrorist impulses associated with radical ideas". Bush did what he did because he believed that "[f]reedom and democracy were the best antidotes to totalitarian ideology whether in its religious or secular form.... The goal of spreading democracy and freedom was then a strategic US interest, not only a moralistic policy". In sum, a wide array of scholars subscribes to the impure idealist thesis.

If impure idealism shaped Bush's decision, there is no reason to doubt the motives imputed to states by Mechanistic Realism. As impure idealism is informed by long-term security considerations, taking one step back in order to take two steps forward, the strategy conforms to a hierarchy of goals of which security ranks highest. Yet, to the extent that impure idealism was in play, it still impugns the assumed strategies of power amassment enunciated in the mechanistic catalogue. Impure idealism implies that the tools of power politics are more diverse than the catalogue would have it. If democracy promotion and other initiatives associated with idealism were considered viable self-help strategies to maximize security, we have traced a mechanism that clearly breaks with the strategies of power enhancement enunciated by Mechanistic Realism.

But even by granting the pursuit of the national security interest a richer repertoire of idealist-looking means, it would be, one could argue, an unwarranted lowering of the anti-idealist barrier if such acts were awarded the idealist label. Acts that can, charitably, be given an idealist interpretation, but which on closer scrutiny are motivated by the pursuit of long-term self-interest, are exactly of the kind that do not lend themselves to idealist explanations.

Yet one may ask, is it pure serendipity that idealist-looking policies serve the long-term national interest, or is it the idealist character of these policies that lends them instrumental utility when it comes to promoting the national interest? On the one hand, one may argue with Bacevich (2003) that the fact that pursuit of self-interest can be associated with idealism, has no real bearing on the long-term utility of these initiatives for the national interest. The implantation of democracy "is just a bonus" and the liberation "theology is largely a pretext" (ibid.: 1).

> That is, the Anglo-American invasion of Iraq in 2003 is about freeing Iraqis to precisely the same degree as the Anglo-American invasion of Europe in 1944 was about freeing those imprisoned by Hitler's death camps. In each instance military action resulted in liberation that was incidental, welcome and admirable, but that was no more than a *byproduct* all the same ... let us take care not to breathe too deeply the intoxicating vapors given off by the rhetoric devised to justify the use of force to advance US interests.
>
> (Ibid.: 2, my italics)

Based on Bacevich's argument, what makes us associate the Iraq endeavor with idealism is merely a welcomed by-product of the pursuit of the national interest, and the idealist content of the policies, while welcome, bears no responsibility for the long-term utility of the policy whatsoever. It had not mattered much for US interests if Bush had instead established a US-friendly tyrant in Iraq, in the belief that s/he would see to it that no WMD were procured, that no bonds with terrorists were forged and that no terrorists were allowed to develop hostile plots. A cynical policy would serve the US self-interest just as well, as the character of the policy has nothing to do per se with its long-term utility. If Bacevich is correct, that it is pure serendipity that the idealist-looking policy in Iraq advances the national interests in the long run, then acts of impure idealism must clearly be subsumed under the anti-idealist thesis.

However, that conclusion is not beyond reasonable dispute as it may be that the idealist character of the policies lends them instrumental utility when it comes to the long-term national interests. How? When foreign policies are viewed by others as having intrinsic value, there is a good chance that they will trigger favorable *reciprocity* of some kind. Idealist-looking acts have the merit of inviting gratification by others. Descartes (in Elster 2007: 102) writes that, those who do nothing save for their own utility, ought also, if they wish to be prudent, work ... for the good of others, [because] one ordinarily sees it occur that those who are deemed obliging and prompt to please also receive a quantity of good deeds from others, even from people who have never been obliged to them.

Such reciprocity, it seems, is conditioned on the premise that the idealist character of the policy is not visibly implanted in order to *bring about* this reciprocity, in which case the positive feedback would probably not *come about*. The reciprocity is an unintended side effect of following the tit-for-tat logic. But, importantly, it is a side effect that renders the idealist character of the policies relevant by its utility to the national interest. It is the intrinsic value to idealist-looking initiatives, even those ultimately instigated out of self-interest, that assures that idealism is rewarding. Judged on the merit of long-term consequences, it is therefore not irrelevant if the US installs a dictatorship or democracy. When the US chose the latter, it lent instrumental merit.

Descartes' prudence is an important, yet implicit, premise for Nye's (2004) argument about "soft power", the view that others might come to want what you want because they approve of your policies. Nye advances an argument to the effect that seducing US polices would co-opt rather than coerce others to act in the US interest (Nye 2004: 5). By this mechanism idealist-looking policies become an asset in and of themselves and it is not pure serendipity that idealist-looking policies, producing attraction, are to the benefit of the national interest in the long run. After all, not all policies are seductive, such as the installation of a US-friendly dictator. By contrast, the example one sets by demonstrating concern for the welfare of others, for example by implanting democracy, bears fruit, so to say, by virtue of the idealist character of such initiatives.

Accordingly, even if US initiatives to spread values like democracy, human rights and individual opportunity are instigated out of concern for the long-term self-interest, that is, the initiatives are examples of impure idealism, whether the initiatives eventually benefit the US self-interest is not immaterial, because of the existence of the mechanism pointed out by Descartes and reiterated by Nye. Even *impure* idealism has an intrinsic quality, making it less clear whether such acts should be grouped with the anti-idealist thesis. Yet, all things considered, impure idealism fails to overcome the anti-idealist barrier as such acts ultimately fail to transcend the self-interest. The existence, and the presumed prudence, of impure idealism ensure that international politics, while pervaded by cynicism, are also characterized by more than brutality and conflict of interest.

5.7 Conclusion

That all claims to the effect that idealism shaped US policies in the first eighteen months after 9/11 are fraught with uncertainty, calls for cautious conclusions. The findings presented here are, on balance, not convincing enough to write Mechanistic Realism off entirely, but suggest the catalogue is short of mechanisms necessary to establish idealist influence. Sensitivity to these six positions on idealism augments our causal awareness and enriches our understanding of how idealism possibly affected Bush's decisions. The categorization offers a more nuanced comprehension of the role of idealism in the wake of 9/11, even if it does not provide a definitive answer.

The six positions on idealism that emerge on scrutiny of the evidence and scholarly analysis introduce some causal patterns that supplement the repertoire of mechanisms offered by Mechanistic Realism. This should come as no surprise as Mechanistic Realism does nothing to explain how non-security motives enter decision-makers' heads and affect their behavior.

Nevertheless, some of the inferences deducted from this case are compatible with Mechanistic Realism. In fact, anti-idealism, idealism induced by security in abundance and (with a reservation) impure idealism square well with realist assumptions. In contrast, pure idealism, weak idealism and over-determining idealism diverge from the assumed motivational structure proposed by Mechanistic Realism. Overall, the evidence warrants a cautious willingness to believe that idealist motives, that were not highest in the US hierarchy goals, had causal impact on the policy.

The fact that there is insufficient empirical basis to conclude confidently that idealist sentiments shaped Bush's decisions in this case, one in which the scrutinized statements are heavily steeped in idealist terms, lends on the face of it credence to the anti-idealist presumption that idealism has negligible impact on foreign policy choice. Inability to establish confidently that idealism gave impulse to decisions in this case, makes one wonder whether we ever shall be.

Still, I think, it is analytically more honest to be sensitive to the various ways idealism might have held sway and regard all six positions on idealism as potential mechanisms worthy of a place in the explanatory toolbox. While the anti-idealist presumption, implicitly heeded by Mechanistic Realism, is a good reminder that all declarations of idealist intent warrant scrutiny, accepting it peremptorily may gloss over too much human complexity, reduce decision-makers to fictional skeletons and lead us to accept invalid conclusions. Bush, at any rate, appears to defy a pure anti-idealist interpretation.

If nothing else, this exploration shows that documenting the presence of causally efficacious idealist motives poses a considerable hermeneutic challenge. The epistemological circumstances surrounding Bush's idealism simply preclude confident ontological claims about its impact. The lack of scholarly agreement, evident in what was written above, testifies to the difficulty of the task. But instead of acknowledging this imperfect epistemological situation, many researchers cited here conclude more confidently than the facts of the matter warrant.

Such hyperbolic confidence, I fear, mars idealist explanations. Without a closer examination, idealism risks ending up as a rather unhelpful explanatory variable. Specifically, I have three concerns. First, many idealist arguments accord, on inspection, idealist ideas a minor role. Weak idealism, security-in-abundance-idealism and impure idealism, while on the face of it idealist explanations, do not make good on the pledge to show that idealist ideas are of anything near symmetrical importance to security concerns. This raises questions about what extra value idealist arguments add to the explanation.

Second, idealist arguments are empirically weak. Typically, analysts who assert that idealism shaped Bush's policies do so in such a bland manner as to defy comprehension. Arguing, for example, like Richard Pearl (in Colucci 2008: 105) that "Freedom. That's where he [Bush] started out and that's where he is now" suggests that Bush was in the grip of ideas, but is far from convincing evidence that the desire to bring freedom to oppressed peoples instigated his actions. The same applies to claims that Bush and Rice "became converts to the messianic 'freedom' mission only after 9/11" and both became "'fervent believer[s]' in peace by democratization" (Record 2008: 81). The imprecision of other familiar buzzwords such as "the freedom agenda", "peace through democratization", "democratic imperialism", "idealistic fervor" etc., which flourish in the literature as designations of the administration's idealist motives, profoundly complicates efforts to evaluate the empirical validity of the idealist variable.

Third, idealist arguments are weak with respect to psychological plausibility. It is often averred by those invoking idealist arguments that "realism cannot capture the liberal character of this expansion" or that realism fails to account for the administration's "missionary take on liberal exceptionalism" (Monten 2005: 143). This is a fair point. Yet despite all the weaknesses of realism, the psychological assumption underpinning it, namely that people are concerned with security, has at least an a priori plausibility, as security is an ultimate human desire (Gat 2006: 667–669). The same cannot be said of the kind of motivation idealist explanations invoke. That it cannot as easily be argued that concerns with the welfare of others are an ultimate human aim implies that idealist arguments inevitably have a more curious character. Alluding to "liberal character" and "missionary take on liberal exceptionalism" does not satisfy our intellectual curiosity without some sort of suggestion as to how this kind of motivation enters into decision-makers' heads. I am aware that this is much to demand and some would think it reflects a bias favoring realist thinking about mental and motivational matters. Be that as it may. Without greater psychological plausibility, idealist explanations will struggle to persuade. Pointing to the "utopian aspects" of Bush's thinking, as Boyle (2004: 99) does, in fact, prompts more questions than it answers.

While it appears that idealist explanations can complement our understanding of foreign policy choice, and indeed complement the one-dimensional realist attention on security, it must be done in a way that defies easy critique, especially considering the strength of the anti-idealist thesis and its psychological plausibility. Exploration of idealist motives must direct attention to at least three tasks. First, the *underlying motive* involved in actions we typically think of idealistic, such as democracy promotion, must be properly scrutinized. It is arguably inapposite to call policies that benefit others idealistic if they are a means to a self-interested end. If this fact had been more closely observed, many authors who now invoke idealism would have had to suspend the idealist label.

Second, attempts to understand *relative impact* must guide all composite suggestions. Only then can we gain insight into whether the invoked idealist motive was necessary, sufficient or neither. Because of insufficient clarity on this matter, it is often difficult to know what some analysts are really arguing or what sort of role they envisage for idealist ideas when they point to the influence of idealism.

Third, statements of idealistic intent must be examined while bearing the crucial difference between *real motives* and *mere rhetoric* in mind. How much significance, for example, is it justified to ascribe to Bush's (in Woodward 2004: 89) insistence in connection with the Iraq war that "I believe we have a moral duty to free people"?

The six perspectives enunciated here come from an attempt to attract attention to these three tasks. Despite imperfections, most will agree that the categorization is analytically clarifying. Yet the end result is still disappointing as analytical clarity is no gratifying substitute for confident conclusions. And ultimately, I am neither confident enough to conclude firmly that idealism shaped Bush's decisions nor do I believe that failure to provide sufficiently convincing evidence of idealism is an acceptable reason to dismiss its impact altogether.

This limbo leads to a depressing conclusion about the possibility of overcoming uncertainty on matters of political motivation. Absent evidence of the highest quality (which is unavailable in the present case), social inquiry reaches its analytical limits in confrontation with such hermeneutic challenges. While it is possible in principle, and arguably analytically rewarding, to subsume observations under anti-idealism, pure idealism, weak idealism, overdetermining idealism, idealism induced by security in abundance and impure idealism, it is far more difficult, perhaps beyond our reach, to establish in practice their respective causal impacts. Since idealist explanations of the Bush administration's policy rest on limited and uncertain evidence and on a curious psychological basis, one probably has to live with unresolved questions of validity on this score.

To complicate matters further, and based on the perplexing variety of statements made by members of the administration, even the involved decision-makers seem unable to dissect reliably the relative impact of various motivational contributions. The fact that the totality of their statements is incoherent underscores the point, and suggests how genuinely torn they must have been between various concerns and motives. I doubt whether an optimal source, say, Bush's personal diary, would have provided complete insight into "the dark labyrinth of human motives" (Wolfers 1962: 70) and dispelled our worries. It may be beyond our reach to know whether Bush used idealist rhetoric as a convenient mask, whether his other-regard was genuine, whether strategic reasons and ethical went hand in hand, whether both concerns by themselves were sufficient to instigate action, whether abundance of security spurred idealism, or whether policies typically associated with realism were instigated due to their believed, long-term strategic utility. The available evidence is mixed and even optimal evidence would presumably not be much different. The mixed empirics possibly reflect the state of the matter. The case may be one of those empirical instances in which "an impression of puzzling behaviour may be truer to the facts than attempts at explaining it away" (Malnes 2006: 188).

If this conclusion offers any insight, it suggests that questions about the motivational precursors to some aspects of the US response to 9/11 defy traditional causal analysis.[6] More confident conclusions would have to rely on cursory conjunctions and I think the lack of scholarly agreement on this issue owes a lot to the role of conjunction. Overall, we would probably fare better by stipulating the possibilities and acknowledge that what we are dealing with here is "the kind of problem men are forever trying to solve but never solving" (Osgood 1953: 1).

Nonetheless, a clarification of the various ways in which idealism *may have* operated is not devoid of value as it suggests various solutions to the motivational pulls that the policymakers presumably experienced. Acknowledging that this discussion brings us to the limit of what social analysis can accomplish implies that we have to abstain both from (bombastic) conclusions about the impact of idealism and from (bombastic) conclusions to the effect of totally dismissing the impact of idealism. However, if this case offers any guidance, any analytical framework ignoring idealist explanations is making an unsafe bet, as is any framework that puts all its bets on it.

6 Conclusion

Although not explored exhaustively above, this book has grappled with the old, but still baffling enigma of why wars occur between states. Like all human acts, wars start in the minds of individuals. But how do minds become bent on war in the first place? Building on well-known realist insights, Mechanistic Realism provides a repertoire of psychologically plausible mechanisms suggesting an answer. Whereas the grand theory of realism explicates in abstract how the social condition of anarchy wedded to an assumption of security-seeking states prompt struggles for power that sometimes degenerate into war, Mechanistic Realism exhibits the psychological precursors in the minds of those individuals who shape foreign policy and steer it into power struggles and wars. The catalogued mechanisms push the boundaries of inquiry to the lowest level of abstraction that realist insights permit.

By spelling out the operating psychological processes at the decision-making level, Mechanistic Realism breaks with two important precepts traditionally adhered to by realist practitioners. First, it has been a commonplace to deliberately ignore the plethora of causal processes taking place within states, analyzing them instead as if they were black boxes, varying only in power, size and position. The assumption, which supposedly justifies this approach, is that the circumstantial constraints facing a state, along with its share of power, ultimately determine that state's conduct, not factors inside the state.

None of the realists adhering to this view deny that individuals with desires, beliefs and emotions reside in the black boxes or that their intents are causally responsible for their state's foreign conduct. Yet they boldly assume that the significant individual precursor to foreign policy is derived exclusively from observations of the systemic constraints facing the state. Like a burning house compels individuals of all inclinations to leave the building, international conditions presumably compel states of all inclinations to employ the same basic arguments about how to act. To explain the rush for the exit, or explain state behavior, there is supposedly no need to analyze the processes inside the black box that produced it (cf. Wolfers 1962: 13).

Second, it has been a common realist presumption that explanations should rest on general laws. Laws provide knowledge of cause and effect explaining why X leads to Y. Yet laws do not help us understand why a produced effect

Y follows a cause X. Law-like statements such as "anarchy causes wars of aggression" do not exhibit the details in the sequence suggesting *why* this is so. Hence, laws are black-box statements hiding the intervening causal processes or connections running from X to Y. By exploring the intersecting causal chains sitting inside realist black-box statements, Mechanistic Realism reduces the time lag between cause and effect and put us in a position to better understand how observations in the social world fit together, thereby reducing the chance of spurious inferences, enhancing explanatory credibility and giving greater satisfaction to our intellectual desire for truth.

By providing a glimpse inside the black box in both these senses, Mechanistic Realism is apt to fill a dual purpose. In the first place, it can be used to analyze the decision-making processes taking place inside black boxes, that is, within states. In the second place, it unpacks the finer causal chains that sit inside law-like black box statements about cause and effect, as espoused by realism, thereby displaying in sharper light the causal sequence responsible for state behavior. By delivering on both these measures, Mechanistic Realism adds value to the realist tradition.

Paying heed to three precepts of social science analysis – scientific realism, a mechanism-based research program and methodological individualism, on which I expanded in Chapter 2 – I proposed a way of increasing the explanatory power of realism by exploring the theory's micro-foundations. Instead of validating realism by assessing its ability to predict non-specific outcomes, say great powers go to war to maximize power, I attempted to validate it by assessing the extent to which its implied causal processes, incorporated into Mechanistic Realism, actually occurred and were responsible for the observed outcomes (George and Bennett 2005: 209). By taking realism apart, by spelling out the more fine-grained psychological mechanisms that realist premises permit, and by confronting it piece by piece with empirical evidence of what happened in one given case, it was possible to examine methodically which building blocks could be upheld and which failed to convey a true explanation.

In order to pass an informed judgment on realism's merit and at the same time stay true to the doctrine of methodological individualism, I had to interpret the theory and present what it implied for *individual* decision-makers. This micro-analytical revamp required theoretical elaboration. The elaboration rested on the supposition that traditional formulations of realism were *preliminary* in the sense that the premises permit us to say more about individual-level psychology than is commonly done. Chapter 3 was an attempt to translate what amounted to a realist *benchmark*, i.e., Mearsheimer's theory of Offensive Realism, into a set of plausible psychological mechanisms suggesting how men and women think and act as decision-makers, based on the assumption, defended persuasively by Jon Elster, that theories are only apt guides to individual-level analysis if the psychological operations implied by them lend themselves to plausible, detailed, descriptions of "frequently occurring causal patterns". The translation resulted in a more specific, less opaque and empirically more incisive framework consisting of explanatory mechanisms more general than the phenomena they subsume.

Although the translated mechanisms differed with respect to psychological micro-level plausibility, they could all stand. Some mechanisms, such as the desire for security and reacting with fear to threatening signals, alluded to frequently occurring mental operations with a very high plausibility, bordering on the obvious. Other implied regularities, such as uncertainty fosters fear, counter-wishful thinking or the primacy of military means, had a less obvious psychological application. On any measures, the detailed account of the mechanisms was an apt starting point for empirical analysis as it, on the one hand, elucidated the causal chains that sit inside postulated law-like regularities (so-called black-box statements), and, on the other, aspired to account for the processes inside states (often regarded as black boxes) responsible for state behavior. The book has peered *inside the black box* in both these senses.

Although Mechanistic Realism pointed to mental operations presumably applicable to all actors making foreign policy decisions, I applied the catalogue to one chosen case, namely the thinking of members of the Bush administration between 9/11 and the beginning of the Iraq war, in order to gauge its explanatory power. I approached the data on what happened within the administration presuming that observations would correspond to the invoked mechanisms, suggested by the tentative judgment put forward by acclaimed scholars of realism as a suggestive truth candidate. Yet wanting to avoid theory-laden conclusions and aspiring to pass the objectivity test suggested by Føllesdal (and introduced in Chapter 2.4), I was open to the suggestion that the data themselves would open one's eyes for other mechanisms, unrelated to Mechanistic Realism. Detection of these would contribute to the project of gathering mechanisms into an explanatory toolbox capable of dispelling foreign policy puzzles.

I identified several difficulties likely to hamper my effort in this regard. In the first place, telling a mechanism from a detailed description is not only methodologically challenging, but tangled up with the philosophical impossibility of observing causality, i.e., the sequence between cause and effect, directly. In the second place, imputation of motives and reasons is always fraught with uncertainty as the evidence on which such imputations are based may be deliberately produced to hoodwink (Elster 2007: 59–65). The sources available in this case did not lend themselves to confident answers as they were *unreliable* on several scores. Most inferences would therefore, on principle, be empirically weak and subject to withdrawal or correction upon the emergence of evidence or reasoning upsetting them. Yet, as Chapter 4 demonstrated, Mechanistic Realism enriched our understanding of the policies pursued, confirming the analytical utility of several mechanisms in the framework, and Chapter 5 on idealism, suggested ways by which causal forces ignored by Mechanistic Realism may operate.

6.1 Empirical conclusions

To begin with I observed with puzzlement the lack of consensus regarding the validity of realism after 9/11 among its main advocates. On the one hand, several realist scholars opposed the Bush administration's foreign policy, suggesting that realist theory was short on explanatory power in this case. On the other hand, the theory had the merit of correctly predicting US conduct after 9/11 ex post, and acclaimed scholars such as Robert Jervis and Kenneth Waltz vouched for its validity. But as both the invalidity and the validity claims, to my surprise, were not based on meticulous empirical investigation on the individual level, I believed it would be required to develop a realist framework up to the task of probing individual decision-makers and their states of mind.

After empirical scrutiny, the validity claim of Mechanistic Realism was neither confirmed nor disconfirmed, but rather nuanced. Chapter 4 documented that several of the posited mechanisms received enough support from the available evidence to vouch for their validity. Although disputed by those imputing hidden agendas to the administration, the evidence suggesting security ranked highest in the US hierarchy of goals was, on balance, more convincing. Fear was fostered by exposure to threatening signals, but also a response to the uncertainty experienced. A strategy for maximizing power, rather than one aiming to preserve the status quo or one aiming to amass power within reasonable limits, was formulated and military means were considered pivotal in this pursuit. Self-help reasoning, observed as unwillingness to transfer autonomy to other actors, was also conspicuous, illustrated by defiance of the UN, and there were several indications of the administration acting to achieve a good margin of safety, suggesting precautionary reasoning had causal impact. Even perplexing observations, such as why signals of conciliation were interpreted with a sinister slant, could be dispelled by invoking the curious phenomenon of counter-wishful thinking. Defying expectations, however, was the fact that the mechanisms presumably taming expansive efforts were, to all intents and purposes, inoperative.

Despite the uncertainty of the sources, one attraction of the evidence was that it rendered plain the requisite mental states that *preceded* the decisions I aspired to explain. The desire for security and the evidence of the fear gripping members of the administration were both plausible *precursors*, that is, plausible *causes*, of the decisions eventually made. This is in contrast to several alternative attempts to validate realist motives by invoking the *consequences* of the administration's decisions. Consider, as an illustration, Jim Holt's (2007: 4) realist-inspired explanation of the Iraq war, where he highlights its beneficial effects:

> One can't say for certain that oil supplied the prime motive. But the hypothesis is quite powerful when it comes to explaining what has actually happened in Iraq. The occupation may seem horribly botched on the face of it, but the Bush administration's cavalier attitude towards "nation building" has all but ensured that Iraq will end up as an American protectorate for the next few decades – a necessary condition for extraction of its oil wealth.... In terms of realpolitik, the invasion is not a fiasco; it is a resounding success.

Since an outcome cannot, without further argument, explain a cause, Holt's suggestion that control over Iraq and its resources validates the importance of the desire for "American geopolitical supremacy" (ibid.) fails to convince. In contrast, the explanation presented in Chapter 4 invoked individual motives, beliefs and reasons present at the decision-making moment, reducing the chance of spuriousness. The mechanisms were efficacious precursors to the US response to 9/11 and since the bulk of observations could be subsumed under the familiar causal patterns exposed by Mechanistic Realism, the framework displayed explanatory power.

Despite this, several of the mechanisms of Mechanistic Realism failed to dispel a lurking suspicion that other mental states gave impetus to the policy as well. The evidence was, after all, more mixed than the above résumé indicates and invoking other factors appeared required to *complete* the explanation offered by Mechanistic Realism, as Chapter 5 made clear.

In Chapter 5, I probed the validity of idealist explanations of US conduct and identified five different attempts to overcome the anti-idealist barrier to which Mechanistic Realism is wedded, i.e., five explanations defying the rejection of idealism. To various degrees, all of the suggestions accorded a role to idealist ideas and the quantity of statements suggesting that the administration pursued goals that transcended the national security interest was indeed impressive. On the face of it, the massive presence of idealist rhetoric upset explanations of US conduct which placed realist motives ahead of idealist ones.

Yet, on inspection, all idealist explanations were weaker than was first apparent. First, the evidence for idealism was uncertain. Although there was no paucity of idealist statements, their authenticity could not be verified. Second, the role accorded idealist ideas in idealist explanations was often smaller than at first glance. Acts we typically associate with idealism, such as democracy promotion, were justified as a means to a self-interested end, and therefore failed to overcome the anti-idealist barrier. Third, idealist explanations were weak with respect to psychological plausibility. Although it is frequently suggested that "the expansion of philanthropy has gone further in the United States, than in any other part of the world" (Aileen D. Ross in Lipset 1996: 67) and "the spread of democracy through American power ... is inseparable from American national messianism and the wider 'American creed'" (Lieven 2003: 8), other-regard of this kind is a priori more curious as it, in contrast to security, cannot be related to an ultimate human aim.

Despite these weaknesses, annulling all idealist indications would require a misanthropic presumption that would offend the vagaries of human motivation observed elsewhere. Even if the epistemic position ruled out a confident answer, the impression of a certain measure of idealist influence appeared truer to the facts than its total rejection. At the end of the day, I am doubtful whether Bush himself is capable of dissecting rigorously how much idealism actually mattered to his decisions, but I doubt he would deny it any role whatsoever. And the five idealist suggestions were a rewarding way of understanding analytically how idealism might have influenced him.

In sum, the administration did make decisions pertaining to national security after 9/11 under the influence of several mechanisms of Mechanistic Realism.

Yet they appear to have acted under a slight influence of idealist mechanisms as well. The available data render an evaluation of the relative impact of each impossible, something which precludes an intellectually satisfying answer. All the same, several mechanisms of Mechanistic Realism made better sense of the choices made; they were both superior to the neo-conservative thesis and truer to the facts than other explanations of a realist cast. In that sense knowledge has progressed.

6.2 Implications for theory

Generality is typically viewed as an appreciated feature of theory. Of two equally tenable theories, most would prefer a general to a less general one. Needless to say, realism's general scope is among its most characteristic properties – compared with other theories, it allows us to explain much with little. Yet, realism's wide scope is also a vulnerability as even one anomalous counterexample suffices to impugn its generalizations. When counterexamples pile up, as many believe they do in the case of realism, one can, conservatively, choose to stick with the theory, arguing that certain anomalies are an acceptable price to pay for simplifying generalizations. Alternatively, one may, adventurously, call for theoretical modifications. But since generality is appreciated even by modifiers, it is often suggested that realism ought to be revamped in a way that increases its validity yet preserves its comprehensive explanatory scope. Brenner (2006: 512), for example, subscribes to this ambition and argues for a "Lakatosian monster-adjustment" that "increases the theory's [realism's] capacity". He aspires to use a discarding counterexample, i.e., the emerging relevance of non-state actors, as a stepping stone to revamp realism.

> This monster-adjustment provides the impetus and opportunity to extend realism's reach into a potentially much wider range of international phenomena where structural homogeneity [i.e., identical state units] is not a prerequisite.... [After the adjustment] a wider range of international behavior and outcomes can be considered under realist frameworks.
>
> (Ibid.: 520)

A central argument of this book has been to dispose of both conservative theoretical fidelity and the project Brenner calls for, in favor of the theoretically less ambitious but analytically more rewarding attempt to accumulate a set of mechanisms and make an explanatory toolbox. This argument, heavily influenced by the works of Jon Elster, implies a modification of realism that robs it of its most characteristic feature, to be exact, its generality. Still, it is likely to benefit the realist tradition if paid heed to. If anything, Mechanistic Realism has demonstrated how much more understanding can be gained by exploring the via media between grand theories and detailed descriptions, i.e., the intermediary between realism's comprehensive propositions and the detailed narratives of what transpired within the Bush administration.

Many will disagree with this project. Hyde-Price (2007), for example, thinks a project along these lines is futile and sees good reasons to uphold the dualist epistemology.

> [G]ood theory is necessarily parsimonious: it involves abstraction and simplification, not descriptive accuracy ... thinking theoretically means that one must be prepared to sacrifice detailed descriptions for broad observations.
>
> (Ibid.: 9, 7)

Yet those inclined to agree with Hyde-Price should appreciate that the project of accumulating mechanisms does not imply that we shall forget about either good theories or detailed descriptions, as they are both eye-openers to behavioral regularities with a degree of consistency among cases. Rather, endeavoring to identify mechanisms of an intermediate degree of generality calls for attempts to decompose the former and aggregate the latter, so that we overall become better equipped to explain the events we encounter. Having a set of mechanisms, to the extent possible analytically tailor-made for specific contexts, is better than having a comprehensive theory with wider applicability because mechanistic explanations are epistemologically more satisfactory in the sense that they provide more complete and more certain answers to our questions (cf. Elster 1999: 6). Whether the mechanisms in question are dependent or independent of more abstract theoretical models, or whether they belong to one school of thought or the other, is of far less importance compared to their ability to dispel local puzzles.

The events encountered in this project vindicated the words of the pioneering realist Hans Morgenthau (1968: 19): "[i]n every political situation contradictory tendencies are at play". And to comprehend these contradictory tendencies, to appreciate the quandaries with which decision-makers grapple, grasping the complexity of their motives, understanding their state of mind, requires a more versatile program that steers clear of both the nomological and the ideographic extremes.

On the one hand, the empirical complexity of this case precluded a general theoretical explanation of the kind offered by realism. First of all, because such an explanation fails to exhibit the more fine-grained processes responsible for the outcomes we seek to understand. Second, because the impact of competing causal factors, such as idealism, is incompatible with unyielding and parsimonious realist fidelity. On the other hand, the detailed descriptions, while indispensible with respect to revealing the sequence of the events, do not seem sufficiently alert to the fact that many of the described occurrences fall into recurring causal patterns that can be located across widely different foreign policy settings. Between the nomological and ideographic extremes, explanation by mechanism rectifies the nomological as well as the ideographic shortcomings. Mechanistic Realism comprehends the fine-grained processes on display better than nomological theories and is less blunt than descriptions with respect to the general regularities under which the observations can be subsumed. Applied to this case, it revealed that Bush and other members of his administration were neither realist automats under the influence of mono-causal forces beyond their control nor autonomous foreign policy revolutionaries, but rather that they acted under the influence of a selection of mechanisms one would expect to be at work in foreign policy decision-making situations.

Snyder (2008: 184) is concerned that rejecting theory in favor of a catalogue of mechanisms commits a "theoretical mistake ... [of] causal underdetermination" and is critical of approaches that acknowledge contradictory causal forces since they preclude the possibility of determinate predictions.

> [C]ircumstances that might plausibly lead towards one behavior (say, gambling on war) might just as plausibly lead to the opposite behavior (say, prudent self restraint), yet no additional variables are adduced to explain why the former is chosen.
>
> (Ibid.)

Snyder's concern is understandable, as prediction and control are at the heart of the social scientific attempt to assess how far theories have "been able to prove [their] fitness to survive by standing up to tests" (Popper 2009: 248). In addition, those, typically practitioners, who would like theories to be prescriptive, would realize that a catalogue of contrary mechanisms is of limited use since tendencies in different directions are acknowledged as a matter of fact. Yet when we take into account the nature of the topics of social science inquiry, understanding after the fact, rather than prediction before the fact, is probably a more pertinent ambition. As argued throughout this book, mechanism-centered research renounces the ambition to identify universally valid causal assumptions required for prediction in order to gain explanatory power after the fact. The elaboration of mechanism 5 in Chapter 3 is a case in point. In abstract, decision-makers in anarchy appear apt to both maximize power (5a), preserve power (5b) and, after due consideration, to amass power within reasonable limits (5c). Thus formulated, the three versions of mechanism 5, while suggesting reasonable unambiguous empirical variation, admittedly defy strict testing. Without knowledge of the triggering conditions, we are, ex ante, not in a position to predict how a decision-maker will act, only that her actions plausibly will conform to one of the three suggested patterns. After knowing the content of the decision, we may conclude provisionally which mechanism was responsible. And invocation of one of the mechanisms is in effect to offer an explanation in hindsight.

By specifying the circumstances that make the activation of one or the other mechanism more or less likely one could gradually move towards a more unified mechanistic theory. This would require a tremendous amount of empirical research. In the meantime, even if specifications of this kind fail, it would be rash to deny the role mechanisms in the explanatory toolbox can plausibly play, simply because they contradict another mechanism that could also plausibly come into play. Our inability to tell ahead of time what to expect, does not prevent us from attempting to explain occurrences, invoking mechanisms, in retrospect. I think this book has demonstrated the viability of this approach.

However, the project of accumulating mechanisms must not be confused with frictionless *eclecticism*, i.e., an unremitting and careless picking of elements from various theories without thinking through whether the elements can be logically reconciled. By being alert to contradictory tendencies, illustrated both by the variations of mechanism 5 and the influence of idealism, while at the same time avoiding mechanisms that are *fundamentally* incompatible, the accumulation of mechanisms is a program that aspires to confront strict theoretical monogamy without falling into the trap of boundless theoretical polygamy. One has to strike a fine balance: on the one hand, to take seriously that human psychology is incoherent and the factors potentially determining foreign policy choices are too complex to allow for fixed answers, while, on the other hand, not assuming that every conceivable mechanism deserves a place in the toolbox.

To exemplify: the mechanisms by which uncertainty fosters fear and the twin mechanism, defying realist premises, by which uncertainty fosters complacency, embody contradictory causal chains that can operate on different occasions. In Chapter 5, it was demonstrated empirically that the Bush administration acted under the influence of both. Both mechanisms are sufficiently general and precise to enrich our understanding of specific instances of the kind. However, a mechanism whereby the common purpose of mankind renders *uncertainty* inconsequential in international politics would be fundamentally incompatible with the other two, and could not be included in a coherent toolbox.

Since Mechanistic Realism offers a repertoire of mechanisms inspired by the realist tradition, I doubt that I have identified all the mechanisms impacting foreign policy decisions. Yet there is no presumption to the effect that the catalogue must be expanded indefinitely to do so. Waltz's (2008: 84) suggestion that "the infinite materials of any realm can be organized in endlessly different ways" is laying it on too thick. The complexity of international politics is not boundless, suggesting that the number of mechanisms required in the toolbox is finite. Although a definite or final answer about the precursor to the US response to 9/11 is missing, the realist mechanisms espoused here have improved our understanding of the various influences under which the Bush administration made decisions. And the resulting catalogue can serve as a set of expectations with which to explore cases not yet encountered.

Of particular significance in this case was the suggestion that the decisive explanatory factors belonged to different "paradigms" that are often viewed and treated as mutually contradictory and explanatorily irreconcilable. Yet my conclusion indeed suggests that an explanation is incomplete without taking the influence of both realism and idealism into account. This fact alerts us to the mechanism-centered research strategy's capacity to "open up what has become a rather stylized debate among contending schools of thought and create space for research that is driven by local puzzles and recurrent policy-relevant problems" (Bennett 2003: 2). When a mechanism demonstrably shapes a foreign policy decision it aspires to a place among several peers in the repertory of social scientific explanations regardless of the school of thought to which it belongs. This attitude deflects the unfruitful tendency in the IR field to cling exclusively to a given "paradigm" and to creatively interpret any observation in light of it.

Countering the tendencies to part the IR field into contending theoretical labels and "isms", and acknowledging only causal forces in one direction, is an endeavor to which I hope this book has contributed. The influence of realist and idealist mechanisms suggest that the precursors to the Bush administration's decisions cut across schools of thought often pitted against one another as fundamental adversaries. But the above conclusion shows that they can be coherently reconciled in a composite explanation. Ultimately, alertness to all "contradictory tendencies" is the only genuine *realism*.

Finally, both the theoretical arguments and the empirical conclusions of this book have undermined the instrumentalist doctrine. Waltz's (2008: 75) suggestion, quoted in Chapter 1, that a "theory cannot fit the facts or correspond with events it seeks to explain" did not describe the epistemological situation in this case study very well. Although Mechanistic Realism failed to identify all the effective causes shaping US policy in the wake of 9/11, some of its micro-level mechanisms clearly "fitted the facts" and "corresponded with the events". That several of the theoretically posited mechanisms were consistent with individual-level observations is telling evidence of the continuing impact of realist regularities in contemporary international politics, and I see no reason whatsoever to abstain from the added explanatory value that a break with instrumentalism implies.

However, breaking with instrumentalism implies splitting up realism into pieces, disposing of its universal features, and instead viewing it as a set of contingent mechanisms that sometimes need explanatory support in order to explain foreign policy in full. The theoretical implication of this micro-analytical turn is that the *grand theory* of realism breaks down. Yet the empirical support some of the mechanisms posited by Mechanistic Realism received in this case indicates their aptitude for being true. So even though realism as a grand theory is gone, the validity of its implied mechanisms gives reason to think that the tragedy of great power politics will linger.

Notes

1 Introduction

1 The idea of explanation by mechanisms employed in this book is strongly inspired by the works of Jon Elster. Many of the ideas developed here originated with him. To my knowledge, there is no other scholarly work on IR attempting to draw on Elster's plea for mechanisms. I would also mention that without feedback from Raino Malnes and Svein Melby, the arguments of this book would have been far easier to upset.
2 Harry Frankfurt maintains, in his serious philosophical examination *On Bullshit* (2005), that bullshit is a product of a particular state of mind, the state of not being concerned with truth. I sometimes find myself wondering if some realist scholars aren't themselves very close to this state of mind when they conduct their analyses. Rather than a concern with truth, their concern seems to be model esthetics and theoretical parsimony. Measured against these criteria they are successful, but to the extent that their attitude deflects a concern with truth, it is unfortunate. As Glenn Snyder (2002: 157) writes, "parsimony and logical elegance may need to be sacrificed in favor of greater 'realism'".
3 This was the topic of three panels at the International Studies Association Conference held in April 2012.
4 Some would find the realist advocacy staggering given the theory's view of policy-makers as, in effect, "prisoners" of the structural circumstances. If they truly believed the scope for choice was constrained to such a degree by the "forces of anarchy", one has to wonder why they attempted to sway the decision-makers, insofar as suggestions of what someone *ought* to do imply a belief in an *ability* to do so, and if the policy-makers cannot help but conform to the dictates of systemic pressures, as realism indeed indicates, advising them to behave differently would indeed be futile. As Little (2007: 222) points out, there is an "unresolved tension between the importance he [i.e., Mearsheimer, but the point applies to other realists as well] attaches to structural forces, on the one hand, and the theories adhered to by practitioners, on the other".
5 John Mearsheimer (2001: 30), a realist who I will return to in Chapter 3, initially rejects the instrumentalist doctrine in acknowledging that "a theory based on unrealistic or false assumptions will not explain much…. Sound theories are based on sound assumptions". Nevertheless, on the self-same page he also vouches for instrumentalism, maintaining that each of his theoretical assumptions is a "reasonably accurate representation of an important aspect of life" (ibid.). Elsewhere he inadvertently adopts the instrumentalist position, maintaining that "offensive realism is like a powerful flashlight in a dark room … most of the time it is an excellent tool for navigating through the darkness" (ibid.: 11) and suggests that theories of international politics offer "useful tools for anticipating what lies ahead" (ibid.: xii). Finally, and this of course is the hallmark of instrumentalism, Offensive Realism is pervaded by useful, but empirically dubious "as if" assumptions, such as the argument that states should be treated "as if" they were identical black boxes, even if we know that they are not; that

states can be treated "as if" they are unitarily rational actors, even if they are not; and that military capability can be treated "as if" it equaled power, even when we know there is more to power than military capability. Note that Richard Little (2007: 220, fn. 8) takes Mearsheimer's rejection of instrumentalism at his word. By so doing, Little overlooks that Mearsheimer, on closer inspection, speaks with two tongues.

2 Foundations for social analysis

1 I assume Hill's doubt arises because these phenomena depend for their existence on human cognition. But it is unclear why we should adopt a different theory of truth when we form beliefs about phenomena conditioned by human thought. While the scope of reasonable interpretation might be wider in such cases, the validity of any interpretation must presumably be judged according to the extent to which it corresponds to the cognitive facts under consideration. A more serious problem for Hill is that his view undoes itself on inspection. The crux of his argument is to deny the possibility of uncovering social scientific truths. At the same time he appears to believe that his own statement refers to a *true fact* about the scope of social sciences, which means that he admits one important exception to his rule, namely his own statement. Skepticism is arguably warranted for proponents of ideas who reserve a superior standard for their own judgments.

2 Here is a telling example: Øystein Tunsjø (2008), whose analytical framework draws on the tradition called critical constructivism, does "not deny the existence of a material world outside ... heads" but asserts that reality "cannot be known purely and directly" (ibid.: 2). He favors "a more modest conception of what knowledge is" rather "than assuming that 'the truth' is out there and discoverable" (ibid.: 7). Tunsjø brings up "national interests" as an example of a phenomenon beyond truthful description and subscribes to Ninkoich's view that "'as objects of study, interests are slippery because they have no objective existence apart from the way people constitute and interpret them'" (ibid.: 5).

Introducing theories of social construction and discourse methodology, Tunsjø aims to reexamine a piece of history "which to date has been inadequately tackled" (ibid.: 7). More precisely, his "study emphasises the comparative advantages of using a critical constructivist method to explain US Taiwan policy since 1949" (ibid.: 8). Based on well-documented archival analysis he questions the interpretation, often inspired by realism, that only geopolitical concerns, strategic considerations and balance of power logic informed US Taiwan policy during the Cold War. On his understanding, a contingent *identity* formed by changing discursive practices within the US made possible and instigated change in US Taiwan policies from 1949 and onwards.

Despite Tunsjø's initial denial that social truths are within the scope of social analysis and that access to an objective reality is attainable, his discourse analysis is disciplined, even constrained, by historical evidence that all social scientists would consider relevant in the quest for the precursors to US Cold War actions. Furthermore, it is an important premise of his argument that all interpretations of the instigation of US policy can be challenged in light of new evidence, perspectives and methodology. It seems reasonable to impute to Tunsjø an acknowledgment that his own interpretation is no different on this score. Accordingly, he needs a standard against which the quality (or "adequacy") of various interpretations can be judged, and I find it very hard to believe that Tunsjø's standard, after all, is something other than correspondence to reality.

His claim that a contingent identity formed by changing discourses can account for US Taiwan policy is one aspiring candidate for truth. It can complete other accounts and is in itself correctable. The merit of Tunsjø's account derives solely from rigorous observations of what took place and sound extrapolations from those observations. Tunsjø's "re-examination" presumably reduces the disparity between our interpretation of US Taiwan policy and what actually went on during those years. Thus, although reluctant to admit it, Tunsjø researches as if he subscribes to the correspondence theory of truth. This lends credit to Wendt's (1999: 47) assertion that "most IR scholars are at least tacit [scientific] realists".

3 Note that scientific realism is a purely *ontological* position. Adherence to the doctrine does not entail the view that scientific inquiry one day will close the gap between our perceptions of the world and the world as it is, only that this is the principal aim and the appropriate goal for science. In practice, any scientific realist would acknowledge that several obstacles of an *epistemological* nature stand in the way (the limitations of our senses and the imperfections of our intellect, the opaqueness and complexity of individual consciousness, the impossibility of describing every detail of a social event), but according to a scientific realist, there is nothing in principle that makes a true description unachievable.

4 A typical misunderstanding is that scientific realism entails an unwarranted enthusiasm about science's capacity to capture the truth. Rather, modest ambitions typically prevail among realists. It is also wrong to impute to adherents of the doctrine the view that some truths are established once and for all. Given the difficulty of acquiring firm knowledge, a scientific realist is rather inclined to underscore the likelihood that established knowledge must be revised. That well-regarded and unanimously accepted theories are proved wrong does not dismiss, but confirms the scientific realist's assumptions. Sometimes even a certain methodology is attributed to scientific realists, but the doctrine is through and through agnostic when it comes to methodology. It is a doctrine that is not associated with any particular school of thought in IR theory and rejects "the very attempt to demarcate a 'scientific method'" (Wight 2006: 19).

5 Elster (1993: 5) suggests it is too demanding for social scientists to identify in advance the conditions under which one or the other mechanism is activated, which is why he includes in the definition of mechanisms that they are "triggered under generally unknown conditions" (Elster 1999: 1). "My own view is that the social sciences are currently unable to identify such conditions and are likely to remain so in the future" (Elster 1993: 5). However, even without explicating the conditions conductive for the activation of one and not another mechanism we would still have identified a "frequently occurring and easily recognizable causal pattern" (Elster 1999: 1), providing a measure of explanatory power after the fact.

6 Think of rain rituals in "primitive" cultures. We know today full well that they are ineffective. Hence, performances of rain rituals puzzle us. Durkheim, however, dispelled the puzzle by use of reason-explanation. According to him (in Boudon 2006: 32–33) the primitives had *reasons* to believe that such rituals had the capacity to produce rain, because they saw no difference between the magic of making fire by rubbing wood and producing rain by dancing. The reasons explain away the puzzle, even if the reasons themselves were objectively ungrounded.

7 This echoes Wolfers' (1962: 13) argument: "General fears of losing the cherished possession of life, coupled with the stark external threat to life, would produce the same reaction, whatever the psychological peculiarities of the actors".

8 It is admittedly not always easy to recognize mechanisms. An important dispute within realist IR theory concerns how states respond to fear. Since behavior is often ambiguous, the very same act, say the production of submarines or the production of a missile shield, can be subsumed under an offensive as well as a defensive causal pattern. Additionally, the two mentioned mechanisms are not particularly good at excluding spurious effects. Offensive and defensive policies may, for all we know, have other motivational precursors.

3 Mechanistic Realism

1 Mearsheimer gives "great powers" a somewhat approximate definition as states with "sufficient military assets to put up a serious fight in an all-out conventional war against

the most powerful state in the system" (Mearsheimer 2001.: 5). The theory's main focus is on great powers because these supposedly "have the largest impact on what happens in international politics. The fortunes of all states – great powers and smaller powers alike – are determined primarily by decisions and actions of those with the greatest capability" (ibid.: 5).That said, Mearsheimer acknowledges in a footnote that the range of the theory is wider in principle because it also "has relevance for smaller states" (ibid.: 403 fn. 5). Given this acknowledgment on Mearsheimer's part I shall use the non-differentiating term "states", even though I agree that the most powerful typically set the scene of action. That the US counts as a great power is, I believe, beyond doubt.

2 One may argue, and Mearsheimer hints at this in a footnote (Mearsheimer 2001.: 414 fn. 8), that it would have been apposite to include a premise according to which states worry that other states are occasionally motivated by non-security calculations or worry that other states behave irrationally. The mere possibility of this eventuality would obviously burden the system with even more uncertainty. Adopting the premise would require an account of *why* this worry arose, and creating such an account would severely hamper hypothesis generation to the effect of making predictions based on the theory utterly impossible. That probably explains why Mearsheimer only comments on it in a footnote. At one point in the main text, however, Mearsheimer maintains that there "are many possible causes of aggression, and no state can be sure that another state is not motivated by one of them" (ibid.: 31). This claim clearly alludes to the possibility of non-security motives, such as religion, ideology, personal gains or irrationality sometimes being causally effective. The claim, though, runs counter to and undermines the core argument of the theory. Mearsheimer cannot have it both ways because it is inconsistent to argue, on the one hand, that states always act rationally to maximize power, and, on the other, put in the caveat that they sometimes behave irrationally and depart from security considerations. What causes Mearsheimer to abstain from clarification on this score is probably his desire to construct a parsimonious framework able to generate powerful predictions despite being well aware of the tendency of states to behave irrationally from time to time. I think this demonstrates an unjustified willingness to sacrifice validity in the name of theory construction, which is why I think a mechanistic approach, which renounces universality, fares better. As I discuss in the empirical chapters, evidence suggests that fear seemed to mount in the US in the aftermath of 9/11 because the decision-makers worried about other states' penchant for irrationality.

3 I am indebted to Malnes's (1993) contraction of Hobbes' theory for the idea of condensing the theory in this fashion.

4 Given that individuals execute foreign policy, the motives imputed to states must be found among the individuals acting on its behalf. It cannot be imputed that security ranks highest in the hierarchy of state goals if the decision-makers rank goals differently. Arguing that fear is the prime emotional impetus of state action is false if the decision-makers are insensitive to fear or if different emotional states are precursors of their actions. Similarly, state reasoning can be nothing but the decisive reasons acted upon after collegial deliberations among the decision-makers; and assumed psychological inclinations, such as pessimism, must ultimately reside in the individuals in command. This, at least, is what the program of methodological individualism suggests.

5 Jervis (2003c: 3) thinks that it is impossible to separate rational from irrational fear. Discussing Bush's statement "We will not live in fear", it would be a mistake, he argues, "to try to characterize this as rational or irrational; it just is and provides a powerful impetus to behaviour". I disagree. If the fear is not rational, we have a negligible basis for understanding how it comes about and even less basis for understanding the behavior it elicits.

6 A more widely read translation uses the word "fear" in this passage.

7 Claiming this psychological disposition sways political decision-making is somewhat bold, given the bulk of psychological research that documents a general human tendency to be excessively optimistic (cf. Sunstein 2005: 52).
8 On numerous occasions, Mearsheimer (2001) displays awareness of the possibility of decision-makers acting under the influence of mechanisms other than the ones he accentuates. Indeed, he tends to be quite categorical, as when he maintains, "There are no status quo powers in the international system" (ibid.: 2). On other occasions he carefully includes subtle reservations. Consider what he writes on the very same page: "They [states] almost always have revisionist intentions" (ibid.: 2) and "dangerous rivalry would probably emerge" (ibid.: 2). Why include the reservations "almost" and "probably" if not to suggest the possibility of alternative and contradictory mechanisms under the influence of which different outcomes could come about? Perhaps Mearsheimer would concede that the non-deterministic mechanistic approach can be helpful, at least in those cases he has in mind when he includes his reservations? In addition, Mearsheimer alerts us to the fact that social science theories "rest on shakier theoretical foundations than that of the natural sciences", "that political phenomena are highly complex" (ibid.: 7), that "omitted factors [in his theory] ... occasionally dominate a state's decision making process" (ibid.: 11) and that "the fact remains that they [states] sometimes – although not often – act in contradiction to the theory" (ibid.: 12). All these contentions are at par with endorsing attempts to cope better with the shaky foundations and contradictory tendencies of the social world and go a long way to identifying and computing the influence of omitted factors that sometimes contradict the theory. The mechanism-centered research strategy appears suited to aid that endeavor.

4 The explanatory power of Mechanistic Realism

1 Quotes in support of this point are omnipresent in all speeches on the topic and in all the relevant security documents. Some randomly picked examples follow. "The President's most important job is to protect and defend the American people" (DHS June 2002: 1). "The purpose of our actions will always be to eliminate a specific threat to the United States or our allies and friends" (NSS 2002: 16). "We must accord the highest priority to the protection of the United States, our forces, and our friends and allies from the existing and growing WMD threat" (NSCMWD 2002: 2). "Defending the American homeland is the most basic responsibility of our government" (NSCWMD 2002: 6). "Combating terrorism and securing the US homeland from future attacks are our top priorities" (NSCT 2003: 1). Victory in the war on terror is defined as a situation in which the population "can live free from fear and where the threat of terrorist attacks does not define our daily lives" (NSCT 2003: 12).
2 Note that Bush's security concerns came into existence independent of his contemplating the survival of the US. What mattered, it appears, was the perseverance of what he refers to as "our way of life", suggesting that the intense preoccupation with security can come about absent threats to *survival*. Higher-order preferences, such as societal values, may be capable of producing the same effect. It is impossible to deny a state's survival as an always present motive, since it is a precondition for the realization of any other value, but it need not necessarily have been the direct instigator of all of Bush's security concerns.
3 Note in his first public appearance after 9/11 how Bush refuted any notion of him experiencing fear; he is always comforted, he says, by "a power greater than any of us [i.e., God]" (Bush 2001a)). He quotes Psalm 23, "Even though I walk through the valley of the shadow of death, I fear no evil, for You are with me". This divine submission is what Bertrand Russell (1938/2004: 10) calls "the sense of ultimate safety". Taken at face value the statement suggests that fear is not a catalyst for Bush's actions. Hence, an attempt to read fear in the minds of individual decision-makers seems in trouble. Robert Jervis (2006b: 15) takes statements like these very seriously,

and argues that "Bush's personal religious outlook and personality, [...] the religious conviction that permeates his way of thinking" has shaped the US response to 9/11. Without rejecting Jervis's claim and the possible influence of Bush's strong religious faith on US policy, I think it, on balance, justified to question the validity of the specific claim that he is, because of his faith, completely insensitive to fear. In that case he would be a biological and cultural exception. Besides, many other statements undermine the claim, and some of Bush's actions; for instance his personal security preparations would be partly inexplicable without presupposing a certain ability to experience fear. On a more philosophical score, Russell (1938/2004: 10) argues that ultimately "all submission is rooted in fear", even submission to a Divine Will. If correct, the biblical quote is self-contradictory and consequently Bush is, at least in some subtle sense, capable of experiencing fear.

4 As noted by terror expert Hoffman (2006: 40), the psychological effect is often the purpose of terrorist attacks and the intent to inflict psychological distress is often imputed to terrorists by the attacked.

5 Three much-discussed examples illustrate the point. Firstly, in the prelude to the Iraq war there were different opinions about whether the weapons unaccounted for by Hussein actually existed. In the early 1990s the UN inspectors had identified a certain amount of biological weapons material. Hussein had accounted for the destruction of much of it, but not all. Blix was reluctant to entertain categorical conclusions over the unaccounted weapons. The failure to identify them "does not necessarily mean that such items could not exist. They might – there remain long lists of items unaccounted for – but it is not justified to jump to the conclusion that something exists just because it is unaccounted for" (quoted in Braut-Heghammer and Riste 2005: 111). Consequently, Blix suspended his belief on the matter. The administration, by contrast, was strongly inclined to believe the weapons were concealed. Powell (in ibid.: 109) asserted that "inspectors can look all they want and they will find nothing ... this in part and parcel of a policy of evasion and deception that goes back 12 years". It was against his wish and departed from the judgment of supposedly neutral weapons inspectors, but the individuals responsible for US national security took it as an alarming sign. When two reasonable interpretations were available, they subscribed to the least peaceful.

Second, so-called "dual purpose" objects were subject to dispute. One example is the reports of aluminum tubes imported by Iraq. The tubes could be utilized for various purposes, but again members of the administration were quick to conclude that such items were most probably intended for illegal weapons production. Condoleezza Rice (in Braut-Hegghammer and Riste 2005: 86) stated that they "were only really suited for nuclear weapons programs". The CIA was less categorical, but also their judgment tilted in the worst-case direction. The unclassified report titled "Iraq's Weapons of Mass Destruction" (quoted in Braut-Hegghammer and Riste 2005: 87) contains the following:

> All intelligence experts agree that Iraq is seeking nuclear weapons and that these [aluminum] tubes could be used in a centrifuge enrichment program. Most intelligence specialists assess this to be the intended use, but some believe that these tubes are probably intended for conventional weapons.

Again, the observations permitted more reasonable interpretations, but the administration arrived at the counter-wishful conclusion.

Third, there was the issue of a strategic decision to disarm. According to Blix's memoirs one of the questions that spurred disagreement among world leaders was whether the evidence suggested that Hussein had made a "strategic decision" to disarm. One indication of such a decision would be if he willingly accounted for the destruction of all items that potentially could be used in the production of chemical, biological and nuclear weapons. Again, the signals were uncertain and again the administration favored the most sinister interpretation.

6 Arguably, this is overshooting the target since the historical record shows that deterrence does indeed fail at times. It could fail vis-à-vis Iraq if the threat of US retaliation lost credit in the eyes of Hussein or if Hussein lost cost sensitivity, both (unlikely but) conceivable prospects. That said, it still stands to reason that deterrence was a palpable *option* in dealing with Iraq.
7 The concern with demonstration can be observed on lower levels of execution as well. On September 19, 2001, Donald Rumsfeld (in Feith 2008: 55) transmitted three objectives to the counterterrorism planners. The first two had an obvious military strategic utility: finding targets and new intelligence sources. The third objective, however, was of a different kind:

> Opportunities to demonstrate a capability or a boldness that will give a pause to terrorists and/or those who harbor terrorists and force them to exercise much greater care, at greater cost or with much greater fear than they otherwise might have.
>
> (Ibid.: 55)

Elsewhere Rumsfeld reiterates this concern. He is skeptical of some of the operational plans exactly because "they will not likely produce impressive results" (Feith 2007: 64) and suggests ways to improve the impressiveness of the measures (ibid.: 66). As he wanted to convey to the terrorist and other states that attempts to defy the US were severely retaliated, military actions that signaled boldness were especially alluring. The suggestion that the US was paralyzed by the 9/11 attacks and reluctant to fight had to be discarded. "It would only make our enemies more aggressive if the United States seemed unwilling to pay a price to defend its interests" (Feith 2007: 55).
8 The presence of collective action problems suggests that Joseph Nye's (2002) argument by which "the world's only superpower can't go it alone" must be qualified. Rather, it appears to be the case that certain US goals, such as regime change in Iraq, because they deviate from their allies' ambitions, could not be initiated and eventually realized *unless* the US did it alone. Concerted action, while desirable on many scores and, according to Nye, on balance the best way to maximize long-term security interests (ibid.: 158), has a limited chance of being initiated when goals are discrepant. In those circumstances, multilateralism is simply not a viable option, and unilateralism the only way to get something done. Despite Arthur Schlesinger Jr.'s (2004: 19) insisting that "joint action may often be the best way to safeguard those [US national] interests", it remains a fact that it is difficult, if not unattainable, to initiate joint action when interests do not coincide.
9 "Strong powers naturally view the world differently than weaker powers.... And these disagreements reflect, above all, the disparity of power ... Americans, being stronger, developed a lower threshold of tolerance for Saddam and his weapons of mass destruction" (Kagan 2003: 27, 29, 31).
10 Still, the administration was interested in contributions, sympathy and acceptance by others as long as they did not require preference adjustments on their part. Bush appeared to be of the opinion that such support would be mustered only if he provided strong leadership. In an interview with Woodward (2003: 340–342) Bush regarded unwavering action as more important than consultations to rally allies.

> Well, you can't talk your way to a solution to a problem. And the United States is in a unique situation right now. We are the leader. And a leader must combine the ability to listen to others, along with action ... we're never going to get people in agreement about force and use of force. But action – confident action that will yield positive results provides kind of a slipstream into which reluctant nations and leaders can get behind.

It is clear that while Bush wanted contributions, he was unwilling to change preferences in exchange for them.

158 *Notes*

11 The unwillingness to forgo autonomy and a critical attitude toward coalitions were both on display in internal deliberations as well. Feith (2008: 51, 90) recalls how

> Rumsfeld dictated us [in the Pentagon] to include a cautionary note about coalitions ... [He] was in favor of organizing a coalition, but not as an end in itself ... if they [partners] insisted on political conditions for their participation, they could limit the President's freedom of action to protect the United States ... So long as the offers of help were useful and not burdened with unacceptable political conditions, Rumsfeld favored accepting them.

12 As Korb and Conley (2009: 237) point out, "Although his administration initially involved the United Nations in assessing Iraq's alleged WMD capabilities, it quickly became apparent that international cooperation was of interest only if it did not hinder the push to remove Saddam Hussein". While the administration decided to garner as much support from the UN as possible, "there was never any abandonment of the broader goal of dislodging Saddam Hussein from power" (Mann 2004: 348).

13 Kagan's (2003: 37) view represents this line of thinking:

> relative weakness has understandably produced ... interest in building a world where military strength and hard power matter less than economic and soft power, an international order where international law and international institutions matter more than the power of individual nations, where unilateral action by powerful states is forbidden, where all nations regardless of their strength have equal rights and are equally protected by commonly agreed-upon international rules of behavior.

14 Substantiating these arguments, game theorists are maintaining that a reputation for restraint can tranquilize others and reduce systemic tensions. This, of course, would be a too risky bargain according to Mearsheimer's reasoning, as restraint may also be exploited. Nevertheless, even scholars who concede that "the incentives for aggression are pervasive", view restraint as crucial because it may affect the calculation of rivals. Inspired by Schelling (1960), Roger Myerson (2006) points out the benefits of committed restraint in cases when rivals cooperate. In such cases restraint might foster a reputation for cooperation. By contrast, "Lack of clear restraint can stimulate others' resolve" (ibid.: 15). Being a great power bully creates powerful incentives for opposition on the part of rivals. In similar fashion, Keohane (1984: 26) argues that there is a "cost to reputation" if international commitments are broken, by which potential rewards of future cooperation are forsaken. At the same time there is a potential cost to reputation if you react with restraint when rivals defy you. In those cases, even if punishment is costly, or rather, exactly because it is costly, a successful long-term deterrer would demand resolve. Without a reputation for restraint when rivals cooperate and resolve when rivals defect, the overall pay-off will be less than optimal.

15 Other Republicans, whose opinions it is impossible to overhear in the US public discourse, including Henry Kissinger (summarized in Pfiffner 2004: 10), argued to similar effect: "a preemptive US attack would undermine conventions of international law centuries old. The treaty of Westphalia of 1648 'established the principle' that nations are not justified in interfering in the internal affairs of other nations".

16 His judgment concurred with the consensus inside and outside government that "Guys in caves can't get WMD" (Tenet 2007: 259).

17 Elsewhere, and independent of Cheney's remark, he puts forward arguments to the same effect: "In the face of such steely resolve [terrorists getting fissile material], the only responsible course of action would be to do whatever was necessary to rule out any possibility that terrorists could get their hands on fissile material" (Tenet 2007: 261).

5 Idealism

1 Mark Danner (2005: 6) writes that "the most reliable way to distinguish the true intentions of Bush and his officials is by looking at what they actually did". While sound on the face of it, his advice is unhelpful in situations where different motives encourage the same action. From a scientific point of view it matters if the Iraq war was caused by security concerns or an ethical duty to free an oppressed people and since those motives are compatible with the same conduct, looking at what the US actually did will not solve the puzzle. By following Danner's suggestion, one also runs the risk of extrapolating a cause from an outcome, which is sometimes warranted, but is also a dangerous analytical path as behavior is an insufficient guide to its own causes.
2 The presumption can be illustrated by how Mearsheimer interprets instances of national unification. National unification typically makes strategic sense as pursuit of power, but may also be favored by desires to redeem the neighboring people of same nationality from a repressive rule. Attempts at national unification thus lend themselves to both a realist and idealist interpretation. In such instances the anti-idealist presumption will favor the first.
3 But they also aver: "America went to war with Iraq for one overriding reason – because it believed Baghdad had weapons of mass destruction and was prepared to use them". So it is hard to know where they really stand.
4 On certain occasions Colucci baffles with his inferences because of their strong idealist slant. One example is illustrative. In relation to the impact of democracy promotion he quotes a summary from a reliable source of what appears to be a significant classified document outlining the goals, objectives and strategy towards Iraq: "It asserted that a free Iraq would eliminate the threat of WMD, the means of delivery the weapons, and prevent Saddam from breaking out of containment. The broader goals of the operation were to eliminate the Iraqi threat to its neighbors, liberate the Iraqi people from tyranny, and prevent Baghdad from supporting terrorists. The United States, the document boldly noted, would help the Iraqis 'build a society based on moderation, pluralism and democracy'" (Colucci 2008: 190).

Here he concludes that "America's main goal was democratic transformation to give the Iraqis their natural law rights to affect the region" (ibid.: 190). This is indeed a surprising conclusion given the content of the memorandum. It puzzles me that Colucci, whose book is arguably one of the most thoroughly documented books I have read on this topic, can conclude that "the Bush doctrine is best understood" in terms of "idealism" (Ibid.: 209).
5 Mearsheimer (2001) invokes two important impediments that typically tame idealist conduct even when the opportunity arises. The compelling power of these impediments justifies, according to Mearsheimer, a total analytical omission of idealist conduct. First, idealist goals will only be pursued when such efforts have virtually no effect on the distribution of power in the system, which is rare. Additionally, it means that very limited resources will be procured to such projects. Second, states will only pursue unselfish goals "as long as the requisite behavior does not conflict with balance of power logic" (ibid.: 46), which is to say that self-interest prevails in all dilemmas. When idealist goals collide with power considerations, the dictates of realism always hold stronger sway and that, obviously, will often be the case.
6 Malnes's (2006: 186–188) argument that explanatory expectations, on occasions, "have to be set rather low", helped me reach this conclusion.

Bibliography

Alexander, Gerard (2007). "International Relations Theory Meets World Politics. The Neoconservative vs. Realism Debate", in Renshon, S.A. and Suedfeld, P. (eds) *Understanding the Bush Doctrine. Psychology and Strategy in an Age of Terrorism*. New York: Routledge, pp. 39–64.

Art, Robert (2003). *A Grand Strategy for America*. Ithaca and London: Cornell University Press.

Audi, Robert (ed.) (1999). *The Cambridge Dictionary of Philosophy (Second edition)*. Cambridge: Cambridge University Press.

Bacevich, Andrew J. (2003). "Freedom is Just Bonus", *Los Angeles Times*, April 13, p. M5.

Barnes, Fred (2006). *Rebel in Chief. Inside the Bold and Controversial Presidency of George W. Bush*. New York: Three Rivers Press.

Beck, Ulrich (2005). *Power in the Global Age*. Cambridge: Polity Press.

Bennett, Andrew (2003). "Beyond Hempel and Back to Hume: Causal Mechanisms and Causal Explanation", lecture at the American Political Science Association, August 28.

Biddle, Stephen (2005). "American Grand Strategy after 9/11: An Assessment", Carlisle, PA: Strategic Studies Institute, US Army War College.

Blix, Hans (2004). *Disarming Iraq*. New York: Pantheon Books.

Boot, Ken and Wheeler, Nicholas, J. (2008). *The Security Dilemma. Fear, Cooperation and Trust in World Politics*. New York: Palgrave Macmillan.

Boudon, Raymond (1998). "Social Mechanisms without Black Boxes", in Hedstrøm, P. and Swedberg, R. (eds) *Social Mechanisms. An Analytical Approach to Social Theory*. New York: Cambridge University Press, pp. 172–203.

Boudon, Raymond (2006). "Are we Doomed to See the *Homo Sociologicus* as a Rational or as an Irrational Idiot?", in Elster, J., Gjelsvik, O., Hylland, A., and Moene, K. (eds) *Understanding Choice, Explaining Behaviour. Essays in Honour of Ole Jørgen Skog*. Oslo: Unipub forlag/Oslo Academic Press, pp. 25–41.

Boyle, Michael (2004). "Utopianism and the Bush Foreign Policy", *Cambridge Review of International Affairs*, 17 (1), pp. 81–103.

Braut-Hegghammer, Målfrid and Riste, Olav (2005). "Were WMDs the Real Issue?", *Forsvarsstudier* No. 4/2005.

Brenner, William J. (2006). "In Search of Monsters: Realism and Progress in International Relations Theory after September 11", *Security Studies*, 15 (3), pp. 496–528.

Bromwich, David (2008). "Euphemism and American Violence", *The New York Review of Books*, LV (5), April 3, pp. 28–30.

Brooks, Stephen (1997). "Dueling Realism", *International Organization*, 51 (3), pp. 445–477.

Brzezinski, Zbigniew (2007). *Second Chance. Three Presidents and the Crisis of American Superpower*. New York: Basic Books.
Bush, George W. (2001a). "Statement by the President in his Address to the Nation", September 11 [online]. Available at: http://georgewbush-whitehouse.archives.gov/news/releases/2001/09/20010911-16.html [Accessed September 19, 2010].
Bush, George W. (2001b). "Remarks by President Bush in Photo Opportunity with the National Security Team", September 12 [online]. Available at: http://georgewbush-whitehouse.archives.gov/news/releases/2001/09/20010912-4.html [Accessed September 19, 2010].
Bush, George W. (2001c). "Radio Addresses of the President to the Nation", September 15 [online]. Available at: http://georgewbush-whitehouse.archives.gov/news/releases/2001/09/20010915.html [Accessed September 19, 2010].
Bush, George W. (2001d). "President Urges Readiness and Patience", September 15, [online]. Available at: http://georgewbush-whitehouse.archives.gov/news/releases/2001/09/20010915-4.html [Accessed 19 September 19, 2010].
Bush, George W. (2001e). "Address to a Joint Session of Congress and the American People", September 20 [online]. Available at: http://georgewbush-whitehouse.archives.gov/news/releases/2001/09/20010920-8.html [Accessed September 19, 2010].
Bush, George W. (2001f). "International Campaign against Terror Grows", September 25 [online]. Available at: http://georgewbush-whitehouse.archives.gov/news/releases/2001/09/20010925-1.html [Accessed September 19, 2010].
Bush, George W. (2001g). "Radio Address of the President to the Nation", September 29 [online]. Available at: http://georgewbush-whitehouse.archives.gov/news/releases/2001/09/20010929.html [Accessed September 19, 2010].
Bush, George W. (2001h). "President: We're Making Progress", October 1 [online]. Available at: http://georgewbush-whitehouse.archives.gov/news/releases/2001/10/20011001-6.html [Accessed 19 September 19, 2010].
Bush, George W. (2001i). "Presidential Address to Nation", October 7 [online]. Available at: http://georgewbush-whitehouse.archives.gov/news/releases/2001/10/20011007-8.html [Accessed September 2010].
Bush, George W. (2002a) "Bush Delivers Graduation Speech at West Point", June 1 [online]. Available at: http://georgewbush-whitehouse.archives.gov/news/releases/2002/06/20020601-3.html [Accessed September 19, 2010].
Bush, George W. (2002b) "President's Remarks at the United Nations General Assembly", September 12 [online]. Available at: http://georgewbush-whitehouse.archives.gov/news/releases/2002/09/20020912-1.html [Accessed 19 September 19, 2010].
Bush, George W. (2002c). "President Bush Discusses Iraq with Reporters", September 13 [online]. Available at: http://georgewbush-whitehouse.archives.gov/news/releases/2002/09/20020913.html [Accessed September 19, 2010].
Bush, George W. (2002d). "President Bush Outlines Iraq Threat", October 7 [online]. Available at: http://georgewbush-whitehouse.archives.gov/news/releases/2002/10/20021007-8.html [Accessed September 19, 2010].
Bush, George W. (2002e). "President Delivers State of the Union Address", January 29 [online]. Available at: http://georgewbush-whitehouse.archives.gov/news/releases/2002/01/20020129-11.html [Accessed September 19, 2010].
Bush, George W. (2003a). "President Delivers 'State of the Union Address'", January 28 [online]. Available at: http://georgewbush-whitehouse.archives.gov/news/releases/2003/01/20030128-19.html [Accessed September 19, 2010].

Bibliography

Bush, George W. (2003b). "The President Discusses the Future of Iraq", February 26 [online]. Available at: http://georgewbush-whitehouse.archives.gov/news/releases/2003/02/20030226-11.html [Accessed September 19, 2010].

Bush, George W. (2007). "The Moment Has Come to Get Rid of Saddam. Transcript of Bush's conversation with José Maria Aznar, February 22, 2003", *The New York Review of Books*, 54 (17), November 8 [online]. Available at: www.nybooks.com/articles/archives/2007/nov/08/the-moment-has-come-to-get-rid-of-saddam/ [Accessed September 19, 2010].

Bush, George W. (2010). *Decision Points*. New York: Crown Publishers.

Buzan, Barry, Wæver, O., and de Wilde, Jaap (1998). *Security. A New Framework for Analysis*. Boulder: Lynne Rienner Publishers, Inc.

Carr, Edward Hallet (1946). *Twenty Years' Crisis 1919–1939. An Introduction to the Study of International Relations*. New York: Harper & Row Publishers.

Cheney, Dick (with Liz Cheney) (2011). *In My Time. A Personal and Political Memoir*. New York: Threshold Editions.

Chomsky, Noam (2007). "Chomsky on Iran, Iraq, and the Rest of the World", *Foreign Policy in Focus*, February 16 [online]. Available at: www.fpif.org/articles/chomsky_on_iran_iraq_and_the_rest_of_the_world [Accessed September 19, 2010].

Clausewitz, Carl von (1989). *On War*. Princeton, New Jersey: Princeton University Press.

Coker, Christopher (2009). *War in an Age of Risk*. Cambridge: Polity Press.

Colucci, Lamont (2008). *Crusading Realism. The Bush Doctrine and American Core Values after 9/11*. Lanham: University Press of America, Inc.

Crawford, Neta C. (2000). "The Passion of World Politics. Propositions on Emotion and Emotional Relationships", *International Security*, 24 (4), pp. 116–156.

Daalder, Ivo H. and Destler, I.M. (2009). *In the Shadow of the Oval Office. Profiles of the National Security Advisors and the Presidents they Served – from JFK to George W. Bush*. New York: Simon & Schuster.

Daalder, Ivo H. and Lindsay, James M. (2005). *America Unbound. The Bush Revolution in Foreign Policy*. Hoboken, New Jersey: John Wiley & Sons, Inc.

Dancy, Jonathan (1998). *Introduction to Contemporary Epistemology*. Cambridge: Blackwell.

Danner, Mark (2005). "'The Secret Way to War': An Exchange", *The New York Review of Books*, 52 (12), July 14 [online]. Available at: www.nybooks.com/articles/archives/2005/jul/14/the-secret-way-to-war-an-exchange/ [Accessed September 19, 2010].

Dueck, Colin (2004). "Ideas and Alternatives in American Grand Strategy, 2000–2004", *Review of International Studies*, 30 (4), pp. 511–535.

Dueck, Colin (2006). *Reluctant Crusaders. Power, Culture, and Change in American Grand Strategy*. Princeton: Princeton University Press.

Dunn, David Hastings (2003). "Myths, Motivations and 'Misunderestimations': The Bush Administration and Iraq", *International Affairs*, 79 (2), pp. 279–297.

Dunne, Tim and Schmidt, Brian C. (2001). "Realism", in Baylis, J. and Smith, S. (eds) *The Globalization of World Politics. An Introduction to International Relations*. Oxford: Oxford University Press.

Elbaradei, Mohamed (2003). "The Status of Nuclear Inspections in Iraq: 14 February 2003 Update", IAEA News Centre [online]. Available at: www.iaea.org/NewsCenter/Statements/2003/ebsp2003n005.shtml [Accessed September 19, 2010].

Elster, Jon (1981). "Snobs", *London Review of Books*, 3 (20), November 5, pp. 10–12.

Elster, Jon (1983). *Explaining Technical Change. A Case Study in the Philosophy of Science*. Cambridge. Cambridge University Press.

Bibliography 163

Elster, Jon (1989). *Nuts and Bolts for the Social Sciences*. Cambridge. Cambridge University Press.
Elster, Jon (1993). *Political Psychology*. Cambridge: Cambridge University Press.
Elster, Jon (1999). *Alchemies of the Mind. Rationality and the Emotions*. Cambridge: Cambridge University Press.
Elster, Jon (2007). *Explaining Social Behaviour. More Nuts and Bolts for the Social Sciences*. New York: Cambridge University Press.
Fearon, James D. (1995). "Explanation for War", *International Organization*, 49 (3), pp. 379–414.
Feith, Douglas J. (2008). *War and Decision. Inside the Pentagon at the Dawn of the War on Terror*. New York: Harper.
Finlay, David O., Holsti, Ole, and Fangen, Richard R. (1967). *Enemies in Politics*. Chicago: Rand McNally
Føllesdal, Dagfinn (2006). "Objectivity", Elster, J., Gjelsvik, O., Hylland, A., and Moene, K. (eds) *Understanding Choice, Explaining Behaviour. Essays in Honour of Ole Jørgen Skog*. Oslo: Unipub forlag/Oslo Academic Press, pp. 75–80.
Frankfurt, Harry (2005). *On Bullshit*. Princeton: Princeton University Press.
Frum, David (2003). *The Right Man. The Surprise Presidency of George W. Bush*. New York: Random House.
Gaddis, John Lewis (2002). "A Grand Strategy of Transformation", *Foreign Policy*, 133 (November/December Issue), pp. 50–57.
Gaddis, John Lewis (2004). *Surprise, Security and the American Experience*. Cambridge, MA: Harvard University Press.
Gaddis, John Lewis (2008). "Ending Tyranny. The Past and Future of an Idea", *The American Interest*, September/October Issue.
Gat, Azar (2006). *War in Human Civilization*. Oxford: Oxford University Press.
George, Alexander L. and Bennet, Andrew (2005). *Cases Studies and Theory Development in the Social Sciences*. Cambridge, Massachusetts: MIT Press.
Gordon, Michael R. and Trainor, Bernard E. (2007). *Cobra II. The Inside Story of the Invasion and Occupation of Iraq*. New York: Vintage Books.
Gray, Colin (2002). "World Politics as Usual after September 11: Realism Vindicated", in Boot, K. and Dunne, T. (eds) *Worlds in Collision. Terror and the Future of Global Order*. New York: Palgrave Macmillan, pp. 226–234.
Greenwald, Glenn (2007). *A Tragic Legacy. How a Good vs. Evil Mentality Destroyed the Bush Presidency*. New York: Crown Publishers.
Gurtov, Mel (2006). *Superpower on Crusade. The Bush Doctrine in US Foreign Policy*. Boulder, Colorado and London: Lynne Rienner Publishers.
Haber, Stephen, Kennedy, David M., and Krasner, Stephen D. (1997). "Brothers under the Skin: Diplomatic History and International Relations", *International Security*, 22 (1), pp. 34–43.
Hacking, Ian (1983). *Representing and Intervening. Introductory Topics in the Philosophy of Natural Science*. Cambridge: Cambridge University Press.
Hacking, Ian (1999). *The Social Construction of What?* Cambridge: Harvard University Press.
Halper, Stefan and Clarke, Jonathan (2004). *America Alone. The Neo-Conservatives and the Global Order*. Cambridge: Cambridge University Press.
Hedstrøm, Peter and Swedberg, Richard (1998). "Social Mechanisms: An Introductory Essay", in Hedstrøm, P. and Swedberg, R. (eds) *Social Mechanisms. An Analytical Approach to Social Theory*. New York: Cambridge University Press, pp. 1–31.

Heilke, Thomas (2004). "Realism, Narrative and Happenstance: Thucydides' Tale of Brasidas", *The American Political Science Review*, 98 (1), pp. 121–138.

Heng, Yee-Kuang (2006). *War as Risk Management. Strategy and Conflict in an Age of Globalised Risks*. London and New York: Routledge.

Hernes, Gudmund (1998). "Real Virtuality", in Hedstrøm, P. and Swedberg, R. (eds) *Social Mechanisms. An Analytical Approach to Social Theory*. New York: Cambridge University Press, pp. 74–101.

Hersh, Seymour M. (2004). *Chain of Command. The Road from 9/11 to Abu Ghraib*. New York: Harper Collins.

Hill, Christopher (2003). *The Changing Politics of Foreign Policy*. New York: Palgrave Macmillan.

Hobbes, Thomas (1968). *Leviathan*. London: Penguin Books.

Hoffman, Bruce (2006). *Inside Terrorism. (Revised and expanded edition)*. New York: Columbia University Press.

Holmes, Stephen (2007). *The Matador's Cape. America's Reckless Response to Terror*. New York: Cambridge University Press.

Holsti, Kalevi J. (1995). *International Politics. A Framework for Analysis*. New Jersey: Prentice-Hall International, Inc.

Holt, Jim (2007): "It's the Oil, Stupid", *London Review of Books*, 29 (20), pp. 3–4.

Hyde-Price, Adrian (2007). *European Security in the Twenty-first Century. The Challenge of Multipolarity*. London: Routledge.

Jervis, Robert (1976). *Perceptions and Misperceptions in International Politics*. Princeton, New Jersey: Princeton University Press.

Jervis, Robert (1997). *System Effects. Complexity in Political and Social Life*. Princeton: Princeton University Press.

Jervis, Robert (2003a). "The Compulsive Empire", *Foreign Policy*, 137 (Jul/Aug Issue), pp. 83–89.

Jervis, Robert (2003b). "Understanding the Bush-doctrine", *Political Science Quarterly*, 118 (3), pp. 365–388.

Jervis, Robert (2003c). "The Confrontation between Iraq and the US: Implications for the Theory and Practice of Deterrence", *European Journal of International Relations*, 9 (2), pp. 315–337.

Jervis, Robert (2006a). "Reports, Politics, and Intelligence Failures: The Case of Iraq", *The Journal of Strategic Studies*, 29 (1), pp. 3–52.

Jervis, Robert (2006b). "The Remaking of a Unipolar World", *The Washington Quarterly*, 29 (3), pp. 7–19.

Jervis, Robert (2010). *Why Intelligence Fails. Lessons from the Iranian Revolution and the Iraq War*. Ithaca and London: Cornell University Press.

Kagan, Robert (2008). *The Return of History and the End of Dreams*. London: Atlantic Books.

Kagan, Robert (2003). *Of Paradise and Power. America and Europe in the New World Order*. New York: Alfred A. Knopf.

Kagan, Robert and Kristol, William (2004). "The Right War for the Right Reasons. The Liberation of Iraq was Abundantly Justified", *Weekly Standard*, 9 (23), February 23 [online]. Available at: www.weeklystandard.com/Content/Public/Articles/000/000/003/735tahyk.asp [Accessed September 19, 2010].

Kaplan, Fred (2008). *Daydream Believers. How a Few Grand Ideas Wrecked American Power*. New Jersey: John Wiley & Sons, Inc.

Kaplan, Morton (1971). *On Historical and Political Knowing. An Inquiry into Some Problems of Universal Law & Human Freedom*. Chicago and London: The University of Chicago Press.
Katzenstein, Peter J. and Okawara, Nobuo (2001/02). "Japan, Asian-Pacific Security, and the Case for Analytical Eclecticism", *International Security*, 26 (3), pp. 153–185.
Keller, Bill (2002). "The Sunshine Warrior", *The New York Times Magazine*, September 22, pp. 48–55, 84, 88 and 96–97.
Keohane, Robert O. (1984). *After Hegemony. Cooperation and Discord in the World Political Economy*. Princeton: Princeton University Press.
Klare, Micheal T. (2003). "For Oil and Empire? Rethinking War with Iraq", *Current History*, 102 (662), pp. 129–135.
Korb, Lawrence J. and Conley, Laura (2009). "Forging an American Empire", in Maranto, R., Lansford, T., and Johnson, J. (eds) *Judging Bush*. California: Stanford University Press, pp. 234–251.
Krasner, Stephen D. (1978). *Defending the National Interest: Raw Materials Investments and US Foreign Policy*. New Jersey: Princeton University Press.
Krauthammer, Charles (2001). "The Bush Doctrine. AMB, Kyoto and the New American Unilateralism", *The Weekly Standard*, June 4, pp. 21–25.
Krauthammer, Charles (2004). "Democratic Realism. An American Foreign Policy for a Unipolar World", Washington DC: *The AEI Press*.
Layne, Christopher (2006). "The 'Poster Child for Offensive Realism': America as a Global Hegemon", *Security Studies*, 12 (2), pp. 120–164.
Legro, Jeffrey W. and Moravcsik, A. (1999). "Is Anybody Still a Realist?", *International Security*, 26 (2), pp. 5–55.
Lemann, Nicholas (2002). "The Next World Order", *The New Yorker*, April 1 [online]. Available at: www.newyorker.com/archive/2002/04/01/020401fa_FACT1 [Accessed 19 September 2010].
Lemann, Nicholas (2003). "Real Reasons". *The New Yorker*, September 22 [online]. Available at: www.newyorker.com/archive/2003/09/22/030922ta_talk_lemann?printable=true [Accessed September 19, 2010].
Levy, Jack S. (1997). "Too Important to Leave to the Other: History and Political Science in the Study of International Relations", *International Security*, 22 (1), pp. 22–33.
Levy, Jack S. (2007). "Preventive War and the Bush Doctrine", in Renshon, S.A. and Suedfeld, P. (eds) *Understanding the Bush Doctrine. Psychology and Strategy in an Age of Terrorism*. New York: Routledge, pp. 175–200.
Lieven, Anatol (2003). "The Push for War", *London Review of Books*, 24 (19), October 3 [online]. Available at: www.lrb.co.uk/v24/n19/anatol-lieven/the-push-for-war [Accessed 19 September 2010].
Lieven, Anatol (2004). *America Right or Wrong. An Anatomy of American Nationalism*. Oxford: Oxford University Press.
Lipset, Seymour Martin (1996). *American Exceptionalism. A Double-Edged Sword*. New York: W.W. Norton & Company.
Little, Richard (2007). *The Balance of Power in International Relations: Metaphors, Myths and Models*. Cambridge: Cambridge University Press.
Litwak, Robert S. (2007). *Regime Change. US Strategy through the Prism of 9/11*. Baltimore: Johns Hopkins University Press.
McClellan, Scott (2008a). *What Happened. Inside the Bush White House and Washington's Culture of Deception*. New York: PublicAffairs.

McClellan, Scott (2008b). "Hardball with Chris Matthews", transcript MSNBC, June 2 [online]. Available at: http://today.msnbc.msn.com/id/24949444/print/displaymode/1098 [Accessed September 19, 2010].

Malnes, Raino (1993). *The Hobbesian Theory of International Conflict*. Oslo: Scandinavian University Press.

Malnes, Raino (1994). *National Interests, Morality and International Law*. Oslo: Scandinavian University Press.

Malnes, Raino (2002). *Materiell og Mental Virkelighet. Metafysiske Emner fra Empirisk Vitenskap* [*Material and Mental Reality. Metaphysical Topics from the Empirical Sciences*]. Oslo: Abstrakt forlag.

Malnes, Raino (2006). "Explaining and Making Sense of Action", in Elster, J., Gjelsvik, O., Hylland, A., and Moene, K. (eds) *Understanding Choice, Explaining Behaviour. Essays in Honour of Ole Jørgen Skog*. Oslo: Unipub forlag/Oslo Academic Press, pp. 177–189.

Malnes, Raino (2008). *Meningen med Samfunnsvitenskap* [*The Meaning of Social Science*]. Oslo: Gyldendal Akademisk.

Mann, James (2004). *Rice of the Vulcans. The History of Bush's War Cabinet*. New York: Penguin Books.

Mann, Michael (2003). *Incoherent Empire*. New York: Verso.

Mazarr, Michael J. (2003). "George W. Bush, Idealist", *International Affairs*, 79 (3), pp. 503–522.

Mead, Walter Russell (2004). *Power, Terror, Peace and War. America's Grand Strategy in a World at Risk*. New York: Alfred A. Knopf.

Mearsheimer, John J. (2001). *The Tragedy of Great Power Politics*. New York and London: W.W. Norton & Company.

Mearsheimer, John J. (2005). "Hans Morgenthau and the Iraq War: Realism versus Neoconservatism", *OpenDemocracy*, May 18.

Mearsheimer, John (2006). "Conversations in *International Relations*: Interview with John. J. Mearsheimer (Part 1)", *International Relations*, 20 (1), pp. 105–123.

Mearsheimer, John (2009). "Reckless States and Realism", *International Relations*, 23 (2), pp. 241–256.

Mearsheimer, John J. and Walt, Stephen (2003). "An Unnecessary War", *Foreign Policy*, 134 (January/February Issue), pp. 51–59.

Mearsheimer, John J. and Walt, Stephen (2007). *The Israel Lobby and US Foreign Policy*. New York: Farrar, Straus and Giroux.

Melby, Svein (1997). *Amerikansk Utenrikspolitikk* [*American Foreign Policy*]. Oslo: Tano.

Miller, Benjamin (2010). "Explaining Changes in US Grand Strategy: The Rise of Offensive Liberalism and the War in Iraq", *Security Studies*, 19 (1), pp. 26–65.

Moens, Alexander (2004). *The Foreign Policy of George W. Bush. Values, Strategy, and Loyalty*. Aldershot: Ashgate.

Monten, Jonathan (2005). "The Roots of the Bush Doctrine. Power, Nationalism, and Democracy Promotion in US Strategy", *International Security*, 29 (4), pp. 112–156.

Monten, Jonathan (2007). "Primacy and Grand Strategic Beliefs in US Unilateralism", *Global Governance*, 13 (1), pp. 119–138.

Morgenthau, Hans J. (1968). *Politics among Nations. The Struggle for Power and Peace (4th ed.)*. New York: Alfred A. Knopf.

Myerson, Roger (2006). "Force and Restraint in Strategic Deterrence: A Game-Theorist's Perspective", conference paper presented at Chicago Humanities Festival on Peace and War, November 11.

Newbold, Greg (2006): "Why Iraq Was a Mistake", *TIME*, April 9 [online]. Available at: www.time.com/time/printout/0,8816,1181629,00.html [Accessed September 19, 2010].
Newbold, Greg (2007). Interview with author, November 2.
Nye, Joseph (2002). *The Paradox of American Power. Why the World's Only Superpower Can't Go it Alone*. New York: Oxford University Press.
Nye, Joseph (2004). *Soft Power. The Means to Success in World Politics*. New York: Public Affairs.
Osgood, Robert (1953). *Ideals and Self-Interest in America's Foreign Relations*. Chicago: The University of Chicago Press.
Oudenaren, John Van (2004). "Unipolar versus Unilateral", *Policy Review*, 124 (April/May Issue) [online]. Available at: www.hoover.org/publications/policyreview/3438956.html [Accessed 19 September 2010].
Parsons, Craig (2007). *How to Map Arguments in Political Science*. New York: Oxford University Press.
Pfiffner, James P. (2004). "Introduction. Assessing the Bush Presidency", in Gregg II, G. and Rozell, M.J. (eds) *Considering the Bush Presidency*. New York: Oxford University Press.
Popper, Karl (2007). *The Poverty of Historicism*. London and New York: Routledge Classics.
Popper, Karl (2009). *The Logic of Scientific Discovery*. London and New York: Routledge Classics.
Powell, Colin (2001). "Seizing the Moment", US *Foreign Policy Agenda*, 6 (3), November, pp. 5–6.
Powers, Thomas (2010): "How They Got Their Bloody Way", *The New York Review of Books* LVII (9), May 27, pp. 6–10.
Prados, John (2004). *Hoodwinked. The Documents that Reveal How Bush Sold Us a War*. New York: The New Press.
Rasmussen, Mikkel Vedby (2006). *The Risk Society at War. Terror, Technology and Strategy in the Twenty-First Century*. New York: Cambridge University Press.
Rathbun, Brian C. (2007). "Uncertain about Uncertainty: Understanding the Multiple Meanings of a Crucial Concept in International Relations Theory", *International Studies Quarterly*, 51 (3), pp. 533–557.
Record, Jeffry (2004). *Dark Victory. America's Second War against Iraq*. Annapolis: Naval Institute Press.
Record, Jeffry (2008). "Why the Bush Administration Invaded Iraq. Making Strategy after 9/11", *Strategic Studies Quarterly*, 2 (2), pp. 63–92.
Renshon, Stanley A. (2007) "The Bush Doctrine Considered", in Renshon, S.A. and Suedfeld, P. (eds) *Understanding the Bush Doctrine. Psychology and Strategy in an Age of Terrorism*. New York: Routledge, pp. 1–37.
Rice, Condoleezza (2002). "The War on Terrorism and the Bush Administration's Foreign Policy", remarks at Johns Hopkins University, April 29.
Rice, Condoleezza (2005). "The Promise of Democratic Peace", *The Washington Post*, December 11, p. B7.
Rice, Condoleezza (2011). *No Higher Honor. A Memoir of My Years in Washington*. New York: Crown Publishers.
Ricks, Thomas E. (2007). *Fiasco. The American Military Adventure in Iraq*. New York: Penguin Books.
Ritchie, Nick and Rogers, Paul (2007). *The Political Road to War with Iraq. Bush, 9/11 and the Drive to Overthrow Saddam*. London and New York: Routledge.

Rodenbeck, Max (2006). "How Terrible Is It?", *New York Review of Books*, 53 (16), November 30, pp. 33–38.
Rorty, Richard (1989). *Contingency, Irony, and Solidarity*. Cambridge: Cambridge University Press.
Rosecrance, Richard N. (2002). "War and Peace", *World Politics*, 55 (1), pp. 137–166.
Rove, Karl (2010). *Courage and Consequence. My Life as a Conservative in the Fight*. New York: Threshold Editions.
Rumsfeld, Donald (2002). "Transforming the Military", *Foreign Affairs*, 81 (3), pp. 20–32.
Rumsfeld, Donald (2011). *Known and Unknown. A Memoir*. New York: Sentinel.
Rumsfeld, Donald and Wolfowitz, Paul (2001). "Testimony before the Senate Armed Services Committee", United States, Department of Defense, December 12 [online]. Available at: www.defense.gov/speeches/speech.aspx?speechid=506 [Accessed September 19, 2010].
Runciman, David (2006). *The Politics of Good Intentions. History, Fear and Hypocrisy in the New World Order*. Princeton: Princeton University Press.
Russell, Bertrand (1938/2004). *Power. A New Social Analysis*. London: Routledge Classics.
Sammon, Bill (2002). *Fighting Back. The War on Terrorism from Inside the Bush White House*. Washington D.C.: Regnery Publishing INC.
Satz, Debora and Ferejohn, John (1994). "Rational Choice and Social Theory", *The Journal of Philosophy*, 91 (2), pp. 71–87.
Schelling, Thomas (1960/1980). *Strategy of Conflict*. Cambridge, Massachusetts: Harvard University Press.
Schelling, Thomas (1966). *Arms and Influence*. New Haven and London: Yale University Press.
Schelling, Thomas (1978/2006). *Micromotives and Macrobehavior*. New York: W.W. Norton & Company.
Schlesinger Jr., Arthur M. (2004). *War and the American Presidency*. New York: W.W. Norton & Company.
Scowcroft, Brent (2002). "Don't Attack Saddam", *Wall Street Journal*, August 15, p. A12.
Searle, John (1990). "The Storm Over the University", *The New York Review of Books*, 37 (19), December 6.
Silverman, David (2008). *Doing Qualitative Research*. London: Sage Publications Ltd.
Snyder, Glenn (2002). "Mearsheimer's World – Offensive Realism and the Struggle for Security. A Review Essay", *International Security*, 27 (1), pp. 149–173.
Snyder, Jack (2008). "Correspondence. Defensive Realism and the 'New' History of World War I", *International Security*, 33 (1), pp. 174–194.
Suedfeld, Peter (2007). "The Bush Doctrine in Perspective", in Renshon, S.A. and Suedfeld, P. (eds) *Understanding the Bush Doctrine. Psychology and Strategy in an Age of Terrorism*. New York: Routledge, pp. 319–328.
Sunstein, Cass R. (2005). *Laws of Fear. Beyond the Precautionary Principle*. Cambridge: Cambridge University Press.
Suskind, Ron (2007). *The One Percent Doctrine. Deep Inside America's Pursuit of its Enemies since 9/11*. New York: Simon & Schuster Paperbacks.
Tenet, George (2007). *At the Center of the Storm*. New York: Harper Collins.
Thucydides (1954). *The Peloponnesian War*. New York: E.P. Dutton & Co. INC.
Trachtenberg, Marc (2006). *The Craft of International History. A Guide to Method*. Princeton: Princeton University Press.

Tunç, Hakan (2005). "What was it All About After All? The Causes of the Iraq war", *Contemporary Security Policy*, 26 (2), pp. 335–355.
Tunsjø, Øystein (2008). *US Taiwan Policy: Constructing the Triangle*. London: Routledge.
Underdal, Arild (1984). "Can We, in the Study of International Politics, Do without the Rational Actor Model?", *Internasjonal Politikk*, Temahefte: Norsk Utenrikspolitiks Institutt (NUPI), pp. 63–79.
Walt, Stephen (2005). *Taming American Power. The Global Response to US Primacy*. New York, London: W.W. Norton & Company.
Waltz, Kenneth (1979). *Theory of International Politics*. Reading, MA: Addison-Wesley Publishing Company.
Waltz, Kenneth (2000). "Structural Realism after the Cold War", *International Security*, 25 (1), pp. 5–41.
Waltz, Kenneth (2002). "The Continuity of International Politics", in Boot, K. and Dunne, T. (eds) *Worlds in Collision. Terror and the Future of Global Order*. New York: Palgrave Macmillan, pp. 348–353.
Waltz, Kenneth (2008). *Realism and International Politics*. New York: Routledge.
Wendt, Alexander (1992). "Anarchy is What States Make of It: The Social Construction of Power Politics", *International Organization*, 46 (2), pp. 391–425.
Wendt, Alexander (1999). *Social Theory of International Politics*. New York: Cambridge University Press.
Wight, Colin (2006). *Agents, Structures and International Relations. Politics as Ontology*. New York: Cambridge University Press.
Wolfers, Arnold (1962). *Discord and Collaboration. Essays on International Politics*. Baltimore: The John Hopkins University Press.
Wolfowitz, Paul (2003). "Deputy Secretary Wolfowitz: Interview with Sam Tannenhaus, Vanity Fair", United States Department of Defense, May 9 [online]. Available at: www.defenselink.mil/transcripts/transcript.aspx?transcriptid=2594 [Accessed September 19, 2010].
Woodward, Bob (2003). *Bush at War*. New York: Simon & Schuster, Pocket Books.
Woodward, Bob (2004). *Plan of Attack*. New York: Simon & Schuster.
Zelikow, Philip (1993). "Offensive Military Options", in Blackwill, R.D. and Carnesale, A. (eds) *New Nuclear Nations. Consequences for US Policy*. New York: Council on Foreign Relation Press, pp. 162–195.
Zelikow, Philip (2007). Email interview with author, October 25.
Zonis, Marvin (2007). "The 'Democracy Doctrine' of President George W. Bush", in Renshon, S.A. and Suedfeld, P. (eds) *Understanding the Bush Doctrine. Psychology and Strategy in an Age of Terrorism*. New York: Routledge, pp. 231–250.

US Government documents

CFA (Presentation – The Case for Action) (2002). September 12 [online]. Available at: www.gwu.edu/~nsarchiv/NSAEBB/NSAEBB254/doc03.pdf [Accessed September 19, 2010].
DHS (The Department of Homeland Security) (2002). June [online]. Available at: www.dhs.gov/xlibrary/assets/book.pdf [Accessed September 19, 2010].
NSCT (National Strategy for Combating Terrorism) (2003). February [online]. Available at: www.cia.gov/news-information/cia-the-war-on-terrorism/Counter_Terrorism_Strategy.pdf [Accessed September 19, 2010].

NSCWMD (National Strategy to Combat Weapons of Mass Destruction) (2002). December [online]. Available at: www.fas.org/irp/offdocs/nspd/nspd-17.html [Accessed September 19, 2010].

NSS (National Security Strategy of the United States of America) (2002). September 17 [online]. Available at: www.globalsecurity.org/military/library/policy/national/nss-020920.pdf [Accessed September 19, 2010].

QDR (Quadrennial Defense Review) (2001). September 30 [online]. Available at: www.defense.gov/pubs/pdfs/qdr2001.pdf [Accessed September 19, 2010].

Index

Page numbers including an "n" e.g. 126n6 refer to notes.

9/11 terror attacks, response to: counter-wishful thinking and fear (mechanism 4) 89–95; descriptions and theories concerning US response 7–10; geographical considerations (mechanism 10) 114; neo-conservatism and US response 70–5; observation and fear (mechanism 2) 80–4; power distribution and deterrence (mechanism 11) 114–15; power maximization, preservation and amassment (mechanism 5) 95–101; precautionary action (mechanism 8) 111–14; primacy of military means (mechanism 6) 101–5; and realism 3–6; regional hegemony (mechanism 12) 115; security, primacy of (mechanism 1) 75–80; self-help thinking (mechanism 7) 105–11; timing considerations (mechanism 9) 114; uncertainty and fear (mechanism 3) 84–9

Afghanistan 99, 103, 109
al-Qaeda 82–3, 112
Alexander, Gerard 107
America Alone. The Neo-Conservatives and the Global Order (Halper and Clarke) 70–2
anarchy 26, 32–3, 43, 64; forces of 7; influence on decision-making 64; offensive realism 41; repercussions of 64; structural 3, 30; uncertainty and fear 51–2
anthrax attacks 83
Art, Robert 58
"as if" assumptions 48, 151n5
Aznar, José María 121, 124

Bacevich, Andrew 135

balance of power 2, 7, 12–13; *see also* power
Barnes, Fred 125
Bennett, Andrew 33
Biddle, Stephen 76
bin Laden, Osama 85, 99
black box 24, 64, 141–2
Blix, Hans 89, 90
Boot, Ken 42, 60
Boyle, Michael 138
Brenner, William J. 146
Bromwich, David 97
Brooks, Stephen 61
Brzezinski, Zbigniew 95
Bush, George W., administration of 5, 14, 76, 77–8, 83, 84–5, 158n10; on Afghanistan 99; anti-idealist explanation of policies 120–1; concern with US strategic reputation 99–101, 104, 158n14; decision to use military force 103–5; dualist arguments in responses to terrorism 98–9, 156n5; excessive pessimism concerning Iraq 92; idealism and security as equal motives 128–9; and impure idealism 132–6; influence of Mechanistic Realism on response to 9/11 69–70; interprets terrorist attacks as war 102; misuse of information 84, 89–91; mixture of security and idealist motives 127–8; neo-conservatism and response to 9/11 70–5; nomological analysis of post 9/11 policies 8–9; "offense is a good defense" attitude 95–8; offensive actions 96; promotion of freedom as an ideal 123–6, 130; rejection of deterrence 93–4; religious outlook 155–6n3; risk assessment and evaluation 111; security

Bush, George W. *continued*
  in abundance thesis 129–31; self-help thinking and attitude to international cooperation 106–11; sinister judgement concerning Iraq 90–1; uncertainty and fear 86; unilateralist inclinations 106, 109, 158n10, 159n12; *see also* 9/11 terror attacks, response to

Cheney, Dick 76, 79, 81, 83, 85, 86, 112, 115
Chomsky, Noam 120
CIA 91, 112
Clarke, Jonathan 70–3, 103
Clausewitz, Carl von 52–3
Clinton, Bill 74, 99
Coalition for a Realistic Foreign Policy 5
Cold War 132, 152–3n2
Colucci, Lamont 126, 159n4
complacency 26, 51–2, 85, 87–8, 113, 149
Conley, Laura 103, 159n12
correspondence theory of truth 21–2; causal relationships 22; descriptions of phenomena 21–2; socially constructed beliefs 22
counter-wishful thinking 52–3, 89–95, 115; *see also* wishful thinking
Crawford, Neta C. 15
critical rationalism 15
Crusading Realism (Colucci) 126

Daalder, Ivo H. 84, 106, 126
Danner, Mark 159n1
decision-making: anarchy, influence and repercussions 64; cost/benefit analyses 61, 62, 63; counter-wishful thinking and fear 52–3; decisions on use of military capability 57–8; fear as a cause of 14–15; geographical considerations 62; limited applicability of mechanisms 64; need for additional mechanisms 64–5; observation and fear 49–50; power distribution and deterrence 62–3; power maximization, preservation and reasonable amassment 53–7, 58; precautionary action 60–1; psychological theory 48–9, 141; regional hegemony 63; self-help thinking 58–60; survival 44–5, 49; timing considerations 61–2; uncertainty and fear 50–2; uncertainty of the intentions of others 42, 45
Defence Planning Guidance (DPG) 71–2, 74

defensive realists 29
democracy 79–80, 120, 124–5, 126, 127, 130–6
democratic globalism 131
Descartes, René 135–6
determinism 43, 44
deterrence 56, 62–3, 92–3, 99–101, 104–5, 114, 157
Dobriansky, Paula 124
Dueck, Colin 107
Dunn, David Hastings 95
Durkheim, Émile 153n6

eclecticism 3, 149
ElBaradei, Mohamed (IAEA inspector) 89
Elster, Jon 9, 26, 28, 34, 142, 146, 151n1, 153n5
explanation 24–9, 34

fear 26, 29, 38, 45, 72, 143, 154n4, 154n5; and counter-wishful thinking 52–3, 89–95; and foreign policy decisions 14–15; and observation 49–50, 80–4; and uncertainty 50–2, 84–9, 149
Feith, Douglas 79–80, 82, 86, 94, 96, 97, 98, 104, 108, 111, 128
Fleming, Melissa 85–6
Føllesdal, Dagfinn 21, 38
Frankfurt, Harry 151n2
Friedmann, Milton 23
Frum, David 104
functionalism 32, 120, 121, 144–5

Gaddis, John Lewis 107, 132, 134
generality 10, 146
geography 47, 62, 114
George, Alexander L. 33
George W. Bush, Idealist (Mazarr) 125
Gordon, Michael R. 74, 100–1
Gray, Colin 4
Gurtov, Mel 83–4, 89

Haber, Stephen 36–7
Hacking, Ian 36
Halper, Stefan 70–3, 103
hegemony 44, 45–7, 63, 115
hermeneutic dilemma 51, 119
Hill, Christopher 22, 152n1
History of the Peloponnesian War (Thucydides) 8
Hobbes, Thomas 8, 54
Holmes, Stephen 77, 105
Holsti, Ole 53
Holt, Jim 144

Hosti, Kalevi J. 27
Hussein, Saddam 86–7, 92–3, 129
Hyde-Price, Adrian 147

idealism 16, 77–9; and abundance of security 129–31; anti-idealism 118–22; assessment of influence on US post 9/11 policies 136–40; compatibility with Mechanistic Realism 137; explanations of US conduct 144–6; as a factor in Iraq war 117–18, 159n1; impure idealism 131–6; over-determining idealism 128–9; and psychological plausibility 138; pure idealism 122–6; reciprocity 135–6; relative impact 139; statements of idealistic intent 139; underlying motive 138–9; weak idealism 126–8
ideographic analysis 7–9, 147
instrumentalism 10–12, 150, 151–2n5; disparity with scientific realism 23
intelligence 84–5
International Atomic Energy Agency (IAEA) 85–6
international politics: continuity, degree of 1–2; cooperation 59; self-help system 44–5, 58–60, 105–11; see *also* decision-making
Iraq, US attack on 4, 5, 71, 75; excessive pessimism of Bush administration 92; idealism and security as equal motives 128–9, 159n1; low number of troops 27, 28; misuse of information by Bush administration 84, 89–91; mixture of security and idealist motives 127–8; neoconservative idea of military regime change 74; precautionary arguments for US attack 113–14; realist-inspired explanations 144–5; reasons for attack 77–8, 100–1; UN agreement for 121–2; uncertainty about future Iraqi capabilities and intentions 88, 90–1

Jervis, Robert 4, 8–9, 42, 83, 88, 90, 91, 95, 108, 118, 134, 144, 154n5

Kagan, Robert 108, 122, 129, 159n13
Kaplan, Morton 24
Katzenstein, Peter J. 29
Keane, Jack 98
Keohane, Robert O. 59–60
Klare, Michael 120
Korb, Lawrence J. 103, 159n12
Krauthammer, Charles 130–1, 133
Kristol, William 129

Legro, Jeffrey W. 3
Lemann, Nicholas 100
Levy, Jack 36
Lieven, Anatol 122–3
Lindsay, James M. 84, 106, 126
Little, Richard 39, 49
Litwak, Robert S. 91

Malnes, Raino 3, 26, 34
Mann, James 109
mass casualties 82, 83
Mazarr, Michael J. 125
McClellan, Scott 78, 79, 83, 125
Mead, Walter Russell 129
Mearsheimer, John 5, 29, 30–1, 39, 40–1, 42, 43–4, 46, 47, 54, 59, 61, 62, 63, 65, 93, 99, 119, 129–30, 142, 151–2n5, 153–4n1, 154n2, 155n6, 159n5
mechanism-centered research strategy 148; accumulation of explanatory mechanisms to dispel observational puzzles 25–6; complexity, levels of 28; disclosure of causal chains 24–5; prediction 26; presumptive mechanisms 28; reason-explanation 26–7; resolving theory indeterminacies and disputes 29; vicarious problem solving 27; wishful thinking 27–8
mechanistic analysis: beliefs 37; choice of theories 36; complexity of historical retelling 34–5; confirmation bias 35; familiarity 34; objectivity 35–6, 38; observations 36–7; precise explanation 35; process tracing 33–4; representativeness 35
Mechanistic Realism: analysis framework 13–16; anarchy, influence on decision-making 64; anarchy, repercussions of 64; causal mechanisms 10, 12, 14; compatibility with idealism 137; cost/benefit analyses 61, 62, 63; counter-wishful thinking and fear (mechanism 4) 52–3, 89–95; dual purpose of 142; explanation of and reasons for use 6–13; geographical considerations (mechanism 10) 62, 114; limited applicability of mechanisms 64; need for additional mechanisms 64–5; observation and fear (mechanism 2) 49–50, 80–4; power distribution and deterrence (mechanism 11) 62–3, 114–15; power maximization, preservation and reasonable amassment (mechanism 5) 53–7, 58, 95–101, 148, 149; precautionary action (mechanism

174 *Index*

Mechanistic Realism *continued*
8) 60–1, 111–14; primacy of military means (mechanism 6) 57–8, 101–5; psychological processes of decision-making 141; regional hegemony (mechanism 12) 63, 115; security, primacy of (mechanism 1) 49, 75–80; self-help thinking (mechanism 7) 58–60, 105–11; terrorism, disregard of 65–6; theoretical benchmark 40; timing considerations (mechanism 9) 61–2, 114; uncertainty and fear (mechanism 3) 50–2, 84–9; validity of 144; weaknesses of theory 65; *see also* offensive realism
Merton, Robert 10
methodological individualism 7, 12–13, 142; individual anchoring 30–2; link between constraints and individual cognition 32; psychological reactions of policymakers 31
military capability 41–2, 45, 57–8, 101–5
Monten, Jonathan 110
Moravcsik, A. 3
Morgenthau, Hans J. 105, 118–19, 147
Moscow Treaty on Strategic Reductions 87

National Security Strategy 76, 81, 87, 98, 100, 101, 103, 107, 109–10, 113, 123
National Strategy to Combating Terrorism 89
NATO 109
neo-conservative thesis 69; climate of fear 72; empirical weakness 73; lack of credibility 72–3; limited sense of explanation 75; manipulation of political agenda 72; military regime change in Iraq 74; pre-existing agenda theory 73–4; spuriousness, problem of 74–5; and US response to 9/11 70–5
Newbold, Greg 106
nomological analysis 8–9, 147–8
non-state actors 65, 89, 146
NSCWMD 103
Nye, Joseph 136, 157n8

objectivity 35–6, 38
observation 49–50
oceans, as a power limiter 47, 62
"Offensive Military Options" (Zelikow) 81
offensive realism 4, 29, 39, 65, 142, 151–2n5; anarchy 41; as a descriptive theory 40–1; hegemony 44, 45–7; offensive military capability 41–2, 45; rationality 43–4; survival 42–3, 44–5; uncertainty of the intentions of others 42, 45
Okawara, Nobuo 29
On Bullshit (Frankfurt) 151n2
One percent doctrine 112

Pearl, Richard 138
Pentagon 77, 102, 110
Popper, Karl 15, 36, 37–8
positivism 23
Powell, Colin 72, 73, 87, 91, 98, 115, 121–2
power 3–4, 45–7; counter-wishful thinking and fear 115; decisions on use of military means 57–8; distribution and deterrence 62–3, 114–15; maximisation, preservation and reasonable amassment 53–7, 95–101, 148, 149; timing considerations 61–2, 114
Powers, Thomas 84
Prados, John 91
precautionary action 60–1, 111–14
prediction 11–12, 26, 148
process tracing 33–4
psychological plausibility 48–9, 51, 53, 63, 138, 145

rain rituals 153n6
rationality 23, 43–4
realism: causal mechanisms 10, 12; generalism and counterexamples 146–7; structural constraints 30; theory-testing procedure 12; and the US response to 9/11 3–6; usefulness of 11–12; validity of 9–10, 12, 142, 143–4
Realist Thought and Neorealist Theory (Waltz) 11
reason-explanation 26–7
reason mechanism 57
Record, Jeffrey 101, 104
reductionism 29–30
regional hegemony *see* hegemony
relativism 22, 36, 152n1
Renshon, Stanley A. 95, 97, 106, 134
representativeness 35
revisionism 54–5
Rice, Condoleezza 77, 80, 81, 86–7, 94, 96, 97, 103, 124–5, 132–3
Rosecrance, Richard N. 65
Rove, Karl 127–8, 133–4
Rumsfeld, Donald 76, 79, 87, 89, 96, 97, 100–1, 108, 157n7
Russia 87–8, 89

Schelling, Thomas 27, 43, 57

Schlesinger Jr., Arthur 103–4
scientific realism 7, 10–12, 21–4, 153n3, 153n4
Searle, John 22
security 43; competition 46; dilemmas 7, 46; precautionary action 60–1; primacy of 49, 75–80; reasoning 28; *see also* idealism
self-help thinking 58–60, 105–11
self-interest 59–60, 118–22; *see also* idealism
Silverman, David 36
Snyder, Jack 46, 55, 148
soft power 136
Somalia 31
spiral model 56
State of the Union Address 2002 76
states: hegemony and power 45–7; non-security motives 43; offensive military capability 41–2, 45; offensive realism 41; rationality 43–4; struggle for power 3–4; survival 42–3, 44–5; uncertainty of the intentions of others 42, 45; *see also* decision-making
structural realist theory 12
survival 42–3, 44–5
Suskind, Ron 80, 85, 100, 112
suspicion 51–2

Taiwan 152–3n2
theory-laden 36–8
Tenet, George 14–15, 80–1, 82–3, 84–5, 86, 94, 112, 113
terrorism 65, 88–9, 102
Thucydides 8, 50
Trachtenberg, Marc 24, 35
Tragedy of Great Power Politics, The (Mearsheimer) 39

Trainor, Bernard E. 74, 100–1
trust 59–60
truth *see* correspondence theory of truth
Tunç, Hakan 105, 134
Tunsjø, Øystein 152–3n2

uncertainty 26, 42, 45, 50–2, 84–9, 149
unilateralism 75, 106–10
United Nations (UN) 37, 109, 121–2
United States (US): Cold War 132, 152–3n2; and exceptionalism 122–3; and Taiwan; see *also* 9/11 terror attacks; Bush, George W., administration; Iraq, US attack on
usefulness 11–12; *see also* instrumentalism

validation 11–12

Walt, Stephen 5, 93, 106, 130
Waltz, Kenneth 4, 8, 11, 29, 39, 51–2, 55, 88, 98, 110, 144, 149, 150
war on terror 8, 88, 96
weapons of mass destruction (WMD) 82–3, 87, 89, 90–3, 103, 111–12, 113–14, 156n5
Wendt, Alexander 30, 36
Wheeler, Nicolas J. 42, 60
White, Hayden 35–6
wishful thinking 27–8; see *also* counter-wishful thinking
Wolfers, Arnold 13, 54, 55
Wolfowitz, Paul 73, 76, 98, 133
Woodward, Bob 76, 77, 83, 87, 99–100, 108, 111, 127
worst case scenarios 61, 89–95, 112–13

Zelikow, Philip 81–2
Zonis, Marvin 117